A FISH FOR ALL SEASONS

First published in November 2010

Edited - Steve Partner, Terry Doe and Rosie Barham

With special thanks for the use of photographs to:
Mick Rouse/Angling Times – pp. 25, 34, 37, 50, 83, 90, 105, 106, 107, 108, 130, 132, 147, 149a, 155, 156, 157, 158, 159, 160, 203, 208, 240, 241, 254, 276 and 282
Lloyd Rogers/Angling Times – pg 332
Stuart Morgan – pg 211
John Wilson – pg 268

ISBN NUMBER 978-0-9560935-4-7

Designed and published by mpress (Media) LTD.

Unit Four, Ashton Gate, Harold Hill, Romford, RM3 8UF

To my wife, Jo, whose love makes me the luckiest man in the world.

ACKNOWLEDGEMENTS

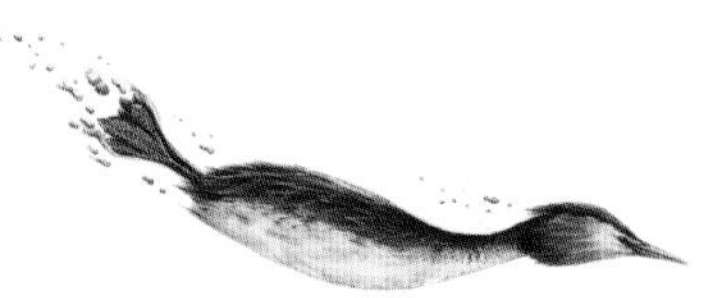

With so many people making the adventures over the last 20 years possible, where do I begin? Can I start by saying thank you to everyone whose path has crossed mine. Friend or foe, each and every one of you has helped to shape my life, which has been more fulfilling than I could ever have imagined. There are, however, individuals who need a personal acknowledgement and a great deal of thanks.

Firstly, my best friend Mick Jackson (Jacko) who has always been there and is blessed with the ability to ignore my incessant talking and at times my demanding nature – thanks mate, and long may our journey continue. As a professional angler, I have received the support of individuals and companies alike. Nick Young was the first to show faith in me at Leeda, followed by Pete Chandler at Dynamite. Peter Drennan has been highly influential, providing not just sponsorship but advice and friendship as well. Richard Lee gave me my first big break with Angling Times and for that chance, I cannot thank him enough. Likewise, Steve Partner at the paper also deserves credit for helping with this book as well as the weekly column I write.

Portraying our sport positively has always been important to me and it would not have been possible to have better mentors than John Wilson, Hugh Miles, Bernard Cribbins and Mick Rouse; even a fool would stand a chance with this group at hand!

Next come the fisheries that have been kind enough to allow me to enjoy their hard work, so for every club or syndicate I have ever wet a line with, you have my gratitude. With people like Roy Parsons, Chris Blunt, Len Gurd, Roo Newby, Mick Barnes, Wayne Little, Chris Logsdon, Pete Orchard, Arnold Zwetsloot, Dave Culley and Seth Johnson-Marshall in control, I should have plenty more fishing ahead of me.

Fellow anglers have also provided lots of highlights so thank you Tim Norman, Terry Lampard, Ray Walton, Stuart Morgan, Terry Theobald, Kev Newton, Neil Wayte, Adrian Smith, John Everard, Chris Yates, Basil Hopkins, John Newlands, Des Taylor, Bob Church, Pete Frost, Mark Harrison, Frank Warwick, Gary Barclay, Gary Archer, Lee Johnson, Adrian Eves, Keith Arthur, Keith Wesley, Owen Jones, Paul Harrison, Pete Reading, Richard Patrick, Terry Hearn, Dave Elliot, Simon Evans, Mike Green, Bob Hornegold, Steve Rowley, Michael Buckley, Ken Wheeler, John Rodgers, Raymond Fisher, Colin Gittins, John Claridge, Kevin Green, Tom Bird, Trevor King and Andrew Allsop - plus everyone else who I have fished with.

Once again, Paul and Cliff Moulder at Mpress have excelled themselves in putting this book together, alongside the proof reading and editing team of Terry Doe and Rosie Barham. I couldn't think of a better group of people to work with. The marvellous drawings that follow are due to the skill of artist Gareth Fareham, so thanks Gaz for your time and effort.

To anyone I have missed, trust me when I say 'thank you', because this book wouldn't have been possible without everyone I have met on my journey. Last, but not least, comes my family – Jo, Ryan, Todd and Natalie. Thanks for your love and understanding.

If the rest of my life can be spent by the waterside in good company, then I will die a rich man.

Any second now...

CONTENTS

FOREWORD

Martin Bowler is simply the best angler I have ever known, and I have been fortunate enough to have fished with the best of the best. In the 1950s and 1960s, I served my own angling apprenticeship with the late Peter Stone, I fished with Dick Walker and the Taylor brothers, and with England's first world champion, Bill Lane; all of them the finest anglers of their time. In later years, I was heavily influenced by the leading matchmen of the day, principally Ivan Marks and Kevin Ashurst. More recently, my association with the England team has given me an inside view of the formidable attention to detail paid by our multiple world champions, particularly to rigs, presentation and feeding. It is against this background that I make the bold statement that Bowler is simply the best!

There is no doubt that the very top men in our sport, those few angling geniuses who consistently outfish the rest of us, are blessed with a range of attributes and abilities which sets them apart. They are so steeped in the sport that they can unquestionably 'think like a fish', and often know with remarkable accuracy when, where and how they will feed. They always seem to know exactly what's going on underwater, to have a clear picture in their minds' eye of just how their tackle or a particular rig is behaving, how it's affecting bait presentation, and therefore what options there are for adjustment and improvement.

This transient sport of ours really is ever-changing, and subject to all the variations of season and climate which can so radically alter the location, behaviour and feeding habits of different species. On top of this, because we catch and return them unharmed, fish in general, and big fish in particular, 'wise up' - get educated, so that last season's successful method may no longer be as effective, or may not work at all. Logging, retaining and constantly adjusting to all these variables requires the true expert to have an almost encyclopaedic knowledge and memory.

There is also a little appreciated physical side to top flight angling - not of pure strength, but certainly of endurance, excellent hand to eye coordination, and perhaps most of all, a dynamic energy that allows the expert to apply himself and really work to catch fish, when we mere mortals falter and tire. Martin is blessed with all of these qualities, and although he has made his name as a big fish specialist, he can do anything. Sea, coarse, game, new species in foreign lands, it doesn't matter; he will adopt, or even invent, any new technique, embrace it, polish and refine it in no time at all, and add it to his bank of skills.

Inevitably, all the top experts become involved to some extent in angling journalism. In Martin's case, the demands of a regular weekly column in Angling Times means that he is literally required to catch something decent every week. It is remarkable that he not only manages to do this, but also spices it up for us avid readers with some really spectacular specimen or other on an almost monthly basis. The expert angling writers fall into two distinct categories; those who write for themselves and those who have their books and articles 'ghosted' by professional angling journalists. Fortunately, for us, Martin Bowler is firmly in the first category, writing all his own material and taking virtually all his own photographs. In this beautiful, landscape format book with so many evocative pictures, he tells us a series of angling stories, which are both educational and thoroughly entertaining.

Peter [signature]

INTRODUCTION

The pages in this book go some way to telling my story over the last 30 years, but I do not possess enough of a grasp of the English language to do it justice. I do not say this in a boastful way, as fish caught can be readily documented; it's the capturing of our natural environment that I struggle with, which has provided such wonder for me. Are words ever enough to describe the sky set alight by a sunset or a harsh winter landscape grizzled by snow? These and many more backdrops of the British countryside supply the canvas on which I merely give the occasional brush stroke. Of course, catching the biggest fish is desirable and there was a time when I would have sold my soul to do it, but even then, if not acknowledged, it was the water itself that provided the true beauty.

Like so many others I began this love affair with a net and jam jar, poking and prodding for hours on end in any brook or stream that crossed my path, and I can honestly say that fishing was never more enjoyable than it was then. The wide-eyed innocence of childhood expected a monster to be uncovered with every turn of a stone, and when I moved on to a rod and reel, every bob of the float brought with it the same excitement. This desire to connect with an unseen world was the catalyst for a lifetime's obsession, trying to unlock the secrets that lie beneath the surface.

Early adventures soon grew in both frequency and length, meaning that most of my teenage years were spent on the bankside. That is where this book really begins; the first steps in pursuit of specimen fish and the path that led ultimately to me becoming a professional angler. Never could I have imagined what I would go on to catch, with record fish and enough specimen captures to turn my life story into something from a Boy's Own annual! Wetting a line with the great and the good of angling whose words and pictures left me in awe as a youngster, meeting the Prime Minister to discuss the issues faced by the aquatic world; this all seems a long way from catching my first gudgeon on the Grand Union Canal. Writing a weekly column in the Angling Times, when those same double pages adorned my bedroom wall as a child, will always be the job I treasure most, while appearing on television to help portray our sport to a wider audience even now seems a surreal experience. Best of all, though, each and every time I wet a line I still have an uncontrollable adrenaline rush that flutters the heart and trembles the hands, as if I was still to catch my first fish.

We are all children of this great country and there is a lifetime of adventures on offer waiting to be discovered, if you let them, and I have had more than my fair share. If I close my eyes I can still see that first carp, set against a lush green set of lily pads, as it supped down a piece of crust, or the huge skate that buckled my back as I tried to prise it off the bottom in 600 feet of water, against a backdrop of the Great Glen. Even the disasters I treasure; a huge barbel lost in the floodwaters of the Kennet, or a night at sea when the small boat was tossed around without mercy over white-capped waves.

Here, then, is my story and while I could never write about every fishing trip, I hope I have done enough to express my love of angling.

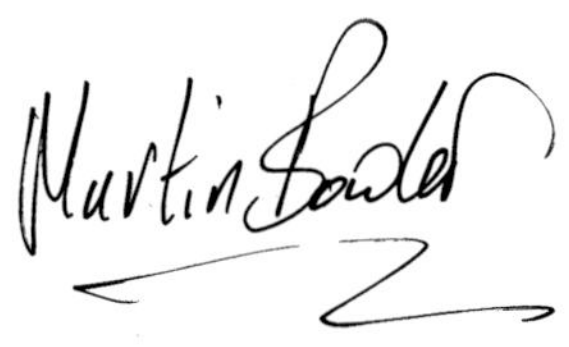

Another adventure awaits.

Camera: Cannon EOS 40D - Shutter Speed: 1/6400 sec - F-Stop: f/8.0 - ISO: 200 - Location: Bedfordshire brick pit.

CHAPTER 01

A GOLDEN DAWN

During the early 1990s, the chain of brick and chalk pits near Bedford looked anything but special at first glance. There was still a rawness to the landscape and the most famous expanse, Elstow, even had a tip situated along one bank. Judging a book by its cover is folly in the world of angling, though, and closer inspection revealed that nature above and below the water was working its magic.

An abundance of wild flowers impregnated the rough terrain giving butterflies and other insect life a perfect home. Closer to the margins, grass snakes were able to feast on the frogs, while their tadpoles happily made the transition between water and air. For me, though, it was the unseen world that captivated the imagination. An incredibly fertile environment, commonplace with newly-created pits, combined with a fast-growing strain of carp, it was not surprising that the words 'Elstow' and 'big mirrors' became inseparable as this news started filtering down the angling grapevine.

For a time a few lucky locals had the sport to themselves and, unsurprisingly, we guarded it under a veil of secrecy. Rapidly growing too were the rudd and pike, two species that would often collide

Bedfordshire's finest.

spectacularly on the tapestry of shallow bars that criss-crossed the 30-acre venue. Huge explosions could be seen as old Esox ripped into a shoal of golden scales, sending them cascading to the bottom. Regrettably, I was still lost to the carp gods when the pike were in their heyday but not, I am happy to report, the rudd. For a few short years, I had arguably the greatest-ever venue for the species at my disposal. Specimens of 2lbs were common in the early 90s but it was in 1995 when I caught a fish over 3lbs that saw the gold rush begin in earnest, and more importantly, a journey through the specimen fishing world which was to shape my life.

On a balmy summer's evening the following year, I arrived to find a favoured swim – The Ramp – free. Given the heat still resonating from the sun and the mill pond surface I guessed that my target could well be in residence, sitting over an old, flooded swim that was now the basis for a plateau. Unfortunately, to reach such an area was not possible with standard floats, so large, loaded wagglers had to be employed. Likewise, a catapult full of maggots stood no chance of reaching the target either, so the use of Horlicks to coagulate the grubs into balls was vital. With preparations complete, I waded out as far as I could before casting two maggots on a size 18 hook to the horizon. Sinking the line, I placed the rod on two rests and began bombarding the float's tip with a ball of maggots every 60 seconds. Holding the rod continuously proved unnecessary given the bold nature of my target once they began feeding.

For the next half-hour, I continued the onslaught until I saw the float slide away without debate. Immediately dropping the 'pult, a sideways strike made the connection and a stalemate occurred momentarily, between bent carbon and an angry fish. Soon though, given the lack of cover, I had gained the upper hand and this resulted in a ruby-finned rudd of 3lbs 2ozs. Greedy to continue the success, another ball of grubs was fired out the moment the fish had kissed the landing net's rim and it was probably less than a minute before the next bite came my way. If purely numbers can judge angling enjoyment, although experience has taught me differently, I was about to hit the jackpot with three rudd over 2lbs and another three over 3lbs to 3lbs 7ozs. It gave me a total of four over the magic mark - all caught within an hour. 'The greatest ever catch' is a title I'm uncomfortable with, mainly because it was not a particularly difficult feat to achieve, but the fishing media did give a true indication of how fortunate I was. Elstow had an amazing population of naïve, giant rudd; I just happened to be in the right place at the right time.

Bars of gold.

A new PB.

Serving my apprenticeship.

Barbel Mecca.

Barbel had also grabbed my post-carp mindset, the Great Ouse being the river that provided me with such an opportunity to tussle with the prince of the river. As yet, Adam's Mill was not on my radar; instead, the prolific stretches of Radwell, Sharnbrook and Felmersham occupied my time. Coming from a carp fishing background it was unsurprising that I brought with me similar tactics, but it was during an all-night session at Bromham when I was able to employ an edge I'd learnt from my former fishing life that proved pivotal. From the moment I arrived and introduced a little hempseed under a far bank raft with a bait dropper, it was obvious that I was sitting on a shoal of a dozen barbel, including fish into double figures.

Eagerly, I cast out a hair-rigged mini-boilie in combination with a bolt set-up and waited for the obligatory rod-wrenching bite. As the sun began to fall from the sky, the barbel began to torment me as they flashed their bronze overcoats in defiance. Occasionally, and through the entire length of darkness, I received savage line bites, which although they indicated the barbel's continued presence, manifested into nothing else. Why couldn't I catch anything? This question puzzled me during the long night-time vigil. To rub salt further into the wound, dawn not only brought with it the sun's colour to the countryside again, but also a view of my adversaries' copper scales twisting and turning over the hempseed I had continued to feed throughout the session.

An 'eureka' moment was required and that's exactly what I had, despite being groggy from sleep deprivation. Every line bite, I concluded, was a spooked fish so why was I legering in a manner I never would have if I'd been carping? A rod erected high in the air with a bowstring line direct to a close range hookbait would be laughable in pursuit of carp, but for some reason it had been deemed entirely acceptable for barbel and river fishing. Like a sheep, I had just accepted this as a correct state of affairs when, in fact, both species find it equally unacceptable. Reeling in, I removed the terminal tackle and slid on a small coffin lead, trapping it six feet up the line with Power Gum stop knots (later substituted for float stops). Connecting the rig and bait back into position below this, I recast the unwieldy outfit into the swim once more, ensuring that the line was kept taut by laying a back lead in a line directly toward me. Now, I hoped, all the line that crossed the gravel run was pinned to the deck, avoiding detection. Within minutes, the answer to the quandary came, with a barbel nearly dragging the rod in. The seven more which then followed only served to show I had at last outwitted the barbel and, more importantly, had an edge which would prove advantageous wherever my adventures took me over the next few years.

Before continuing, I would like to make it quite clear that I am not claiming to have invented this technique for barbel fishing. Sure, I had never witnessed its use before and subsequently wrote about it in monthly magazines, but assuming to be its originator would be presumptuous. No doubt, other people would have worked this edge out and kept 'mum' about it. Claiming to be the first in anything associated with angling is highly questionable.

Ureeka!

Every tactic used has been adapted and refined from the generation before, so if you read an angler claiming to be the first you should, quite rightly, question his level of arrogance. Nevertheless, with my new found method, barbel became far more accommodating, allowing me to push up my personal best to just over 13lbs; a fish caught from the Vauxhall Angling Club controlled, Felmersham stretch. Here, the best swim was the final one in the section, where a cast upstream to the private water above would see the bait land under a near bank bush. This was the only place on the Ouse that I found it possible to catch a quantity of barbel in one sitting. Up to 15 fish in a morning was possible and for a while, I milked this to the full, posting numerous impressive scores. In hindsight though, all I was doing was recapturing the same barbel time and time again, regardless; as with all prolific venues, giving up such a heady cocktail of success can prove difficult. The barbel's, and my, only respite came as the curtain fell on the season for a couple of years.

For a few weeks each spring, all thoughts of angling were put on the back burner as I made my yearly work pilgrimage to the Belgian town of Ypres. Working as a polymer technologist, it was my responsibility to run a team of men, including divers, to repair and install massive floating covers which housed anaerobic digester systems (methane waste converted back into energy) which powered the factories. As much as I've always loved fishing, this was one of the best times of my life, all without a rod and line in close proximity. I was a young man, free of any shackles, who partied and drank a little too much at night while being given responsibility at work! I look back on those six consecutive yearly trips with as much fondness as any angling adventures I have taken part in and, importantly, it gave me a balance to my life.

When I returned toward the back end of April one year in the late 90s, it wasn't long before the lure of late spring drew me once again to the banks of Elstow and its goliath rudd. It was a scene where I was about to experience the pinnacle of my angling for these magnificent creatures. Every year, as winter gave way to warmer weather, the shallow water of a bay fringed with reeds was a magnet to all the species inhabiting the pit. Celebrating a return to milder temperatures, big, grey torsos of mirrors and yellowy flanks of leathers could be seen pushing in and out of the vegetation. For nearly every angler this was enough of a reason to fish here. However, I desired a much smaller sign, equally as special, made up of burnished gold scales and trimmed with blood-red fins. By now this generation of rudd had reached their peak in weight, although numbers had decreased to no more than 40 individuals. Catching them was easy, location on the other hand was an altogether different matter, and frustratingly, more often than not, I would find the swim occupied by a carp angler. Fortunately, I knew many of them well, and often they wouldn't object to me fishing alongside them. I'm sure I was viewed as a little sad, targeting such a diminutive fish compared with their own goals but as far as I was concerned, their lack of vision was a bonus.

When I peered into the reeds from a raised path, I saw what I was looking for; seven fish in total, all sizeable, with a couple of specimens whose proportions were enough to get the pulse racing and heart pounding. First, I needed to be able to wet a line in the swim directly opposite and, given the bivvy erected in it, that could have proved somewhat tricky. Fortunately, a good friend was in residence and despite ridiculing me as a failed carper, he raised no objections to me fishing for the rudd. Mission one completed; on to the next phase - getting them to eat. Spraying maggots was always the answer and to be quite frank switching them into feeding mode was a foregone conclusion, as was hooking one. This had nothing to do with any skill on my part as an angler and all to do with a trait common with the species; naivety combined with a voracious appetite.

Within five minutes, I could see the seven shadows darting around, eagerly devouring each and every grub presented to them from my catapult. It was time to make a cast. A crystal waggler trapped on 3lb line, with bulk shot around its base, was then followed by a 3-foot tail and size 16 hook on which two maggots were impaled.

Action under moonlight.

I cast out and followed it closely with another pouch of maggots fired six feet in front, before reeling the float back into the free offerings. Tense with anticipation, I knew what was about to occur and that only served to increase the adrenaline surge. Directly beneath the waggler, a rudd rose to intercept the hookbait and without the slightest hesitation sucked it in; a moment that was transmitted to me by a sharp dip on the fluorescent orange tip. I struck in response to such an invitation and this, in turn, set the hook home and caused the rudd to shake its head violently.

As the fish surged for the reeds, I needed to make an immediate calculation between a hook pull and line strength. With a prayer that I had made the correct decision, the length of carbon in my hand arced before, thankfully, relenting a little to give me time to crank the reel's handle and gain a few vital turns. The main body of the reeds may have been avoided but I still had to navigate the treacherous individual stems that had grown away from the bed. I knew only too well of their amazing unhooking properties, levering the hook out of a mouth better than any disgorger.

For the next few minutes we played cat and mouse with each other, neither of us sure who would be the victor. Even close to the net, I still knew a loss could easily occur and given the magnitude of a defeat, my disposition remained a nervous one. Shining brightly in the pit's crystal clear water, I could see a rudd that, even by Elstow standards, looked special.

Maybe adrenaline had affected my imagination but it looked the size of a dinner plate and it was definitely a fish I did not want to lose. With every twist and turn, I knew the hook-hold would be strained so I continued to pray that it had found a sound home in the underslung mouth.

Eagerly, and perhaps a little prematurely, I slipped the landing net into the water while increasing pressure on my prize. Up it rose, until the sun was able to magnify its golden overcoat, and the first gulps of fresh air subdued any further urges to test the tackle. With a final turn of the reel handle, it was now my landing net that became illuminated and as I peered inside, there sat not just a rudd but a fish of a lifetime. Gently, I popped out the hook from the corner of its mouth and observed its shape, perfect for supping down flies trapped on the surface film during balmy summer evenings. I then lifted her priceless body and slipped it into a sling for the obligatory ritual of weighing. Without hesitation the 3lb mark was passed and the needle continued to sweep around the dial, reaching the impossible 'four' before slipping back the tiniest of fractions and settling on 3lbs 15oz. I knew that I could travel the whole country and never find another creature like it. Elstow had been more than generous; in fact, I had won the lottery, and still she wasn't finished with her gifts. Two more rudd came my way that afternoon of 3lb 3oz and 3lb 2oz but I'm afraid to say, with the passing of time, I remember little of either. The monster's memory though, will never fade; it burns as brightly as ever.

I feel insincere, given today's nationwide lack of the species, not to recount another tale of the following week when a brace weighing 3lb 5oz and 3lb 11oz fell, and to account for them with no more than a number would be disrespectful to one of nature's finest creations. Once again, The Reeds was the swim in question, but this time I had drawn the shoal into the shallow corner affording me a grandstand view. Now I could watch their movements at close hand and although it provided a spellbinding spectacle, the vision ramped up the pressure and dried the mouth still further. I could literally lower the hookbait under the rod tip, using only the smallest of floats to retain tension rather than for bite indication. Instead, I watched the maggots and by using a simple dodge, I could guarantee not to lose them in a handful of free offerings. The freebies were red, while the hook held two white ones. A take was inevitable and a rudd veered right, straight on to the offerings before it began scooping up each and every one.

In such situations, eye, hand and brain coordination tend to work in slow motion and it's only when the fish fights back that real time resumes. For two more marvellous moments I was happy to play such a game, landing these huge specimens. They were incredible creatures in pristine condition, which had grown huge in a rich, gravel pit environment. On the surface, everything looked rosy at Elstow but even then, I guessed the stock was dwindling rapidly and without any backup rudd coming through, the angling for these specimens was beginning to draw to a close. Strangely, the rudd successfully spawned every season filling the margins with thousands of fry each summer but during the winter, they just vanished, never to appear again.

I guess they simply perished but it was puzzling as to why. On many gravel pits with a range of species, it appears that the first generation are always the ones to thrive the most. Maybe it's because they have the benefit of a virgin, highly fertile environment that diminishes as they grow, or could it be a weakening of the gene pool?

Once in a lifetime.

Early Adams.

With brothers and sisters breeding with each other, perhaps this incest creates a fish unable to cope with the rigours of winter. Whatever the truth, in this Bedfordshire brick pit today, the monsters are just a memory and when they passed away over the couple of years following my success, it reinforced to me that 'making hay while the sun shines' is of paramount importance in successful specimen hunting. A golden era was drawing to a end.

However, as one door began to close another was firmly flung open. The Great Ouse was about to provide a bonanza for perch and barbel anglers. After serving my barbel apprenticeship on various sections of the Ouse, I felt ready to move on to its jewel - the Adam's Mill and Kickles Farm stretches, both of which, over the ensuing years, would well and truly tear up the record books.

An angler named Adrian Busby had tempted a fish of over 15lb the previous season and that was enough to give him victory in the Angler's Mail Specimen Cup. The capture finally saw me buy the correct club cards and maybe, in hindsight, this was prophetic, as 1998/99 would prove to be my year in the very same competition.

Taking a first walk across the cattle bridge that spanned Adams Mill was, I'm afraid to report, not a memory that befits such a legendary water. At little more than a weedy ditch, I found it hard to comprehend that the place had produced huge barbel, or any barbel, come to that, and as I continued my wander around I was convinced that I had been wound up. The high ground of the banks provided a good vantage point for an area of deeper water at the end of a sweeping bend and I stared down, disillusioned, at the gravel bed below. Then a huge glint suddenly lit up the river, convincing me that the sun above had been the cause of the shimmer. I looked up to the sky before re-focusing on the water and this time I saw what was responsible; a barbel and a bloody massive one at that, followed by another, flashing its overcoat at me. 'Ditch? What ditch?' I thought as I rushed back to the car to get my tackle. How shallow we anglers can be when presented with such an opportunity!

Armed, of course, with my back leads and boilies I set about my new found friends with gusto. After a mainly meat, hemp and corn diet, such an offering proved too tempting for not one, but three of the residents who were all amazingly big for the time between 12 and 14lbs. The bond was well and truly formed between me and this marvellous water and over the season I enjoyed many more wonderful days in her company. I had arrived at the perfect time because record-breakers from the Mill were within reach and it was only a matter of time before they made history. The Ouse was out of the doldrums it had experienced in the 1980s and while most of the spotlight fell on its barbel population, another species had found a perfect home in the upper reaches. Like so many times in my career I just happened to be in the right place at the right time.

Happy days.

Camera: Canon EOS 300D - Shutter Speed: 1/60 - F-Stop: f/5.6 - ISO: 100 - Location: The Upper Ouse, Buckinghamshire

CHAPTER 02

PERCH PARADISE

The rise of the Great Ouse as a barbel Mecca had been well documented during the 1990s but another species had slipped under the radar for a while, and it had also reached monstrous proportions. Growing fat on a rich larder of easy food, in splendid isolation, it was missed by all but a few locals and it took a huge slice of good fortune on my behalf to find myself at the forefront of such wonderful fishing.

Frosty.

Dunstable angler, Pete Frost, had run a syndicate on the upper reaches for many years and during the 60s and 70s, it was a prolific venue for large roach and chub. Unfortunately, it didn't last. The building and expanding of Milton Keynes demanded more and more water and with boreholes sunk, the surrounding waterways were drained away, relieving Pete's stretch of its once clear, weed-fronded, fast-flowing characteristics. In its wake, silt suffocated all life and it seemed as if the river had been given the last rites. A drastic step was called for, namely the dredger, and although depth had been restored to the waterway, the other characteristics were never to return. A canal-like environment took its place and anglers deserted Pete's syndicate in their droves. Now the situation had reached a critical point, and without fresh blood, the syndicate would have to be disbanded and the fishing lost forever. Not wanting to see a local venue in such a perilous state, I decided to join more out of friendship than self-interest, unaware that I had made one of the best moves in my angling career. For once, doing the right thing would pay me back tenfold.

Unbeknown to me, an unscrupulous band of entrepreneurs had been introducing the red signal crayfish to the river with a view to harvesting them at a later date. At the time, I believe, a high price was being fetched on the Continent for these crustaceans. Given this, and the now benign waterway, one species had begun to thrive on the protein-rich diet and was able to reach monstrous proportions. Better still, this fact had slipped under the radar of most specimen hunters, which is vital to a successful growth rate, as with all predators. Not, I should add, that I could lay claim to spotting its potential immediately. When I first laid eyes on the stretch, I was unconvinced, proving correct the old adage 'you should never judge a book by its cover'. After paying the joining fee, I forgot about the place for a few months as I had barbel fever and was enjoying myself downstream at Adam's.

The next time our paths crossed was during a late summer Sunday afternoon stroll with my little boy, which saw me wandering down its banks more as an excuse to get out of housework than anything else. Although it was nestled in lovely Buckinghamshire countryside made up of a patchwork quilt of arable and grazing fields, the river itself looked anything but

Never judge a book by its cover.

enigmatic, being almost stagnant in appearance and fishless. For me, it wasn't captivating and I can clearly remember telling my friends that I couldn't ever see myself fishing there. With Mill barbel, I had bigger fish to fry - or so I thought!

It wasn't until September that I returned to the place with a few hours at my disposal to investigate a little further. Rumours in the local tackle shop centred around the capture of a 4lb perch to a long-standing member, which due to my nature was, at best, viewed with a high degree of scepticism, but not enough to prevent me from reaching into my stock of lobworms and making the decision to go the following Saturday morning.

I arrived at 5am; the river steamed and low mist hung in clusters across the fields, its dew saturating the grass in testimony to the onset of autumn, a traditional time to catch my quarry. The dawn chorus had only just commenced when I began the long walk to the area that local intelligence had suggested I visit. Tackle, I'd been advised, should be kept to a minimum because to reach my destination required a good degree of sweating and worn shoe leather!

Not once during this stroll did I contemplate catching much; in fact 4ozs was more likely than 4lbs! Still, I was outside and I hoped the fresh air would clear a heavy head caused from a little too much fun the previous evening. With each deep breath, I could feel myself coming to, an all too common feeling from my younger days.

At last, the seemingly never-ending walk came to a conclusion and it wasn't just an end to the physical effort that I was pleased about, but also reaching safety from a rather angry bull that had taken an instant dislike to me. With nothing more than a gut instinct to go by, I pitched myself up on a deep bend with a fallen tree offering a snaggy sanctuary; its roots penetrating the surface and reaching down to the bottom. If the text books were to be believed then here in the gloom would sit a shoal of stripeys, hidden until the last moment by the camouflage afforded in the branches and waiting to ambush any poor soul who dared to pass by.

The fish received little or no pressure so tackle was an uncomplicated affair made up of an Avon rod and 4lb line fished directly through to a size 6 hook. For casting weight, a single swan shot was pinched on the line, while a large, juicy lobworm was impaled through its saddle, giving a writhing offering scented heavily with pungent amino acids. Flicking it out over the far bank, I prepared to watch the slack line between rod tip and water for any indication, dispensing for the need of a quiver tip. Were the stories true or, as is common in angling, was it a figment of an over-enthusiastic imagination? The answer came when a twitch grew into a slow but certain draw on the mono, forcing me to respond with a strike that met pleasingly with success as a decent fish tried its best to tangle me in the branches. After a short but frantic battle, I took control and though its proportions of 2lbs 14ozs may seem unremarkable today, it was the catalyst for a quest for giant perch that would surpass all my dreams.

Tiger stripes.

Perch paradise.

In many ways, this was the most important fish I ever caught from the Ouse. Suddenly, the place was transformed from a lifeless ditch to a perch paradise, proving how fickle I am; especially given my first impressions of Adam's Mill, as well! A couple more two-pounders were to come my way that fateful morning, and as I made my way home, all thought was of what else may be lurking in the shadows. Was the 4lb fish true, after all? I just had to find out and the best part was it would be a voyage into the unknown as the pages of the Ouse perch story were still to be written.

Unsurprisingly, I became a regular visitor for the remainder of the season and during that campaign I did tempt a few more fish to 3lb-plus but as the cooler weather arrived, so my catches dwindled and, in hindsight, swim selection and the hours I fished were the main reasons behind this failure to tempt any bigger specimens. Following considered opinion, I arrived at dawn, when the light levels were low, but this is, of course, the coldest part of the day in winter. I should have concentrated my efforts at dusk in the deeper water when the light conditions were favourable and the water temperature was at its highest point. This was a lesson that would be learned eventually, but I continued to potter away for now, albeit a little unproductively. However, the season did end with proof that true leviathans existed. Another member of the syndicate landed a magnificent 4lb 3oz specimen, which, to someone like me who had never witnessed such a beast, was truly breathtaking. Somewhere very special had been found and I couldn't wait to return although, once again, the 14th of March had beaten me to it for a while.

Eager to catch my own giant perch, I counted off the days until the start of the new season which, sadly, didn't arrive until July; a month after the traditional June 16th. The hay in the fields had to be cut before I found myself heading for the same deep bend I had fished on the first visit. This time my mindset was completely different and demonstrated by the brisk pace I made down the riverbank. Could I tempt a 4lb fish myself this season? I was about to find out.

Flicking out a worm, I concentrated on the line hanging from the rod tip, just as I had done the previous year, the lack of tension testimony to the

Come what may.

minimal amount of flow. It fell completely slack as touchdown on to the bottom occurred; immediately, it stabbed once and then re-tightened smoothly in a delightful manner normally reserved for Mr Crabtree. With a sideways strike, I made a connection to the perpetrator of these events, causing it to make a surge for the fallen tree in a series of heavy lunges. I refused to give line and although the tackle strained it didn't fail, and the perch boiled on the surface before flicking its blood-red tail in defiance.

I was left in no doubt as to what was at stake now, and this only served to make the situation even more fraught. Up she came again, this time showing an angry, erect dorsal fin that cut across the surface in front of me, before making another wild lunge for some near bank reeds, which forced me to thrust the rod forward. Fortunately, this worked and the fish's trickery was to no avail, then with a final heave, thankfully, I bundled the beast into the net and let out a sigh of relief. Boy, that was exciting!

It looked so big it didn't seem possible that it was the same species I had caught as a young lad on the canal, but this one had stripes more suited to a tiger, and at a weight of 4lbs 3ozs, I had indeed caught a super-sized specimen. I now knew that Richard Walker was right when he described the species as the 'largest of all fish.' I placed the monster safely into a carp sack, as the day was still young, and readied myself to make a second cast after I had calmed down enough to stop shaking.

The junction.

Once again, it was just seconds before the worm was snatched, only this time, my late reactions almost saw the rod wrenched in. The culprit, a fish of 3lbs 14ozs, was closely followed by two more specimens of 3lbs 10ozs and 3lbs 2ozs. By now my head was well and truly spinning.

Then, to add to this amazing generosity, the river decided to give me a fifth and final bite. In a trip where nothing could go wrong, the perch was on to a loser the moment it became hooked and despite its valiant efforts to reach every snag it was soon beaten, once again, displaying a huge length and girth wrapped in a thousand shimmering scales. One four-pounder was more than enough but I had now become the proud captor of a second; this fish weighing 4lbs 2ozs. The floodgates had well and truly opened on catching enormous perch, not only for that day but the next few years. Later, I nearly flew home. The smile stayed on my face for hours and it wouldn't be the last time. I felt so ecstatic.

As crazy as it sounds, three-pounders became commonplace and with every trip there was a distinct

possibility of a 'four' which outlines the amazing sport, given that only two years before such a fish was impossible for me to comprehend. The onset of the second winter also brought with it a better approach than before, my arrival rarely ever being earlier than midday.

While a cool dawn was beneficial during summer, falling water temperatures reversed this situation so the best time to angle was when the sun had been given a chance to do its warming best.

A bite was never forthcoming until 3pm and more likely than not, at dusk. I lost count of the number of times I sat fishless for a few hours, only to catch a hatful in the final minutes of daylight as the beta-light flickered and the rod bent. They had been sitting still as stone in the swim all along, uninterested in any offering until the trigger suddenly came as the day faded away and an urge to feed arrived.

The only time the perch didn't follow this rule was in coloured water and then the middle of the day proved the prime time. I can only surmise that the light levels crucial to the feeding response acted in reverse. With the sun's rays peaking during lunchtime, they penetrated the colour enough to remind a perch of its normal dusk feeding spell. In this situation, the catch rate began to reduce as the afternoon wore on, with a reduction in visibility more akin to the arrival of night-time.

Armed with this information, and with the end of the season fast approaching, the chances of a super-sized specimen laden with spawn looked a good possibility. It was, therefore, hardly a surprise when I found myself pitched up in the favourite bend swim on a mild, March afternoon, eager to make the most of the final days.

Legering tactics had been replaced by a loafer float lying over-depth in a stret-pegging fashion, combined with a 20-foot float rod to maximise control, and 5lb line. A single, double swan shot sat on the deck while a large bow was allowed to form between this and the loafer until it lay flat. If a perch did pick up my lobworm hookbait, no resistance would be felt, with the float slowly cocking as the signal to strike.

The biggest of all fish.

Bite time.

Beyond belief.

This method had proved superior to quiver tipping and by mounting an adaptor for a beta-light on the end of the float, I could easily fish right up to the last minute of dusk, which was vital, as I've already explained; not that such patience was going to be needed on this occasion. I had only just fed the swim with a dozen broken worms, when the loafer suddenly stood to attention before slowly vanishing from view, leaving a momentary, wonderful air of anticipation. I struck, the spell was broken and replaced by a rod-arching connection, and then the long length of carbon in my hands bucked continuously.

Not, though, with a series of head shakes characteristic of a perch but with a heavy, ponderous motion. Pike had proved a problem in the past and I suspected that one had again snaffled the bait, as they adore lobworms.

With this in mind, the approach I used was a little bolder than usual, bullying the fish without fear of breakage or hook pull. A final heave saw the fish hit the surface and it was at this point that a wonderful metamorphosis took place. A polka dot flank was no longer there, instead it was replaced by big, bold stripes highlighting an enormous body which was much bigger than any other I had battled with in the past, even those specimens of early season. Understandably, my mindset changed somewhat at this point and I allowed the perch to sink from view once again. A fight that should have been all but over if I had been brave enough, continued for a few more minutes, the fish angrily trying to bury itself under the near bank vegetation, until at last it reappeared and gulped in a mixture of air and water, killing any more plans to smash the tackle.

Gently, the net was shipped out to take possession of my prize - and what a prize! I literally had to blink to ensure I wasn't dreaming. With the net safely staked out, I went to fetch a fellow angler as a witness and he, like me, was blown away by its proportions. Her belly was, of course, slightly bloated given the time of year, but that wasn't the sole reason for her size. The width and length were equally as impressive, presenting a creature that appeared more mythical than even the wildest of dreams.

I laid her in a damp weigh sling and we watched the dial tumble round before bouncing either side of the 5lb mark. With a wind blowing across us, an accurate reading wasn't possible, so with such an important fish we decided to erect a brolly to carry out the procedure again. The outcome was a 4lbs 14ozs specimen and as I posed for pictures, I could never envisage holding a bigger perch again. There was no doubt in my mind that crayfish, with their protein-rich flesh, had been responsible for the creation of this Mecca, proving that Mother Nature has amazing resilience to diversify and flourish, no matter how hard we try to cock it up!

More 'fours' were to fall my way even before that season ended and over the next few years, despite other adventures grabbing my attention, it was hard not to succumb to the lure of such amazing sport the like of which, even then, I knew I would never experience again. Time after time, magazine column inches were filled with incredible perch from this place. I felt that the river owed me nothing and I had reached the pinnacle – how could it get better? The Ouse, though, has a habit of trumping itself but those tales were still to be lived.

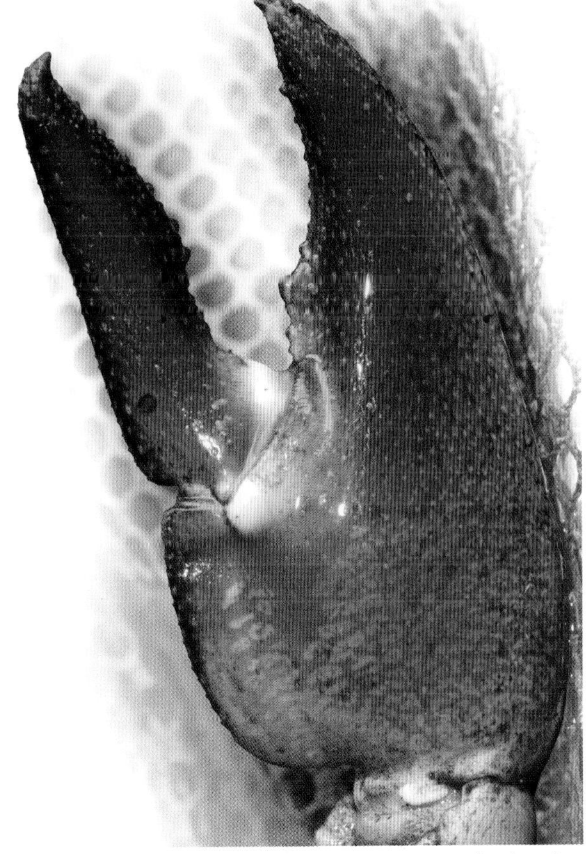

An alien invasion.

Camera: Canon EOS 40D - Shutter Speed: 1/250 sec - F-Stop: f/8.0 - ISO: 200 - Location: Oxfordshire gravel pit.

CHAPTER 03

SEASONAL STRUGGLES

I would class myself as an all-round angler, employing a range of tactics to tempt a variety of species throughout the year. By adjusting to the seasonal changes, there is rarely a time when a fish can't be tempted, be it a carp off the surface on a hot summer's day, a barbel in a raging flood, or a dace at dusk after a bitterly cold afternoon. It's these constant adjustments that make my angling so interesting; every trip is an exciting, new adventure.

Tench time.

Learning to become a competent all-rounder is a long apprenticeship which, dare I say it, is far more complex than that of a carp angler or specimen-hunter. There is a range of fish to study and a huge list of methods and tactics to master. Combine this with an endless amount of variables, be it weather conditions or venues to compute, and you begin to see the challenge. Personally, it's taken 30 years to come to the point of graduation and even now I regularly regress, which I guess will continue for as long as I wet a line. There is no shortcut for replacing time on the bank and whether that is successful time or not, it should be looked on as part of the learning curve. Without my own personal trials and tribulations of trying to understand nature's lessons I wouldn't be the angler I am today.

In 1998, I took my first tentative step toward trying to catch a double-figure tench and my attention was drawn to the magnificent Sywell Country Park in Northamptonshire. In hindsight, the chances of such a fish from the venue during this time was almost impossible, but without this knowledge I prepared excitedly for the new season, hoping to do battle with a species that had enthralled me as a child. I can still remember clearly the first time our paths crossed on a stormy lake in Kent. An electrical storm raged in the sky above as my uncle, elder brother and I sought refuge under just one 45-inch brolly. Our endeavours didn't go unrewarded, though. At dawn, two soaked and bedraggled boys were the proud captors of *Tinca tinca* and we had been given a memory that remains more vivid than any tench tale that has followed.

Back to Sywell; I avoided the first week of the season purposely, as tales of running for swims at dawn filled me with horror, and still does. To be fair, by the time I arrived, and for all the subsequent sessions, I very rarely saw any other anglers in the car park which I guess is one of the benefits of a 3am alarm call! At this time, there were two hurdles to overcome if success was to be ensured; namely the ban on night fishing and the ban on legering. The first proved no issue whatsoever and in fact, experience has taught me that darkness is a waste of time for the species. Float fishing at range was a different matter altogether and one I needed to brush up on. So without any tackle I decided to go on a reconnaissance mission to find out how anglers were not only managing to fish two floats at distance, but also keeping their baits stable on the bottom and maintaining concentration for long spells of time.

At this stage in my career, I was a little naïve but it still came as a shock to find out that 99 per cent of the anglers fishing there were legering! Sure, they had a float on their line but this was a token gesture. Yes, strings of swan shot replaced bombs, but they still gave enough resistance to make a bolt rig work. I really couldn't understand the purpose of a legering ban with this carry-on, especially as some of the rigs were even more lethal to the tench. A row of swan shot bitten hard onto wire trace between two swivels is a death rig if ever I saw one, and this seemed to be a common practice. As I left Sywell that day, I began to formulate my own rig that would allow for self-hooking but remain safe should I get lucky. A trifle ruthless, I admit, but it seemed a case of 'when in Rome…'

Spring.

Summer.

So, it was on a gorgeous, late June morning when I arrived back at the lake to make a closer acquaintance with its inhabitants. Pigeons cooed and a noisy woodpecker did his best to get a headache, banging against an oak tree. The wind was negligible and the day, despite still being early, was already humid, with a fly hatch skipping across the smooth surface. Being an anti-social angler, I had earmarked a spot down the south arm on the far bank, which was previously identified as an area that regularly produced fish and due to the long walk involved it received little attention. Even with the minimum of tackle, I felt as if I was on the brink of a heart attack by the time I collapsed in the long grass, with burning lungs and sore feet. However, the rolling of green shapes accompanied by thunderous tail slaps soon restored my energy levels with a shot of adrenaline. The bay below was alive with fizzing bubbles and I felt justified in putting my body through the agony of such a long hike. It was now time to put the plan I had formulated into action.

Avon-style rods with 1lb 4oz test curves were combined with 8lb line that I hoped would combat the weed that infested Sywell, and prevent losses. Next, on to the main line came a stop-knot that I had positioned two feet over-depth to hold a large and heavy carp-style waggler in place. This not only provided a bite indicator but also enabled me to cast vast distances if required. Two float stops then came into play. The first separated the float's fragile body from the bulk shot (preventing it from being smashed), with the second employed behind the shot to create a bolt rig. Instead of pinching the weights onto the line, I superglued three swans shots onto a length of tubing which I then slid down the mono and semi-fixed at one end, while butting up against the hooklength swivel at the other. This creation also had the bonus of being able to carry a ball of tacky groundbait around it, in effect, giving me the opportunity of fishing a Method feeder. A stretching of the rules it might have been, but I would like to think of it as being innovative! All that was then left to connect was six inches of 10lb Double Strength line and a size 10 hook that had a small sliver of cork fixed to a mono hair, providing the base for the gluing-on of four maggots.

Next, a clear area needed to be located and by casting around, I managed to find a suitable spot at 30 yards. This was marked on the main line with pole elastic, so I could fish very accurately during the session. Once the two rods were out in position, I began to wield the spod, an instrument that I have always found favour with since my early carp fishing days on Elstow, the birthplace of this contraption. I duly put down a bed of hempseed and maggots that would provide, I hoped, a banquet for any tench. Fourteen of the species was to be my reward that day, giving me confidence in the method I had formulated. I was up and running. This catch was to be the prelude to some marvellous fishing over the next few months, culminating with a fish of 9lb 3oz. Sywell had given me that all-important confidence factor and after she had graciously allowed me to plunder her rich waters, I felt ready to achieve the specimen hunting challenge of catching a double-figure tench.

Sensational Sywell.

Autumn.

The pursuit of such a large fish had led me to a gravel pit in the famous Colne Valley where, if reports were to be believed, tench to a monstrous 12lb had been recorded. It is wise, though, not to believe everything you are told - especially when carp anglers are telling you these tales! They might be anal when it comes to weighing their favoured species, but they seem incapable of doing the same with bream and tench. I am sure guesswork replaces any use of scales when these creatures are returned dismissively to the water, cursed for stealing the bait. Anyhow, the water in question showed enough promise to require serious investigation and it was a lovely place to visit, no matter what the reality. The harsh landscape, after gravel extraction for the M25 many years previously, had been replaced by mature trees and birdsong, a testimony to the benefits that anglers bring to the natural world.

Gravel bars that were illuminated on sunny days rose to just beneath the surface, indicating the highways followed by the fish. The tops were unappealing, made up of large, coarse lumps of flint and stone, and the sides were equally unwelcoming, being so steep that they prevented a lead from getting a grip before sliding away into dense weed. No, it was where the bars ended that provided the best substrate; fine gravel that slipped slowly into deeper water.

Action from session one confirmed not just this fact, but also the benefits of using particles over the more traditional groundbait approach. In fact, as already mentioned, I have never been a fan of a method that sees mounds of feed scattered through the swim and have always preferred a nice, even carpet produced by using a spod. The terminal tackle also seemed to be working. I chose to use a Method feeder, short, mono hooklength and size 12 hook combined with three artificial casters, although I have to admit regular mishaps with bent hooks during this period. At this point the perfect model for the tactic had yet to be created, but more of that later. Tench to just under 8lb came my way but double-figure carp proved to be a nightmare, angrily ransacking the area. They had escaped from a netted-off section of the lake when someone forgot that the bottom isn't always flat in a gravel pit! Anyway, the upshot was that any feeding tench would quickly be bullied off and, worse still, I had no idea how I could resolve the situation. This scenario continued throughout the next session but at least I was getting bites.

Trip number three was to be a two-day affair and coincided with early June. A strong south-westerly was blowing in rain clouds that scuttled across the sky in a foreboding manner. Predictably, I made my way to the windward bank to erect base camp before everything got sodden and was rewarded for this decision by the sight of a big, green back rolling 40 yards out. A marker float identified the area as the end of a bar, sloping down from four to eight feet, and it was mercifully free of weed. Thirty spodfuls of feed containing hemp, pellets and casters soon touched down where the fish had shown, quickly followed by a couple of rigs.

Breaking the barrier.

Clipping on indicators was the next task but I never got to complete this exercise before the alarm began to warble. Unfortunately, it was a carp once again, the first of which was tolerable but not the 11 that followed. By 7am the next morning, I'd had enough and was less than impressed when the alarm sounded again. Unconcerned whether I won or lost the battle, I tried to wrench it to the surface as quickly as possible which, given the alarming curve in the rod, I achieved with some haste, but my mindset changed in an instant. Where I had expected to catch sight of the scattered scales of a mirror, instead I saw a huge, great, green flank and bulging yellow underbelly. My mood suddenly changed and the carefree attitude was replaced with complete focus. Back-winding was suddenly the order of the day and I did my very best not to lose it, reducing the tension and taking my time. Fortune was on my side, the tench soon fell into the landing net mesh, and my goal had been realised. A double had become a reality at 10lb 3oz, its impressive proportions trapped inside a shimmering, emerald overcoat. More importantly, it was another step taken on the road to becoming a competent all-rounder but not all the lessons that needed to be learned could be done with the sun on my back – winter also needed to be tamed.

A big pike in Bedfordshire, even today, is a rare creature and in the 1990s, when I wanted to catch such a fish, my options were very limited indeed. I had squandered my best chance when Elstow produced several 25lb-plus specimens but, blinkered by carp, I watched on and never partook, foolishly waiting for another mirror when the real rarity tore into the rudd shoals in front of me. As in most counties, cormorants had already taken their toll on the chain of brick pits that cut through the spine of the county, leaving no baitfish and in turn, fewer pike. I was pleased then, to hear news of an upper-20 being tempted from a venue called Airman Pit, near Shefford. This reed-fringed lake of only a few acres was more famous for its carp and that suited me fine, as the minimum amount of pressure on a predator is of paramount importance to ensure its survival. The first couple of trips served not only to acquaint myself with the venue but also to confirm the pike's presence. More tall stories get told about this species than any other and going off on a wild goose chase is an easy thing to do. Luckily, in this case, after grilling witnesses for information, the story of the big fish did seem to have some credence so the hunt was well and truly on.

January had been a particularly cold month and most sensible people would have stayed at home, but common sense and anglers rarely go together. So despite temperatures which barely rose above zero even at lunchtime, I loaded up my Mk2 Escort and headed off to the pit. The atmosphere was oppressive and greyness shrouded the water, while a cruel wind bit through my thermals as it blasted in off the east coast. However uncomfortable this made me feel, it acted as a blessing too; the acreage that took the brunt remained unfrozen, the rest was locked under an inch of ice. Without further ado, I cast out a smelt and a mackerel, more in hope than expectation, and then huddled behind a brolly hoping against hope that something else was awake.

Unsurprisingly, the afternoon passed by quietly and I really should have beaten a retreat to a warm fire and brought an end to a testing session, but through a combination of madness and keenness, I soldiered on anyway, and decided to stay another hour into dark, which once again proved far from productive. At last, I admitted defeat but still I followed a habit of mine by packing up the alarms before the rods. While addressing the outfit with the smelt on, I caught the main line on the Optonic's ear, dragging the bait a few feet across the bottom, which seemed insignificant but was the trigger for an attack. In the 30 seconds it took me to pick up the rod, a vast set of jaws had taken ownership of the smelt and didn't want to give it back.

As I wound in, I became convinced that I had snagged a weed bed, as it seemed like a dead weight was hanging on the end. I started to gain line until, to my surprise, it hit a surface obstruction ten yards out which forced a halt to proceedings. Due to the wind dropping at dusk, ice had begun to take a grip on the rest of the lake and this was now the obstacle that wouldn't budge. My problems were about to become much worse. The weed exploded in anger as it morphed into a pike and the surprise left me helpless. Within seconds, line had been stripped from my reel and the fish dived under the ice sheet. Confused as to what was going on, I panicked, put on the head torch and watched a big fish cruise by just feet away, but blocked from my net by the icy tomb.

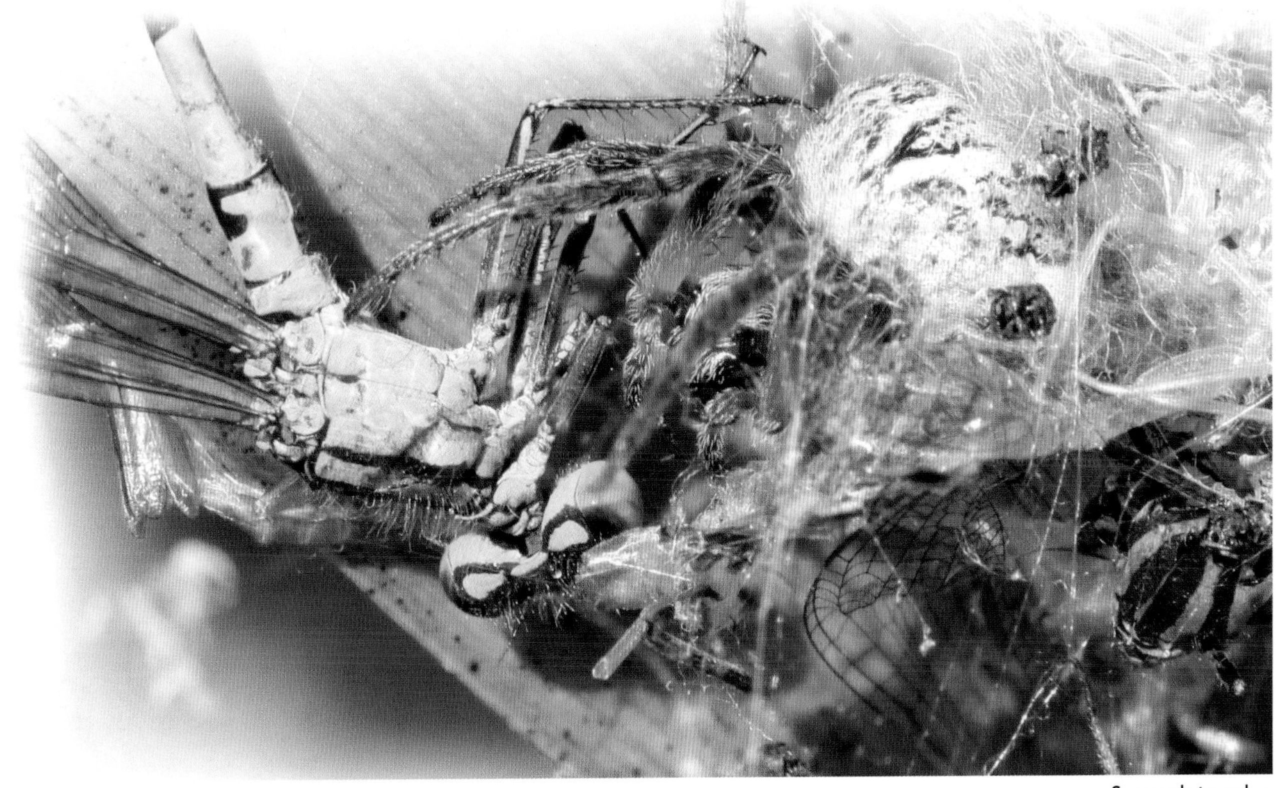

Seasonal struggles.

Winter.

All the time, the main line was still entering the lake some distance away. Madly, I spun the net around and began smashing the handle against the ice trying to fracture it, which I can assure you wasn't done in a controlled manner! With the rod dropped beside me, I used both hands to wield the net handle with even more force, breaking away a tiny chunk at a time. Five minutes of demented behaviour followed, and after throwing rocks in too, I finally cleared a path and only then could I begin to consider regaining line; but would the pike still be on the end? Amazingly, it had stayed sulking under my feet and such was the shock of being caught that it just simply came to the surface and fell into the net. At 26lb 4oz, she was a little smaller than I had hoped for but was a new personal best nevertheless, and proof that a persistent angler can always tame the season.

Living as I did at the time on the eastern side of the country, grayling were a very rare commodity and I hadn't even seen one, let alone caught my own 'lady of the stream'. That was until a friend, Pete Reading, invited me to enjoy the delights of the Dorset countryside. Being an arctic species, these fish are ideal to target in the coldest of conditions and as long as the river runs clear, they are usually a viable target. So it was, that in February 1999 I headed to the Frome where I was about to learn that a willingness to travel is of paramount importance to catching when winter takes a grip.

I was met with a river that was flowing at the kind of pace I wasn't used to on home venues like the Ouse, and there was no place here for either stick floats or wagglers. Taking advice from Peter, I used a 7AAA Avon-style float to trot with and, for once, my centrepin seemed essential. Under guidance, I was led to a run that fed into a deep hole on the outside of a bend. Here, I was told, sat the quarry; all I needed to do was to feed a constant stream of maggots and success would follow. It sounded straightforward but in this alien environment, I wasn't expecting too much.

I can take little credit for what happened next but over the years I've come to learn that it's better to be a lucky angler than a good one. Third trot down, the float no longer remained in contact with the surface and sank from view. Naturally, I struck, only to become overawed by a force trying to break the line. I had been well versed in the grayling's fighting qualities but this was another matter altogether. Had I hooked a double-figure salmon? It might sound like a daft question now but at the time it was the only logical conclusion I could draw given the extreme bend in my float rod. On my local patch, only a barbel could exert that kind of pressure.

Ice breaker.

Beginner's luck.

Rarer than a Dodo.

Perplexed, I did what I could for a full 15 minutes but failed to make any headway and not once did I feel like I was close to overcoming the fish or the flow! Convinced by now that a grayling couldn't possibly be the culprit, I went for broke, straining the 2lb 8oz line beyond all reasonable limits until it whined in the wind. With gritted teeth and a buckled rod, something began to give and at last, a shape started to manifest itself. The gunmetal grey may have turned black and the dorsal fin was no longer like a peacock's tail but it was beyond question a grayling – and an enormous one at that. Now I just had to pray my tiny size 18 hook would hold firm. Fortunately, for the next few minutes my naïvety put paid to any concerns of losing it at the last minute. At that point, I was blissfully unaware that grayling, of all species, truly are the Houdini of fish. A good dollop of luck was with me on that day and the net at last ended the duel. At the time, unappreciative of its proportions, I was just grateful to have caught a grayling but the scales reading 3lb 5oz sobered me up quickly. I had, in fact, landed a colossal fish. It had been a fortunate episode, of that there was no doubt, but it did prove to me that putting myself in the right place at the right time was key to catching - and for my next challenge this really was vital.

Returning to the Great Ouse and milder conditions, I had no reason to expect any more favours from the river given the string of big barbel and perch that she had blessed me with that season, so I was really pushing my luck when I strolled along the banks of Adam's Mill wanting to catch a 2lb roach. There was probably as much chance of achieving this as there was of seeing a dodo! I had spotted half-a-dozen big fish under the cattle bridge during the summer, though, so I admit my decision wasn't based entirely on blind faith. What I needed was a warm, coloured river - in fact perfect barbel conditions – and only now, when all my targets had been achieved with this species for the season, was I prepared to go in search of silver.

A slack had been formed along the nearside of the bridge wall, which on its reconnection with the flow created a crease and here, I surmised, would be the ideal place to cast my maggot feeder. If I had got my calculation correct, the double maggot to a size 16 hook would be intercepted in this zone as the small roach shoal avoided the full rage of the river. Pulsing to the rhythm of the flow, the quiver tip bounced under tension and I began my mission, re-casting with fresh feed every 40 minutes. I received no bites for two hours and that was strangely pleasing because this showed that the chub were unwilling to feed given the coloured water and this would give time for the more timid roach to gain confidence. So when, at last, the tip began to jag with impatience, I suspected who the culprit would be – something that was confirmed by the continuous head-shaking that resonated up the rod.

The fight was unspectacular but nonetheless nerve-jangling, especially when the coffee-stained river started to shine with a thousand silver scales, before a roach flank lay before me, twisting and turning in the flow. This, I assumed, was the only opportunity I would ever have of catching such a creature from the Ouse and I didn't want to throw it away. Ever so gently, I began the gut-wrenching task of increasing the pressure, while straining all the time to reach it with the landing net. It seemed to take an eternity, but patience told as the head, then body, and finally tail, fell over the rim. At 2lb 10oz it completed an amazing period that saw me awarded with the Angler's Mail Specimen Cup. During that season, I had beaten off some of the country's finest anglers to claim the prize but I knew there was still plenty to learn and over a decade later I still feel the same.

In nature's grip.

Camera: Canon EOS 300D - Shutter Speed: 1/60 sec - F-Stop: f/4.5 - ISO: 100 - Location: River Marden

CHAPTER 04

ON THE DROP

During the hot, still, lazy days of summer, enticing a fish to feed can be a tricky affair but one bait above all others exhibits a magical property when it comes to inducing a bite during such conditions – maggots. These tiny grubs can produce a response when the best, designer-made super-baits fail to register even a sideways glance. Why? Well, unlike any paste, pellet, or boilies, it is alive and I believe this signal is too strong to ignore - especially when amplified by the introduction of vast quantities.

You see, the key to awakening any fish from its siesta is a continuous bombardment of grubs, and once your quarry switches on to this food source, catching them really is child's play. The tactic is equally at home on rivers and stillwaters and over the years has accounted for some memorable trips when I'm sure any other approach would have failed.

The Hampshire Avon provides perfect, summer maggot conditions - it runs crystal clear and has a hungry population of chub. Catching this species from the river had never been an issue with over a dozen in a day possible, but despite the numbers I'd banked, a real specimen had eluded me.

I was woken from my slumber by the shrill scream of my alarm clock at an ungodly time but within half-an-hour I was making my way across Wiltshire. Passing the patchwork quilt of fields that are stitched together by the primrose-laced hedgerows, which make up Salisbury Plain, I drove by the Bronze Age creation of Stonehenge and into the neighbouring county of Hampshire.

By the time I had arrived outside the tackle shop in Ringwood, and completed my voyage through the West Country, the morning cloak of mist had been all but burnt off and given way to a beautiful blue sky – perfect spraying weather! With the grubs purchased and safely stashed in the van, I was on the road once more, making the short, five-minute journey to the majestic river. Eagerly, I took my first look at its condition. It was crystal clear, with lush green streamer weed wafting in the flow, while the sun danced and sparkled across its width. A coot then straddled the vegetation and tiny dace pimpled the surface, eager to sample the fly hatch. It provided the most idyllic and tempting of locations and I needed no excuse to wet a line.

Unloading the tackle, I began rigging up my rod in the car park. A strong 13-foot float rod was vital for landing the chub that inhabited the fast-flowing waters of the Avon and I combined it with a stout main line of 3.2lb that had been sprayed with a line floatant. This was vital because it would allow me greater control over the float, the spray preventing the line from being dragged below the surface film. To start the session, I opted for a bottom end only model, a 2.5g Puddle Chucker to be exact, with the bulk of the shot around the base. This left a series of small No 8 droppers to create a natural fall of the bait through the water column. The tail was 4 feet long, with a 2lb 12oz bottom to a stout size 20 barbless hook, removing, I hoped, any suspicion on behalf of the chub. The tackle may have seemed light, but the key is balance and if your outfit adheres to this principle then it's amazing what you can land, even in the weediest of waters.

With everything ready, it was now just a case of grabbing the bait, a few bits and pieces and the Polaroids, before heading off in an attempt to find my quarry's lair. One hundred yards upriver I found a lovely, clear run down the nearside bank, the weeds on either flank providing cover to any chub in residence. Although no fish were visible, I felt certain they wouldn't be far away and that a constant trickle of maggots would draw them from their hiding place. Fifteen minutes later and the feed had indeed begun to work its magic, gradually stirring up interest from under the canopy. Appearing from nowhere, two chub then came flying upriver with their large white mouths working overtime, greedily devouring every maggot as if they had lost their minds. The moment chub start to behave in this manner is not the time to cast out though. By constant feeding for another half-hour, I knew I would have the whole shoal under my feet going wild as they threw caution to the wind. Then, and only then, would it be possible to pick out the biggest fish.

Sitting on your hands while this process unfolds is a testing task, but it was to prove worthwhile. Half-a-dozen chub were going absolutely mad, 'sharking' on each pouchful of grubs in a manner that indicated a fear that they wouldn't get a share of the food. There was even a barbel rising off the bottom to intercept them, such was the commotion going on. Sitting at the tail of this frenzy, though, was a big, dark brute of a fish that even now hung off the main shoal and remained feeding in a rather cautious manner.

A sport for summer.

Chub chasing.

Fooling him would be more by luck than judgement. The time had come to cast and the secret here was to feed a handful of maggots at the same time. It meant my bait went down inside a group of free offerings and prevented individual inspection of the grubs. As I flicked the rig out, I held back momentarily, straightening out the hooklength, ensuring that it wafted off downriver in front of the float. Keeping control, I allowed my maggot to enter the swarm of chub before flicking the rod tip gently so that I forced the bait up in the water and avoided the attention of the smaller fish. It was bang on line for the biggest specimen - then suddenly it was gone, engulfed by a huge pair of white lips. A strike drove the hook home, instantaneously alerting him to the danger, and he took off looking for cover and the bed of streamer weed.

"No, you don't," I muttered, applying full side strain and clamping down hard. This wily old fish knew the game well and decided to switch tactics, charging upstream and appearing under my feet in what might have appeared to be a silly move. There was method in his madness though, and relentlessly, he bored under the reed bed searching for a weakness. For a couple of minutes I was convinced my line was going to part at any moment – the creature's strength was incredible and unforgiving. I could only hope the mono would resist the abrasion of the stems and remain intact. Straining the rod well beyond its comfort zone, at last, I began to make headway and each time I forced the chub to gulp down a mouthful of air its energy slowly sapped away. Back up to the surface came the chainmail-clad brute, its white, rubbery lips connected to me by a tiny piece of metal. The fast flow of the river probed at this most tenuous of links but it wasn't to be found wanting and the chub's path continued toward my waiting net, a frantic swish of the mesh sealing its fate.

When I parted the folds, I took stock of the situation, trying to calm down the nerves which are commonplace for me after such an encounter. Suitably recovered, the moment of truth with the scales came and at 6lb 11oz the Avon had given me a big chub at last. Then all too soon, I paddled into the cool margins to release him, taking care that he regained his energy in an area of slack water. After the time I had invested in his capture, such a short connection would seem mad to any non-angler but for me a kick of the tail as a fish melts back into its natural environment always provides the most joy and as I clambered back on to dry land there was nowhere I'd have rather been.

After my encounters with the gigantic rudd of Elstow I doubted whether I would ever experience such magnificent fishing again. The thought of golden flanks flashing in crystal clear water as they gorged greedily on maggots falling through the layers provided such special memories and remained imprinted on my mind.

It was with excitement, then, that I received a 'phone call from a good friend, Jacko, telling me of a 3lb rudd that had fallen to his carp bait. Even better, he had spotted a dozen other fish in a reedy bay that were all over 2lb, with a few even bigger examples among them. Cambridgeshire was now on my radar and a chance to catch rudd again was too good an opportunity to miss. Plans were hastily made to visit the venue on the next warm, sunny day; conditions that I hoped would provide ideal spotting weather. Luckily, less than a week later I was heading east towards the pit, armed with a bucket of maggots and a float rod.

When I pulled into the car park I was greeted by Jacko, who had kindly offered to show me the spots he had seen the fish in. Making our way around the lake, we soon arrived at the reed-fringed bay he had described to me on the 'phone when recounting his own success. The sun glinted on the surface and the clarity was as clear as tap water, filtered by the chalk banks to create an aquarium-like environment. Dark shadows did drift below the surface but, sadly, they were not that of my target but instead every rudd fisherman's nightmare – marauding carp!

In my experience, carp love sprayed maggot and can prove a major problem when trying to tempt anything else, so understandably, I was wary of their presence. We carried on around the bay and I could then see a few smaller shadows sitting below the carp, which I felt could possibly be rudd. With a tree overlooking the bay, it seemed a perfect vantage point so I scuttled up its trunk post-haste and perched high in the canopy. I could then see that the fish were indeed rudd; there was even a couple of possible 'threes' on show, and another that I put at a much bigger weight. The trouble was, they were surrounded by carp, and I needed a plan to extract the wheat from the chaff.

Crack! The branch my foot stood on suddenly snapped and a frantic grab at a handful of leaves did little to stop my fall. My left leg had become trapped by another branch and although it had halted my descent, there I was, eight feet above ground, hanging upside down like a bat! Luckily, Jacko had seen the whole debacle and was able to help me out of my predicament. God knows what I would have done if he hadn't been there. Fortunately, nothing was broken, just a few grazes, and at least I'd spotted some fish. Shaken, I eventually regained some composure and began rigging up my float rod while formulating a plan as to how I could get the rudd away from the carp. As a rule, rudd seem to switch on to sprayed maggot falling through the water a lot quicker than their competitors, and the idea was to lead the target away by carefully catapulting only the minimum bait in a line, back toward me, until they were out of the danger zone. A bit like coaxing a dog on a lead, or so I hoped.

Five minutes after the first pouchful of grubs cascaded on to the surface, I could see the rudd flashing just below, devouring the bait with gay abandon. It was now time to shift them away from the carp before they became switched on, too. Slowly but surely, the rudd were drawn closer and closer to me – trouble was the carp were also starting to take notice, with an occasional fish charging through a shower of bait with its mouth greedily working overtime. I grabbed my float rod, knowing it was now or never. A 'pult of maggots was closely accompanied by the float and I stared intently at the orange tip that soon bobbed once before sailing under. A sweeping strike resulted in the flash of a large, golden flank just under the surface, followed by a thump on the rod as the fish began to battle.

At last.

The fight with smaller species isn't about stripping line from the spool but can be equally exciting. Frequently, prayers are sent skyward in the hope that the hook doesn't come out. This encounter was exactly that – the fish twisting and turning as it tried to prise itself free, forcing my heart to skip a beat time and time again. The final moments were fraught, as a huge bar of gold popped to the surface, and with the net outstretched, I slowly guided the monster over it. With a swish and a scoop, she was mine. Yes!

After lifting her on to the unhooking mat I opened up my present and was greeted with one of the finest sights in angling – a specimen rudd, the colour enriched and saturated by the clarity of a chalk pit. They surely are one of nature's finest jewels. The scales read 3lb 2oz and it provided me with both the perfect start, and the knowledge that at last I had found a venue that could rival Elstow. Carefully, I placed her in a barbel tube and made sure she was comfortable before calling Jacko, who had disappeared to stalk carp, to organise a picture. While waiting for him, I picked up the catapult again and fired out some more maggots. To my surprise, the other rudd hadn't been disturbed and immediately began feeding again as if nothing had happened. This was too good an opportunity to miss and soon my float was once more sailing out into the taking zone. The bait had hardly begun to fall through the water when it was devoured with relish by a big upturned mouth. Another game of cat and mouse was played out before, once again, I was staring at a large fish on my mat – all 3lbs 10ozs of it. It was the biggest of the bunch I had witnessed from the tree. I would have loved to say that it was a true rudd but, alas, it had more than a hint of roach in it. Nevertheless, it was a cracker and soon I was grinning from ear to ear, and smiling at the camera unconcerned with its heritage.

Over the next couple of years that followed, I continued to have occasional trips to my new found rudd venue, each time practising the enjoyable art of spraying maggots. One trip stands out though, that began on a particularly warm morning. It got off to the perfect start when I managed to

Cambridgeshire cracker.

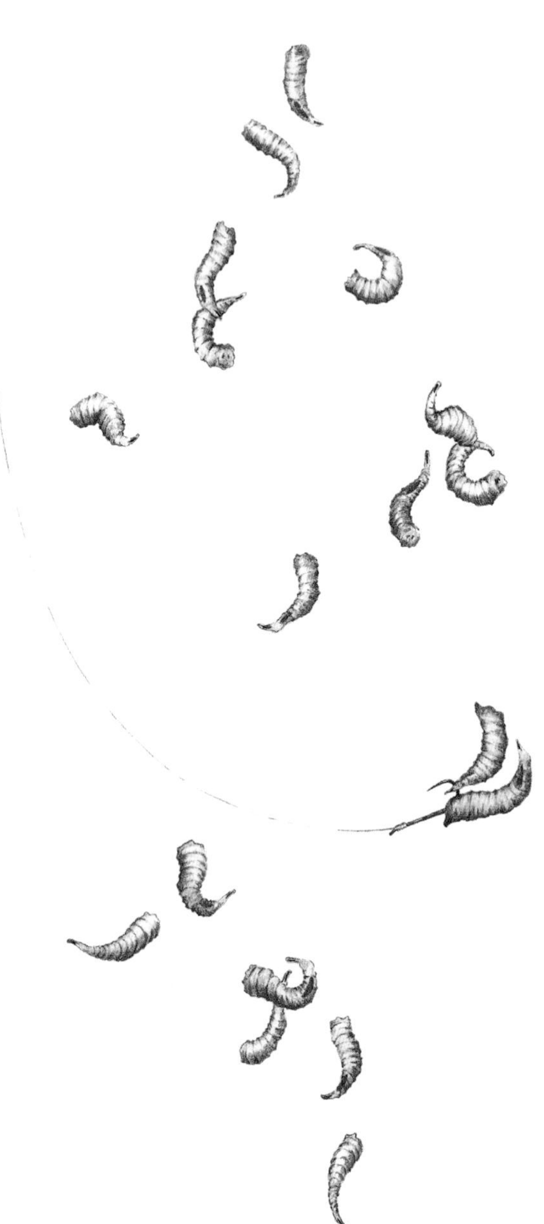

tempt a cracking 3lb 2oz specimen and after the remainder of the shoal had disappeared, I was contemplating what to do for the rest of the day when Jacko appeared again. After a quick chat, he suggested another lake near his home that contained a few large chub; indeed a record-breaker of 10lb had been claimed from it recently and splashed across the angling press.

With both of us jumping into my car, we made the 30-minute journey required but on arriving I became convinced that I was having my leg pulled. This wasn't a lake, more like a garden pond! When I walked through the gates I looked into the water and was greeted by a couple of golden orfe swimming by – this place really did have an ornamental feel.

At that point, I told Jacko that it was like fishing in the neighbour's back yard and, to be honest, it felt embarrassing being there. Then, out of the blue, two large chub, their proportions of mouth-watering size, suddenly appeared, and swam right past us. Hmmm...perhaps I could have one cast, I thought, back-tracking as rapidly as possible. Handing over £10 to the owner, he disappeared to get me some change while I grabbed my float rod and tub of maggots and walked back over to the pond. The big chub were still clearly visible - well, there weren't many places they could hide! I catapulted a couple of pouchfuls of bait over their heads and was surprised to see their reactions. They switched on to them straight away, but the trouble was so did the orfe, trout and carp in the pond. How was I going to pick out a chub?

Let us spray.

Identical twin.

Before the chub knew what was happening, I bundled it into the landing net. Everything had happened within 10 seconds and the chub lay there in complete bemusement, probably still in a state of shock. As I lifted the net, I saw that it was very big indeed, with gorgeous, dark bronze flanks, and broad shoulders of which a bodybuilder would have been proud. On the scales it went 6lb 11oz, an absolute corker, although substantially less than the 10lb claimed by its identical twin! With photos complete, I chucked the rod into the car and was back on the road within 10 minutes of arriving. The owner could keep the change!

Once again, I tried the 'dog on a lead' technique and began drawing all the fish close to me. After I had achieved this, it was then down to a far from simple task of picking out a chub. On dropping a handful of white maggots into the swim, I followed them in quickly with a single red maggot impaled on the hook. This allowed me to know exactly which one was my bait. From the left, a big, white mouth moved in eagerly, devouring all the feed in its path. Closer and closer it came, until...bang! Hand to eye coordination kicked in and I had hooked it! Given that the swim was festooned with snags, I had no choice but to hook, hold and pray.

Fishing on the drop does not always require maggots to be successful, and the deadly bait combination of caster and hemp also fools its fair share of fish. It's especially useful when the venue in question supports a large population of lesser specimens that devour maggots with relish. In this situation, hemp and caster has an uncanny knack of producing bigger fish, therefore it came as no surprise that this was the bait required when I accompanied Guildford specimen hunter, Adrian Smith, on a quest for giant roach.

Set deep inside the New Forest, Sway Lakes offered us what we had been looking for; a narrow, three-acre venue, swarming with silver fish, and home to the Holy Grail of coarse fish, roach over 2lbs. Leaving home in darkness, my excitement reached fever pitch when Wiltshire was swapped for Hampshire. I love racing the dawn to the horizon and today was no different. As the light levels lifted in the west, I applied more pressure on the accelerator – I couldn't wait to get there. When night and day begin to mix under a clear sky, mist is the inevitable consequence, and it swirled down the roads into the lanes and finally the lake that I pulled up next to. Adrian was already there and he introduced me to Sway. To be honest, I was a little taken aback by its proportions. It was narrow, almost canal-like, and certainly not a daunting affair. The fact that it was clad in lilies and reeds did provide it with a good degree of charm, though, despite its lack of stature.

Eagerly, we wandered down the path in the hope of our quarry giving away its location with a dawn roll. Firstly, half-a-dozen bivvies had to be bypassed, their owners keen to tussle with the water's numerous 20lb and 30lb carp, before an expanse of open water in which we could fish presented itself. Standing still in the cool morning air, we awaited a sign and as if by magic, a silver back porpoised across the millpond surface, sending out ripples that rushed towards us in an engaging manner. We had been given the sign and neither of us was going to ignore it. Five minutes later, we were back in the area

They lost all self-control.

with all the paraphernalia required for a day's fishing. Adrian went in the left-hand peg, aiming to fish between two overhanging trees, while I went to his right in an area where the lake widened slightly as it formed a bay.

When choosing to float fish one swim all day I learned a long time ago that behaving like a match angler, as opposed to a specimen hunter, will always pay dividends no matter what size of fish you are after. Trying to cast and feed correctly from a low chair, with tackle sprawled across the floor is completely ineffective. It's far better to be organised and in a position to attack the water in front of you, so my first job was to organise myself to facilitate this. A 13-foot float rod was combined with a small fixed spool reel and 2.6lb line that had been treated with washing-up liquid to ensure that it sank. A loaded float would provide the bite indication, a string of No 12 shot strung out, shirt button style, along the 4-foot drop, giving far better presentation than just a couple of heavier weights. Given the specimens we hoped to land, I stayed with a sensible 2.4lb hooklength and combined it with a size 18 barbless hook. If I fed correctly, I felt sure that more fragile tackle wouldn't be required.

'Little and often' was to be the mantra of the day, and equal proportions of hemp and casters were catapulted across to the far bank reed bed. At first, tiny roach were the only fish to show any interest but as the shoal's chaotic movements increased so did the attention of the shapes which drifted below. Up they rose, despite the sun already blazing down upon them, keen to investigate the confusion. Here, they found something too good to ignore – a caster and hemp combo. My game plan was working and now hunger only needed to overtake caution and I would have my reward. Gently sliding away without the slightest hint of panic, the float was no longer visible. A sideways sweep of the rod made a connection and this was reinforced by a series of heavy thumps, characteristic to the species I was targeting. I needed to give line momentarily, before the arc of carbon regained an upper hand and I began the process of subduing the roach's power. For a minute, it stayed deep before I started the gentle task of coaxing it to the surface. Boils then replaced a taut line, with a silver-blue, livery-rich reward for my patience. The game was nearly up, I just needed to keep my nerve, and fortunately, I did. Very shortly, 2lb 4oz of perfection lay as a heavy handful within my palm.

Sometimes, for no rhyme or reason, the textbooks can be thrown out of the window. There was a high pressure sitting over us, and dawn should have been our only window; the roach, though, lost all control. Following a constant, nine-hour, rain of feed, 15 roach over 2lb to 2lbs 11ozs fell to my tactics, while Adrian plundered nine over the magic mark. Indeed our catch rate only declined due to a combination of bait shortage and fatigue. Proof, if it was ever needed, of the potent pulling power of 'fishing on the drop'.

Camera: Canon EOS 5D - Shutter Speed: 1/30 sec - F-Stop: f/13.0 - ISO: 100 - Location: Adams Mill

CHAPTER 05

MONSTERS AT THE MILL

A chance meeting with Pete Reading and Stef Horak on the Newport Pagnell road bridge, once again put Adams Mill at the top of my 'to do' list. Both anglers had been very successful on the venue that summer by feeding in large quantities of maggots and their finest hour had arrived the previous week. The same 15lb barbel had fallen to each of their rods just days apart and understandably, both wore huge grins.

Monstrous.

Night fishing wasn't allowed, with access to enter the property strictly controlled by a set time that was printed in the club book. However, this didn't stop many from flouting the rule and there was nothing worse than praying, with a knot in your stomach, that you were first to arrive, only to find a car already in situ. Fair enough if it was within the rules, but when you arrived bang on time to find an angler, already fully laden with tackle and just waiting for another car to turn the corner, greeting you with a wave as if to say, 'just got here, mate', it was far from relaxing. This was especially true when a bailiff was the main culprit and a touch of his car bonnet revealed it to be stone cold! On this occasion though, I didn't see another angler disappearing over the horizon. The Mill was empty and I would have first pick of the swims.

Given that this was 1998, maybe you can understand why I was so captivated by their tales, even if I struggled to believe that I could possibly catch a barbel of such proportions. Stef, in his usual manner, was overly keen to tell me the exact swim where it had been caught, information I duly ignored as this was an accepted part of the game and there wasn't a chance he was telling the truth! Still, the Mill wasn't very big, so wherever I wetted a line it wouldn't have been far away from the beast. I congratulated my friends, we went our separate ways, and for the next couple of days I mulled over the situation. Predictably, I came to the conclusion that bream fishing could wait; I wanted a big barbel!

The worst part of any day at Adams Mill was the drive down the old farm track that led to the fishery car park.

On the horizon, the rising sun burned with intensity and was a certain precursor to the predicted heat-wave. I wandered along the steep-sided bank and took my time to inspect the river closely with the aid of Polaroids. Like a fool, I even poked my head over Stef's swim to see, of course, that it was empty. Given the river's clarity I knew that fishing blindly was an error, as somewhere there was sure to be a shoal of monsters flashing their bronze torsos in appreciation of dawn. I crossed over the cattle bridge and headed down the opposite bank until I reached a heavily foliated tree protruding halfway across the river. Its branches kissed the surface, creating a barrier which allowed a raft of fence posts, carrier bags, and footballs to form. Was it here that I would find what I was looking for? As I lay on my stomach, I strained to view the dark water at the back of the obstruction and through the entanglement of debris, a couple of tails swayed to and fro. Then, as if to confirm their presence, a further big barbel swept downstream, momentarily holding station in the pool below before working back slowly to his friends. He had broad shoulders, a long body clad in copper and I had seen all I needed to.

I intended to fish the swim from the opposite bank where I had spotted the barbels' location. Given the angle of the line, by fishing across to the raft I would stand a far greater chance of landing my quarry; that was, of course, if I could fool one in the first place. Knowing that the fish had been targeted and caught with maggots, I reasoned that a fresh approach would pay dividends. This meant boilies, a bait that was new to a barbel angling scene still awash with luncheon meat and hemp. A rig was constructed using a semi-fixed set-up and a size 10 hook, combined with two, 6mm offerings that were produced from the number one mix at the time, the pungent, cheese-smelling 'Grange'.

Heart pounding.

To increase the attraction still further, I also added a stringer of freebies. This set-up was then placed just downstream of the raft where the gravel sloped away into the pool giving four feet of water and a nice clean substrate. To make it less conspicuous, a coffin lead had been positioned on the line between float stops six feet away from the rig, pinning the taut mono to the deck, far from harm's way.

As an additional precaution, a further back lead was then slipped down from the rod tip, ensuring that my presence was completely concealed. Next, came the cunning part of the plan and it required me to spook the barbel! They were sulking under the raft after slipping up to Pete and Stef's maggot attack, and I reasoned that the last thing they would want was another dropper load of grubs, let alone 20 more, so I began to bombard the water upstream of the bush. A little lateral thinking can sometimes really work and I just hoped it would on this occasion. If I could force them out of their safety zone, I knew they would come to rest in the pool below where, of course, I had set my trap.

For half-an-hour nothing stirred under the bush or in the open, so with an 'in for a penny, in for a pound' mentality I recommenced the droppering, only to see the barbel become highly agitated, zooming around and leaving cover. Was it working or were they actually feeding on the maggots?

The answer came, as slowly but surely the fish left the raft over the following couple of hours, resulting in eight hefty, bronze torpedoes taking up residence in the pool. The time had come to let them regain their composure and with it their confidence, so all disturbance was ceased and I tried my best to melt into the background. Then as they began to creep back to the raft, I would be waiting in ambush with a tasty trap.

Fishing Adams Mill was an exciting affair because I so often remained in visual contact with my quarry during the summer months, and at times the river's diminutive size and clarity really tested my willpower. It was hard not to keep poking your head over the swim to check what was happening. This could easily scupper well-made plans so I needed to be patient and wait for the rod tip to tell me the ruse had worked. It was exactly an hour before the first barbel fell to my cunning plan. I think that the word 'bite' is an injustice to what happens when a barbel makes a mistake, and this time was no different. The rod was wrenched savagely from the rests and all hell broke loose to ruin the serenity of the day.

Predictably, the fish sought sanctuary in the branches of the overhanging tree and with the rod compressed to full capacity I tried to thwart such an attempt by using maximum pressure. As I reached the brink of losing control, I clamped down even harder against the spool, trying to stop it singing to the barbel's tune and hoped, no prayed, for the best. The fish's will broke before the 10lb line and it mistakenly headed back downstream and out into the open water which would, all things being equal, result it seeing the inside of my landing net. For a time she resisted the inevitable, defiantly thrashing her tail on the surface before a huge, white belly waved in surrender and slid toward me. The end game had come and I took possession of my prize. Immediately, I knew I had caught my largest ever barbel. Its proportions were of mind-blowing magnitude to an angler still ecstatic about 10lb fish! It was thickset, muscular, and monstrous. Lifting her, I peered inside her mouth and there, clear as day, were two old hook marks alongside mine, confirming immediately that she would weigh over 15lb. It was a new personal best of 15lb 6oz, to be exact.

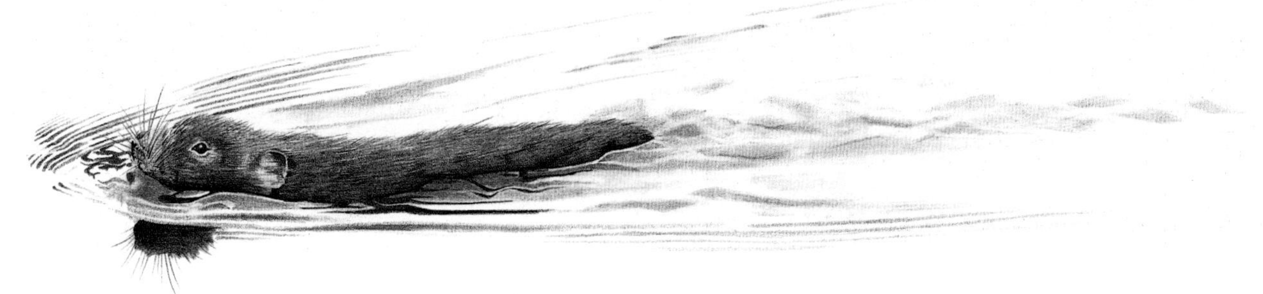

I was euphoric, the pictures were completed and the beast safely returned to its rightful home before I sank back in my chair with a smug smile. Little did I know that it would soon be wiped off my face in the best possible way. With a bait back in situ, another leviathan made the same mistake and I was forced to relive the battle all over again as the fish surged against tree roots that did their best to grasp the line and break it in two. Once again, this fight needed me to remain calm and have faith in the tackle, and only then did it conclude in the same manner. Open water and 12 feet of buckled carbon soon drains the energy from even the biggest of fish and as the boils grew bigger, I knew another beast was close to being beaten. When the net ended the bout, I was rewarded with another barbel weighing in at 14lb 3ozs. This magnificent brace meant I had taken the biggest duo ever recorded, proving the fishery was peerless and that an individual record-breaker wasn't far away. For the time being though, my adventures here would cease but winter had already been earmarked for a return when surely the British best would tumble to one of the monsters at the Mill.

Biggest brace.

It was January 21st 1999 to be precise when my date with destiny arrived. Heavy rain and gale-force south-westerlies had battered our country for the past week but surprisingly, the river had hardly risen and I strongly suspected that it was being held back at Milton Keynes. On this occasion, though, with the passing of the storm, some bright spark had decided to let the lot through in one go, resulting in a scene that even Noah would have been proud of. On arrival at the Mill car park, I was greeted with the sight of a two-mile-wide river. It had well and truly burst its banks and filled all the surrounding fields, while dense fog hung menacingly overhead. A veil of muddy water had swallowed up the countryside. Just getting to the original river bed was going to be a challenge but fortunately, I was parked on the side of the Ouse situated on high ground, leaving my car safe and a small piece of land still exposed in the distance. If I could wade to this point, I had a platform from which I could fish, albeit like a tiny island marooned in a sea of swirling confusion.

As I unloaded the tackle, another car came speeding down the track, obviously, like me, in anticipation of a spot of fishing. As it pulled up next to me, the window was wound down, and the driver made a comment about my mental state before heading back home. I knew from experience, though, that this was the ideal condition in which the biggest fish came out to play. With a rucksack on my back and a sling across my shoulder, I began wading across the flooded field, taking one careful step at a time, feeling my way with a long rod rest. Luckily, the island that had formed was accessible without too much hassle and fishing would be possible from the elevated vantage point. In fact, the river looked great and I was full of confidence, especially as this was the exact area where I'd had a hook pull on a very big fish only a couple of weeks earlier.

Stig of the Dump.

As I looked back to the car park, I saw that two more cars had pulled up containing the familiar faces of Guy Robb and Ray Walton. I waded back to greet them with a handshake and we began to discuss prospects. Ray was beside himself with excitement over the conditions that were perfect for rolling meat tactics.

He soon had the thermometer in the river and even given the mild conditions we were all a little shocked when he read out a whopping 50°F. Wow! It was like a jacuzzi! The barbel would surely want to join in the fun; something that was almost immediately confirmed when a fish crashed in the slack water between the car park and bridge.

"That will do for me," said Ray, as he scuttled into the boot of his bright yellow Mk1 Escort in search of his rod and reel, a task that was easier said than done given the mountain of rubbish inside that enabled him to do a better than average impersonation of 'Stig of the Dump'. Meanwhile, I invited Guy to fish upstream of me on the island and with no further ado we both waded back to the strip of land, confident that someone would catch. Tackling up, I threaded a 4oz sea watch lead on the line, which I hoped would be heavy enough to hold bottom. Bait was a large piece of Grange paste moulded around a boilie of the same flavour, both heavily soaked in an additional amount of corn steep liquor. All of this was suspended off a woefully inadequate 1lb 4oz test curve rod because floodwater fishing was in its infancy and the tackle I needed was still to be perfected. I cast out into the main flow and felt the weight hit bottom before a 'tap-tap' on the rod tip saw it dislodged and then grip once again after finding a more sound footing on the river bed.
I suspected it had come to rest against the line of rushes that filled the margins during the summer and now, although they had died back, they would supply an excellent shelter for a barbel to hide from the turbulence which raged above their heads.

It's hard to explain but I just knew I was going to get a bite. Call it gut instinct or a lucky guess but as I sat perched on the seat watching the rod tip nod in time with the flow, the feeling was overwhelming. Conditions really were extreme, with water continuing to pour over the fields, making the scene one of biblical proportions. Although the river looked unfishable to most, I knew that in these temperatures every barbel in the river would be gorging themselves. It was just a matter of getting a bait to them and I felt sure a take would be on the cards. Through the fog, I could make out the silhouette of Ray rolling his meat hookbait, and as he was on the short side, I hoped that he was especially careful when wading – a wormhole could spell disaster!

Moments away.

A time to reflect.

The scales of history.

For a moment, I took my eye off the ball and 'wham' the rod butt nearly hit me in the mouth as an unseen force did its best to drag my tackle into the river. I grabbed the handle as the rod took on its full fighting action and then a little more besides. To be honest, the barbel down below was more in control of the situation than I was and panic spread across my face.

With little immediate concern, the fish moved downstream with line steadily ticking off the spool and there was very little I could do except hang on and hope to stay in contact. Ray and Guy were soon by my side giving encouragement and guidance. I decided then that I would be better off moving downstream and getting below the fish instead of trying to pull it back to me.

Firstly, in such heavy flood conditions I didn't think it would be possible drag a fish upstream and secondly, I felt that the barbel would wedge itself against the dying reed bed that the lead had originally lodged against, even if I could turn it. If this occurred, the soft test curve would be unable to get it on the move again and disaster would surely follow.

Decision made, I began to wade gingerly down the flooded field, keeping the rod high until I was below the fish and in the relative safe area of the deep pool. Fortunately for me, all went to plan and I was soon ready to recommence the battle from a better vantage point.

The fight was far from over, though, and every lunge had me praying I would remain in contact and that the hook hold was a firm one. Ray didn't make the situation any better with his constant commentary and insistence that I had the 'big one' on.

"Please, Ray give it a break – we've not even seen it yet!" I muttered trying to keep a lid on my excitement. And then we did, as a bloody huge, bronze flank appeared out of the coffee-coloured water.

Britain's best.

It was indeed the 'big one!' To know you are connected to a British record in the most horrendous river conditions possible is scary and my heart was in my mouth. For a while, I became a religious man praying for divine intervention and from that point on, every dive by the fish was met with a wince as I hoped for the hook to remain embedded and the line to stay strong. What was probably only another five minutes seemed to last a lifetime until finally, she was ready and rolled over to reveal her girth.

Record breaker.

'Hook,' I thought, 'please hold, please.' Such was the force of the flow, it was impossible to pull her upstream and into the waiting landing net so Ray ran downstream and positioned the net below her as I let the beast glide slowly towards it. Yes! She was mine and I proceeded to hug Walton. Boy, was I happy!

We rested her and readied everything while wondering how big she'd go. Soon, the scales gave their verdict – 16lb 13oz. I had a new British record and at that moment, I concluded that life didn't get much better. The world seemed a perfect place and even the sun came out for the photos. It is every young angler's dream to break a record and I had done it. The biggest UK barbel ever had fallen to me and for the rest of that day I felt like I was walking on air.

My time at the top was to be short-lived. Only a couple of weeks later, my good friend Kev Newton broke the record with the same fish at 17lb 1oz. Was I disappointed? I can honestly say I wasn't. I'd had my time in the sun and it was good to watch Kev have his day too. Ray's time was also to come, finishing a remarkable spell when the fish kept growing and the record kept tumbling. Despite its critics, it was a special place and a very special time in my angling career.

Kev's time.

Well deserved.

Breaking the bank.

Camera: Canon EOS 300D - Shutter Speed: 1/200 sec - F-Stop: f/9.0 - ISO: 100 - Location: Colne Valley pit

CHAPTER 06

NEVER TO BE

This journey started 20 years ago on the banks of Startops, one of Tring's famous reservoirs. At the time, there was only a limited population of carp although that didn't deter my mate Jacko, his girlfriend Pam, and I; we still made an attempt to catch one or two. The first day of the season saw me wading out in the weed-festooned shallows to investigate the fish that continually rose in and out of the tiny clearings, like seals seeking air holes among a bed of ice. If I stood dead still, the carp would happily swim almost within touching distance, the vegetation becoming sucked under the surface as it tangled around their rudders before rising in these clearings.

There in front of me sat a big, purple back and a set of pulsing white lips. Excitedly, I lowered a piece of bread flake next to its mouth and watched as it was slurped in with great gusto. Striking resulted in an explosion of water that left me soaked but I held on for all I was worth. Luckily, the carp now connected to me was a rather portly specimen, no doubt still full of spawn, and it was unable to vacate the scene of the crime given the strong mono that did its best to stall the surge. This capture of a 22lb common proved, ironically, to be the biggest I would ever catch from the venue, although at the time I had hopes of something much larger and it was this delicious air of mystery that saw a summer's campaign commence.

Starting at Startops.

Two days later, I headed for the shallows once again, only to find, to my horror, two other carp anglers encamped in the area. Our initial meeting was a cold, brief affair and little did I know that I would form a lifelong friendship with one of the anglers, Keith Wesley. Over the next few months, relationships defrosted, and a comradeship was formed that resulted in some great times which I will always treasure more than any fish captured.

As I've alluded, on the angling front the water never did live up to expectations with, I guess, the nuisance fish providing the highest quality of specimens. Roach to 3lb and double-figure bream fell to my rods but it was Pam who really struck gold. While fishing a shallow bay with a stream which cut a deep channel through the centre of it, she made tench history. A 7lb and 9lb fish came first, followed by a true goliath of 12lb 8oz, which was the biggest of the species landed by a woman at the time. It may have been heavily spawn-bound but even to a group of carp-crazed anglers, it cut an impressive figure. Amusingly, it almost caused one of the many specimen anglers who frequented the venue, to cut his own wrists, especially when Pam declared, 'Oh no, not another bloody tench!'

Many of the specimen boys, though, were very friendly and this afforded me the opportunity to bump into the legendary Alan Wilson; and a nicer man you couldn't wish to meet. It did puzzle me, however, why none of them chose to fish along the weedy bank where we were most successful. In fact, I distinctly remember Alan visiting me only to declare, 'I never knew it was like this over here!' and that was from a man who had spent years at Startops! Mind you, it never did affect his results, and it was with great amusement that I would watch weekend anglers arrive and pitch their bivvies either side of the great man, forming long lines.

Nuisance fish.

A journey begins.

Alan didn't need to move because conditions would always eventually change in his favour. He had an infinite amount of time on the bank at his disposal, a point lost on his friends who would have been a lot more successful following the weather and not him!

Eventually, all good things come to an end and it was time for us all to move on to new challenges but years later I would once again go carp fishing alongside Keith.

Following a set of secret instructions and promising to tell no one, I rendezvoused with my friend before we made our way in convoy for the final few miles to the entrance of the private estate. Through the electric gates and up the path we went before pulling up alongside the lake he had spoken about in hushed tones. At about two-and-a-half acres, it was tiny and made to look even more so by a big island smack-bang in the middle. A little taken aback, I consoled myself with the thought that Redmire was only small, although I already doubted my friend's promises of monsters. Keith would have none of it and told me of two mirrors – the dark and the sandy one – both easily over 40lb. Hmmm. Had Keith been drinking, I wondered while I set up the tackle? We were to be joined by another friend of Keith's, Steve Reeve, who

Hidden away.

would also share the honour of fishing the lake first for these virgin whackers. The time had come, then, to stop the chat and see if this water could really deliver on the promises.

With the rods out, we began to reminisce about our old trips together on the reservoir, Keith taking great delight in reminding me that I was a spotty 17-year-old back then! Cutting through this banter, the scream of an alarm indicated almost immediate action, although not to our rods but to Steve's, who was fishing round the corner in a reed-fringed bay. We arrived in the swim to find him already landing a 21lb common, which was fin and scale perfect, testimony to its first ever capture. Yes, a cracking fish but not a 40. Keith must have been getting his weights muddled up, surely, and I took great pleasure in returning the mickey-taking. He simply shrugged his shoulders and told me to wait and see.

Ten minutes later, we were back in Steve's swim, as once again a carp was doing its best to drag his tackle into the reeds. It was hard to get a good view of the fish but from what I could see, it looked like another low-20, and nothing particularly special. A few minutes later, she was ready to net but at this point, her bulk seemed to grow rapidly and she literally spread across the surface. A common with a huge gut presented itself to the net and I made a scoop – the 20 was easily a 30, I now concluded, a fact confirmed when I went to lift it from the water. Placing the beast in a sling, she slammed the scales down to a stunning 38lb of virgin carp. It was simply incredible and I felt somewhat ashamed of myself for ever doubting Keith, a point not missed by him for the remainder of the trip. This was the beginning of a relationship that would see the common's path cross mine every time she came to the bank - but in the most bizarre of fashions.

A year later, it was just Keith and I who returned to the lake, although its tiny acreage wasn't a stumbling block now. I knew for certain that a large common called this place home and it hadn't been caught since our last sortie, so it was definitely overdue a visit to the bank. I hoped my turn had come to make its acquaintance.

We walked around the perimeter until we reached the reed-filled bay that had last produced the beast and, sheltered from the wind, it felt noticeably warmer. We donned our Polaroids and took a closer look. Sure enough, two shadows could be seen gliding over the silt-filled bottom and then a huge, frothing cauldron of bubbles fizzed to the surface as a fish nosed the mud in search of lunch. That was more than enough of a sign for both of us, and we quickly headed back for the tackle; prospects of an early success were looking good. For Keith though disaster was to strike. He had left his rods at home and it would take a good few hours to retrieve them. Old age, I told him, was a terrible curse! Graciously, given my abuse, he told me to get fishing the swim while he set off for home. It was an offer too good to refuse.

Virgin monster.

Getting ready.

After creeping back into the bay, I quickly set up a couple of rods that incorporated 15lb line to 2oz leads, semi-fixed with a 25lb sheathed hooklength and a size 8 hook. For bait, a simple tiger nut would suffice, balanced with a small piece of cork. This was then fished alongside a PVA bag of 3mm Marine Halibut pellets. With both rods ready, I flicked them out little more than five yards and slackened off the mono to minimize alerting the fish to my presence. Before I could reach for some hemp and pellets to catapult over each rod, I noticed one of the lines twitch before the tip wrenched round and the clutch screamed. Incredibly, I was already in! After a spirited fight, I netted a gorgeous, chestnut-flanked, mid-double common, which was a great start but it wasn't the prize I was after. An hour later, a huge patch of bubbles appeared over the other rod before that, too, was away sending the freespool into overdrive. Another double made its way in and I couldn't have hoped for a better start. Surely, the beast would be hungry as well?

On Keith's return, I told him the good news and, given the action, suggested that he sat on the opposite end of the bay. By now, I had noticed that down to my right was a pipe through which water flowed beneath the surface and out into the lake. This, I concluded, was to be my next ambush point. A handful of peanuts was sprinkled into the margin here, before a single nut on a hair rig was lowered in position over the scoured gravel. It wasn't long before a couple of shadows appeared over the area and upended on the nutty treats. Gauging their size was difficult because the flowing water displaced the surface and inhibited my view, but they were certainly worth catching. Occasionally, an oily slick popped to the surface, suggesting that the peanuts were still being devoured and giving rise to the thought that a mistake would soon be made. 'Zzzzzzzzz' the clutch screamed in agreement!

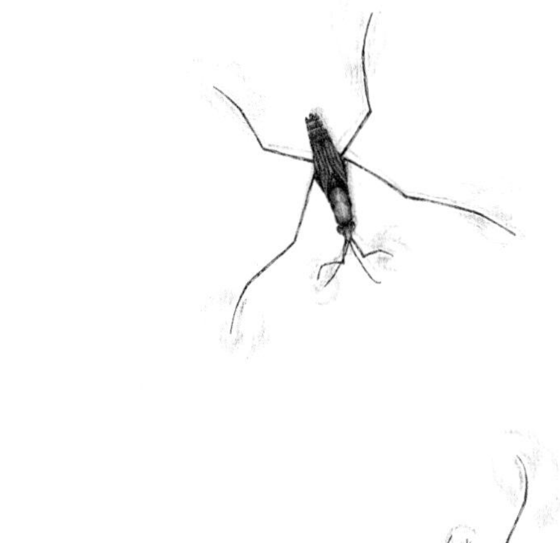

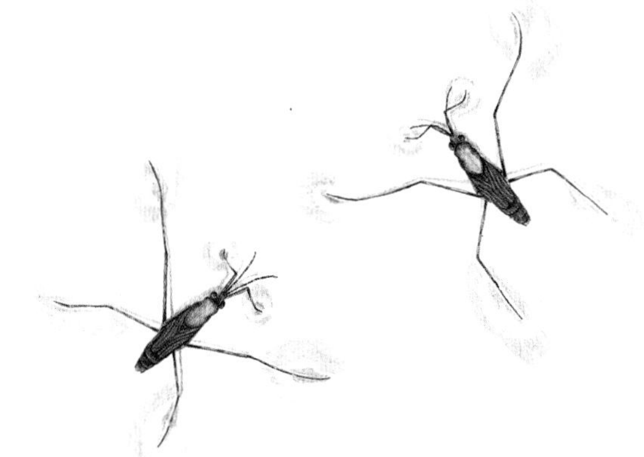

As I grabbed the rod, a wake appeared on the surface and line was stripped from the spool without consideration or control. Ten yards out, I regained the upper hand as the fish smashed head first into the weed and from that point on the carp's fate was sealed. At 24lb, it was a corking common and when the fish and chips supper that evening was washed down with a glass of wine, it had rarely tasted better. What of the big girl, though? That predictable chatter accompanied the meal, and with the sun setting, it was soon time to head for the warmth of our sleeping bags to wait for the night's events to unfold.

At around 3.30am, a buzzer screamed across the lake and woke me from my slumber; Keith was away and in need of assistance. I put my boots on and headed off in his direction, finding him with rod bent and a carp rolling on the surface no more than five yards out. By the lack of fight, we both felt sure a low double was attached to his hook and, like a dog on the lead, he drew it toward the waiting landing net and me. At the last moment, I realised our mistake but fortunately, the net had now safely secured it and there was no time to panic.

'This is one big kipper', were my first words. I struggled to lift her, but she was placed on the mat and our torches illuminated the huge golden flank of the big common again. We had both left our heavy-duty scales in our vehicles so my 40lb Avons would have to do for now. These proved totally inadequate, spinning round until the colour dial turned black and off the scale; an epic angling moment if ever there was one! We placed her in a sack, secured it in deep water, and stuck the kettle on to help regain our composure.

Our scales couldn't be reached until dawn because the vans were parked next to the owner's security-tight home, so there was little we could do but guess her weight and ensure that she was comfortable. We were like kids on Christmas Eve, desperate to open our presents, and as you can understand, no more sleep took place that night. Eventually, the sun rose once again in the sky and we could fetch the scales for the moment of truth. The dial swung round to an impressive 41lb 4oz. Truly incredible – especially as she was a common! I congratulated Keith on a new personal best and hoped it would be third time lucky for me.

Once again.

Twelve months later, we met up for what had become our now annual social trip. Once again, we waited for the electric gates to swing open, drove up the pathway, and strained to gain our first glimpse of the lake. I was prepared for the weed as my companion had warned me of its growth but I must admit I was a little taken aback when we drew up alongside the venue. Where was the water? The entire surface was covered in duckweed. I think the words 'I should have stayed at home', came from Keith first but I was thinking the same. Still, we were here and the 'who dares, wins' attitude was required; it sure beat traversing the M25 once again.

Walking along the margins, we had taken no more than a couple of steps when the lime green surface heaved as a carp bow-waved in panic up the lake. Well, they hadn't gone anywhere. We just needed to get a bait into the water but that was easier said than done. Fortunately, along the far bank the weed appeared a little looser and as the wind blew, small clearings formed giving us a doorway to the aquatic world where a series of golden gravel spots shone out.

"That will do for me," said Keith, quickly.
"Thanks mate, I think I'll cast into the trees for squirrels, then, as there's not as much vegetation up there!" I replied.
Keith laughed and told me to respect my elders!
"Anyway, it would be a waste putting you in this swim as you can't catch the common!" he added. Prophetic words indeed.
'I'll show him', I thought. Dynamite sticks and heavy leads would crash through the weed breaking the surface stranglehold. Having picked the bay from where the fish had originally spooked, I prepared myself to cast. The rod formed a beautiful arc and the bait sailed out perfectly. Thud! The green mass rippled slightly but did little else and my rig sat on the surface. Keith nearly choked to death laughing and shouted something about 'flying fish'. Back to the drawing board.

Having regrouped, I wandered round the lake and arrived at the inflow pipe. It hadn't dispersed the duckweed, but it certainly had made it loose enough to part with the rod tip and with this huge blanket covering the surface, anywhere giving extra oxygen had to be of interest to the carp, I reasoned, especially the big girl. My time was about to arrive!

Gently, I waved my landing net handle around to make a couple of holes. Although over deeper water, the bottom I could see was made up of clear gravel and I laced it liberally with 3mm and 6mm Marine Halibut pellets, one tin of hemp and two pints of maggots. With room for only a couple of baits, I dispensed with the third rod, as an extra line in the water doesn't always equate to extra bites; in fact, it can cost you fish. Braid of 20lb, a small semi-fixed lead, and a hookful of maggots was the basic principle behind both set-ups and I was, at last, ready to fish. Meanwhile, Keith had liberally baited three spots with 14mm Smoky Mackerel boilies and when his alarm duly sung out shortly after casting, it confirmed that he had a successful strategy. A corking double graced the net, quickly followed by two more fish of a similar size; understandably, I was beginning to question my own tactics. Still, it was nice to tuck into the traditional fish and chip supper, washed down with a bottle of wine, with an old friend once again.

The night was a fitful affair and I was constantly dive-bombed by bloodthirsty gnats. My shallow water swim rocked as carp gorged on the bait, their tails occasionally illuminated by moonlight as they broke the surface of the water. What was going wrong? How come I hadn't hooked a fish?

Daybreak arrived, and I reassessed my approach. The carp had now forced the weed away from the inflow pipe and by crawling on all fours, I could observe their behaviour. From my vantage point, it was evident that something was amiss with my rigs because every time a fish ghosted over them its pecs would twitch with anxiety. I waited for the swim to clear of carp and swung the terminal tackle in quickly. Everything looked fine. Could it be, though, that the sheer numbers of maggots presented on the hook made it look unnatural? I'd seen it before with barbel when too many grubs appeared to be off-putting, so I tied up a new hooklength with a size 14 hook, nicked on just three maggots and carefully lowered only one rod back down.

Soon, a shadow blocked off the golden gravel clearing like an eclipse and I stared intently at the slack line. It made a movement, pulling the slack taut and then a huge eruption hit the surface wrenching the line tighter than ever. Grabbing the rod, I clamped down hard and heaved the carp to the surface; I'd rather have the hook pull than lose it in the weed, I reasoned. With a 'do or die' bend of the rod, I bundled it into the net and a gorgeous, scaly mirror of 21lb was my reward for such a swashbuckling approach. You wouldn't have thought removing a few grubs would have made that much difference, but to reinforce the point two more carp fell quickly afterwards. Alas, there was no sign of the common, though.

Everything but...

Anticipation.

Boring by now.

Keith's alarm broke my daydream and I don't know why, but I just knew what the conclusion would be. Yes, you've guessed it - always the bridesmaid but never the bride - the big common wallowed in his net! It pulled the scales down to 39lb 12ozs and I pronounced that I wouldn't have wanted it anyway, because it wasn't 40lb! Keith knew the truth, though, and chuckled before offering his wisdom that the only way I could catch it was if he didn't bother casting out. It was getting boring now, but could it be fourth time lucky?

Another year had passed and here we were again, following the same old routine, playing the same old game. The big girl had even been christened 'Bowler' much to Keith's amusement. Amazingly, over the last three years she had only been caught three times, with each visit to the bank coinciding with mine. We took our places once again beside the lake, and I began to catch a string of carp from the off, while Wesley's rods remained quiet. I knew the clock was ticking and I had to get to the big girl first. It seemed destiny was impossible to deny, no matter how hard I tried, and at 4am the following morning, the victor had taken his spoils. At 41lb 2oz, the common lay at the bottom of Keith's landing net, completing one of the most incredible angling journeys I have ever experienced.

Unfortunately, a few months later she passed away. She certainly wasn't a good-looking carp but one I would have still loved to catch. Somehow, though, my affection for the fish is greater because of my failure, showing me that it's impossible always to win, and without that degree of uncertainty between nature and fishermen, the sport would be meaningless. Why did I lose out so many times? Was it coincidence or was I just plain unlucky? Maybe the real key was my obsession with always wanting to catch as many as possible. While Keith used boilies and, dare I say, a cruder approach, I busied myself with particles and margins, which did indeed produce more carp but was in no way selective. The old girl just wanted an easy meal and that's what boilies provided. The heavier terminal tackle used also helped with selection; it had to be less obtrusive to a 40lb carp than a double, weaning out the lesser fish. For an example of this, a 2lb roach may turn its nose up at a size 10 hook, while to a double-figure barbel it would be quite acceptable, due to scale. In a similar way, I believe this is why the chod rig has been so successful at capturing big fish. It actually eliminates captures of smaller carp and therefore leaves the swim undisturbed for longer. Of course, this is all just theory and one simple fact remains; Keith will forever have the bragging rights over me because 'Bowler' the carp has shed her mortal coil and it's now a case of 'never to be'.

Bowler, the carp.

Camera: Canon EOS 40D - Shutter Speed: 1/2700 sec - F-Stop: f/4.0 - ISO: 400 - Location: Dauntsey Vale

CHAPTER 07

GO WEST

With the beginning of a new millennium so came a big change in my own life. Bedfordshire, the county I had grown up in and been rewarded by with countless big fish, would be left behind as I headed west to the Wiltshire town of Chippenham. It's funny how fate changes your life. Never before had this area been of any interest to me, but with a new page in the book turned, my wife Jo and I set up home together, and somewhat predictably I started making enquiries about the local fishing! For the first time I would live close to a river; but what did the Bristol Avon have in store for me?

Rising near Chipping Sodbury, in Gloucestershire, the Avon begins life as two streams before merging near Malmesbury. From this point on, continually energized by tributaries like the Marden and Frome, its pace quickens as it winds through a captivating West Country landscape. Broad-leaved woodlands, hay meadows and pastures, the river passes them all but this single burn really captured my imagination when its path through the Dauntsey Vale reached the outskirts of my new Chippenham home. Barbel, and lots of them, proliferated in many stretches and despite their top weight falling a little short of their southern competitors, doubles were without doubt thick on the ground. Cue Stuart Morgan, a fellow barbel enthusiast of some repute and a local expert, who kindly took the time to show me the delights of Lacock, Avoncliffe and Limpley Stoke, to name but a few stretches, giving me what I had never had before – barbel on tap.

A boom in interest for the species was also kicking into top gear throughout the nation at this time and by combining ideas with Stuart during this period, we really did ride the crest of the wave. Floodwater fishing was in its infancy and while most anglers stayed at home during the worst the winter had to offer, we loved it. Coffee-coloured water breaking through the river's confines and saturating surrounding fields was our signal to catch barbel, regardless of how hard it was raining. The tackle to cope with such conditions was no longer woefully inadequate Avon rods, but stout 2lb test curve models capable of hurling 6oz sea leads. Fifteen-pound line and strong carp hooks were also the order of the day as we enjoyed a huge amount of success and fun, for I find few things more exhilarating than a savage battle while waist-deep in water

On my doorstep.

The river didn't contain a large quantity of fish over 12lbs, so this target was always the aim and, once I managed to lure a fish over 13lbs, the odds on catching a 14lb specimen got even longer. I was confident, though, that if I ever had the good fortune for one to cross my path I had bait and rigs at my disposal good enough to fool it!

Three days of mild, south-westerly winds accompanied by clouds laden with rain made me smile, even if the weatherman looked gloomy at his own forecast. Initially, the river being spate in nature would rise dramatically, bringing with it all manner of debris before settling down over a day and becoming perfect for catching barbel.

The following morning, a first glimpse of the river confirmed this prognosis with more froth than you would find on a cappuccino. A wall of water fought to stay within its own banks.

The Avon awaits.

Keeping mobile.

Barbel time.

Surface side it may not have looked a good proposition to get a bite from, but I had learned not to judge a book by its cover; down below, barbel would be on the prowl. If I could locate a fish in this maelstrom I knew a bite would follow, so mobility was the key to success. It was crucial that I kept on prodding the River Avon throughout the session along a series of stretches.

With such a mindset, I carried only a small rucksack, lightweight chair, a single rod, and the obligatory landing net as I squelched through deep puddles and muddy gateways, regularly becoming stuck in the cattle-fuelled swamps before I eventually overcame the obstacle course and reached my destination.

The river before me had to be assessed first, as surface flow patterns can be a giveaway to a barbel's lair. By watching carefully as rubbish was pushed along in the flow, I could discount many spots, for if it backed up on itself I felt no fish would want to live in a washing machine. I continued my meander as the clouds gathered above my head and once again dispatched their contents, forcing me to pull up my hood, wipe droplets from my glasses and consider my sanity. I pushed on until a sharp right-hand bend kicked the flow across to the far bank, creating a distinctive crease down the centre, which formed a lovely, smooth, glass-like glide. It was here that the quest would begin.

I cast into the middle of the river where six ounces of lead and a solid 'donk' gave me confidence that the hookbait was presented correctly, even as the rod tip bent round immediately as the line became festooned with weed and all manner of flotsam. The secret here is never to recast until you either want to move, or the lead is physically shifted by the build-up of pressure. Constant casting to remove odd strands of debris only serves to disturb and ultimately destroy the swim. So, after half an hour I found myself in the usual position of holding the rod with it compressed into a full arc, and unable to put it in a rest as it would have been dragged in.

The time for a move was fast approaching, but this thought was never to be put into practise as the strain suddenly relented, only to be replaced with something twice as strong. The power of the bite was transmitted to my hands, which duly responded with a strike. My initial reaction was to think that a small barbel was the culprit then slowly but steadily the pressure began to mount and to prevent disaster, my clutch was forced to yield line. A heavy weight hugged the bottom, unimpressed by my efforts to tame it, and the mono cut upstream as I applied more tension. Fortunately, this time it had the desired effect and turned the force tethered by my rod toward me. Slowly, it began to rise until a tail flapped on the surface.

Bristol's best.

My immediate verdict was a low double but as I began to get more glimpses, it was obvious that I was connected to a very special Bristol Avon fish. Another dive had me holding my breath and loosening the clutch slightly; this was not a time for mistakes and the gravity of the situation forced a tamer response than usual.

I stretched the net as far as I could out into the river and waited for the right moment. She rolled, side on, and lay beaten as I gave a final heave until the mesh took possession of her. This was indeed a moment worth treasuring as one of the biggest fish in the river lay before me. She was muscular and powerful and it wasn't hard to understand why this fish enjoyed the rigours of floodwater life. As she weighed in at 14lbs 7ozs, her special place in the Bristol Avon barbel hierarchy wasn't lost on me.

Over time, other big fish were to grace the landing net with their presence and each winter would see me doing a rain dance, which seemed to work as it was rare that a couple of weeks would pass without a deluge filling the Avon, until it could no longer contain itself and sent water across the fields. Many tales could be told but one which saw a good friend strike gold sticks in my mind.

Shell-shocked!

Since becoming sponsored by Peter Drennan, I had regularly extolled the virtues of floodwater fishing to him, and eventually he decided to test my confidence in the method by agreeing to join me on a jaunt. I was happy to act as a ghillie for the day, while Peter wielded the rod, as I took us from one hotspot to another. Of course, the predictable happened and despite me promising a bite with every cast, all the reliable swims failed to materialise even a knock. Time was running out and while my job wasn't on the line, my pride certainly was. Being a Richard Walker disciple, the crude tackle and conditions I professed to love were alien to Peter. I wondered what he really thought as I identified a tiny slack against the nearside bank, which sat in an area where the depth increased.

With a heavy splash, the lead touched down on the surface and the thick rod tip cranked over in response, now engaged with the river. To the uninitiated, such unwieldy tackle can seem a strange affair although this is soon forgotten when a barbel tears off with the bait. So, in the gathering gloom of a midwinter afternoon I was relieved to watch the very same thing manifest itself in front of Peter. Given the lack of head shaking, the perpetrator of this event was immediately identified as a big fish, which was further, confirmed by an explosion on the surface and a sizeable copper flank twisting in defiance as it shone in the half-light. I don't know who was happier as Peter made the final adjustments and I scooped away with the net. At 12lb 5ozs it was a new personal best and, for me, justification of my methods. To add to the excitement, he then received a phone call giving him the news that he was to be a granddad to twins. Shell-shocked, he headed back to Oxfordshire with a huge smile across his face.

Barbel in Bath.

Wiltshire's waterways.

My new local patch was not all about winter fishing, though. For the first time in my career, fish could be stalked on a regular basis during the summer, and as I peered over gravel clearings among thick weed beds, it was a common sensation to feel my heart pounding with excitement while watching barbel, and a few other surprises, feeding.

From alongside a set of reed stems bouncing in the flow, two shapes made their way upstream, gorging on prawn-flavoured boilies. Their unusual form made me think that these fish weren't barbel as I would have expected, but carp - a chestnut-coloured mirror and, even more surprisingly, a ghosty. Both were big, but how big? I hoped to find out. With these two in the swim, all thoughts of barbel went out of the window even though I had tempted a double from the exact same spot the previous day.

As a shadow moved over my hookbait, I held my breath. Slowly, the mirror rose off the bottom and began shaking its head from side to side and I could see clearly my boilie hanging out of the corner of its mouth. Without thinking, I grabbed the rod, struck, and slid straight down the vertical bank into the river. Line screamed off the reel as a submarine charged upstream, ploughing through weed beds and reeds in an unstoppable surge serviced by pure anger. Quite simply, it was chewing up and spitting out the tackle. With a defiant roll on the surface it reached the tree branches trailing in the river and smashed me up; not a great outcome and I cursed my incompetence. Waist deep in water, I looked to the skies and screamed 'damn it!', or maybe something similar beginning with 'f'! Like a drowned rat, I clambered up the bank and lay on the grass, wallowing in self-pity and trying to regain a degree of composure. I vowed to return with stouter tackle and hoped that the carp wouldn't have been too alarmed by our encounter. To help regain their confidence I deposited a kilo of boilies into the swim. I'd be back!

Two days later, and I was again peering into the water that, importantly, contained no bait. Something had been feeding. Another handful of boilies was introduced and my eyes remained fixed on the gravel bed where they landed. Within minutes, shadows began dancing in front of me and from what I could make out, the culprits were two barbel and three small carp. The monsters had yet to show; maybe I just needed to be patient. With heavier tackle at my disposal of 15lb mono, a leadcore leader and a Stiff Rigger hook, I decided to place my hookbait into the swim, anyway. If they did come back, I wanted to be ready for them and not raise any suspicions with a cast. Over the next five hours, I kept the smaller fish at bay by flicking pellets on their heads every time they approached the bait, which seemed to do the trick. Unsettled, the fish would drop back but without spooking the rest of the swim, or indeed themselves, for very long.

By mid-afternoon, I was starting to lose faith when my attention was drawn to a grey shape upturned and feeding, to my right in the slacker water. I looked a little closer and could see the flank of a mirror, twisting and displaying a set of shimmering scales. This was neither of the big fish that I had seen previously but judging by its frame, it was certainly one worth catching.

Do or die.

For the first time, I allowed the fish to move out into the flow and above the hookbait. Immediately, it upturned and a puff of silt wafted downstream; then it rose sharply looking very agitated. There could only be one cause for this behaviour – my hook.

As I grabbed the rod, a huge explosion hit the surface and line began spinning from my reel. Once again, and without consideration for any safety, I jumped some six feet into the river. I didn't intend to suffer another loss but this carp wasn't going to make it easy. With the rod at its full arc, I turned my foe, spinning it on its back. 'Do or die' was the only option; I just couldn't let her reach the snags. The leadcore leader performed its task admirably, scything through a bed of reeds until the carp rolled in front of me. Still full of anger but toppled by the strength of the tackle, it was now within reach. I slipped the fish into the net and took a while to compose myself before hoisting her back up the bank and on to dry land. A gorgeous, scaly flank greeted me as I parted the mesh. She weighed in at just over 21lbs and I felt that I had put right my failure of a few days before.

With all the commotion, it was unsurprising that the swim was now devoid of fish so, still keen to enjoy more of the day, I decided to head downstream to try to extract a barbel from another spot that had also received a pre-baiting a few days previously.

I switched back to more appropriate tackle and lowered it on to the gravel glide, a PVA bag full of pellets with

Putting it right.

Next, a double.

my half-boilie hookbait hidden inside. Soon, a set of whiskers began twitching downstream attached to a long, bronze shape moving in and out of the flow. With a single flick of the tail, it propelled itself against the river looking to search out the source of the fishy aroma. From my vantage point, I could observe everything clearly and as it reached the bag's contents, it upturned and seemingly sucked up all the bait in one go. For a moment, it stayed motionless, before reality kicked in and a copper torpedo launched downstream with my rod doing its best to follow suit.

Fortunately, the fight was carried out in the deeper pool sitting directly below the swim and apart from the odd surge was a relatively relaxed affair. At least I hadn't needed to jump in again! With its white belly upturned in surrender, I netted my second good fish of the day – 11lbs 2ozs to be exact - making me one extremely happy angler.

Contently, I sat back on my chair and, almost as a second thought, placed a fresh hookbait on the hair. It was unlikely that anything else would feed but another hour on the riverbank would be a joy nonetheless, and I could revel in my success while smoking a cigar and watching the world go by.

Again, the bait was lowered on to the gravel strip, but before I could take a seat and relax I was gob-smacked to see a shoal of carp passing by. As they sensed my bait, the group came to a dead stop and a series of mouths began turning over stones in a bid to relieve their obvious hunger. Now I was in a quandary. Did I remove my barbel tackle and replace it with heavier gear or leave it where it was? The former would mean not spooking them but, then again, I ran the risk of another loss. In the end, I decided to leave the swim in peace and take my chances. It wasn't as snaggy, so I prayed everything would hold and hoped luck would continue to shine on me.

The ghosty of two days previously was one of the fish in attendance and it pushed forward up the gravel looking the most eager; well, that was until a large chestnut-coloured carp barged it out of the way.

Reacquainted.

Could it have been the one I lost? Before I had time to think any further, all hell broke loose and I found myself hanging on to a very angry fish. The first run was unstoppable, as it crashed into a set of far bank pads at full speed. Their stems ripped up from the bottom and reconnected to my line, and in Jaws-like fashion they were dragged under as the carp headed for deeper water. The barbel had shown the area to be snag-free, so I sighed in relief but I still only had a size 14 hook holding us together so it was going to be far from easy.

Five minutes seems an eternity when playing a fish and neither of us was prepared to lose. Then the seemingly relentless lunges began to subside slowly and the surface boils grew bigger and bigger until a pair of lips hit fresh air, gulping for water, and the fish, sapped of energy and with its tail now limp, admitted defeat. She was mine – a carp full of browns, greys, and purples. I pulled open her mouth and could see my hook sitting snugly in the corner, while opposite, another small red tear could clearly be seen. Yes, you've guessed it – it was the carp I had lost.

Living by the Avon during this time was a real joy but not once did I ever consider the old adage that 'nothing lasts forever'. As I write this, the spectre of otters has become a reality and the river, once so accommodating, has had its big fish larder stripped bare. No longer does *Lutra lutra* behave as a wild animal with a vast domain for a single creature, allowing a balance to be struck. No, these reintroduced, semi-tame animals hunt in packs, stripping the Avon and many other rivers of their aquatic jewels. Cormorants have already taken the silver fish, now our specimens are going the same way, and I ask what will be left? Surely, before any reintroduction programme commenced, the ecosystem from the base upwards should have been assessed, and with only a fraction of the otter's natural food, the eel, running the rivers today, devastation was the only conclusion.

Environmentalists and their hypocrisy make me sick and I can only hope that one day nature finds a balance, albeit at the expense of many rare creatures, even if they're not cute and cuddly. Maybe, putting a few of the people responsible into a cage with a bear would make them see sense. After all, this creature is indigenous as well!

Fortunately, Chippenham does afford a great gateway to many of our major waterways and as such, it does allow good sport still to be found within an hour's drive. One such place is the mighty river Severn, and a fishery I soon got my teeth into after moving west.

The lower Severn begins as it leaves behind the cathedral-filled skyline of Worcester, and the craggy outline of the Malvern hills fills the horizon with their patchwork quilt complexion made up of woods and grassland. Here, the average size of the river's barbel population grows, and within its constantly stained water, a monster becomes a possibility. My own introduction to the river came while working for the tackle manufacturer Leeda, and a friendship formed with colleague, Nick Young. As a local match angler, he knew the river well and took time out to show me around, which provided an oasis of great sport for years to come.

The Severn is the heart of caster and hemp fishing, so boilies and bolt rigs were very new when I first arrived on the scene, but it didn't take long for the barbel to seek out my offerings; in fact, the action was incredible. I can remember clearly, streams of bubbles cutting up the river as fish ripped up the sandy bottom, and my rods never stopped bouncing with line bites. A normal trip would see me open proceedings by catapulting two kilos of bait out and while this was left to work its magic I rigged up the tackle, giving the swim half an hour to stew. Two-pound test curve rods and freespool reels, similar to my floodwater tackle, were combined with 15lb line and bolt/hair rig terminal tackle. Unlike when fishing the smaller southern rivers, backleads proved impossible to use as these only doubled the odds of becoming snagged, so line bites were an occupational hazard. Not that this was much of an issue given the populations' naïvety, as they really were like lambs to the slaughter with this hi-tech approach. I was so confident, that if I was not playing a barbel within half an hour of casting out, I would move, as there obviously were no fish in residence.

This tactic worked well come summer or winter, although holding station in a flood of the magnitude that the Severn can throw at you was an interesting learning curve. No matter if 8oz leads were required and you only got ten minutes fishing time before being swept away, it was always better to cast into the middle than in a quieter slack. Contrary to popular opinion, the barbel wanted to be out in the full force of the flow, no doubt enjoying the food being brought down to them.

Sensational Severn.

Big river barbel.

Below Worcester.

If memory serves me correctly, for every ten fish I caught, one would be a double, which meant there were plenty of big fish on offer, as to catch this number in a single sitting was straightforward. With many specimens being 11 or 12lbs, a season's tally looked very impressive indeed. What I really desired from the river, however, was a truly big fish and my chance came on a dull and damp October afternoon.

Traversing a ploughed field made the walk a difficult affair as mud clung to my boots, sapping energy with each footfall. The corn had long since been harvested but the geese still sought to extract its remnants from the sodden earth. The river itself remained swollen from heavy rain in the Welsh mountains, but at least the leaves that blighted an angler's taut line seemed to have abated. To reach the swim I intended to fish meant abseiling a steep and treacherous muddy slope before a stable platform could be found on top of a series of large boulders. Quite why fish were so prolific in this area was up for debate, although I believe it was due to a very subtle narrowing of the river and the flow switching its force to the nearside. Other than that, it was a straight, unremarkable section of water but, interestingly, in the days of big open matches it was always viewed as a flyer.

A big prize.

I adopted my standard routine and it wasn't long before a barbel dragged the rod round, followed by another and another. When dusk arrived, the sport had been brisk although, unusually, every bite had come on the upstream rod, so it came as no surprise when once again it became engaged by a fish. However, the rapid surges generally associated with a shoal-size barbel didn't materialise this time, just a heavy pressure that cut upstream forcing the clutch to submit. Promisingly, there was a distinct lack of head shaking, just a constant, unrelenting force. How I love that sensation of carbon being flexed to the point of failure and mono being stretched without consideration; then, as the tackle's power begins to turn the tide, the first tail slaps arrive before gradually more and more of the barbel reveals itself.

This time was no different as realisation hit home that my original assessment was justified and a big, white undercarriage displayed itself against the tea-stained river. All I needed to do now was keep my composure and allow the landing net to end the battle; in she swung, out of the flow, until her head touched the spreader block. There, safely inside, was one of barbel angling's biggest prizes – a Severn monster weighing 14lbs 7ozs.

My move to Wiltshire had opened up a plethora of angling opportunities and provided me with a new set of challenges that only served to hone my abilities as an angler, all played out against the magnificent West Country landscape so, for now, Bedfordshire wasn't missed.

Camera: Canon EOS 300D - Shutter Speed: 1/320 sec - F-Stop: f/11.0 - ISO: 100 - Location: Linear Fisheries

CHAPTER 08

OXFORDSHIRE ESCAPADES

First, the delicate yellow petals of daffodils saturate the stark, colourless landscape and then the decoration explodes with a haze of bluebells alongside the sweet scent of blossom-filled trees. Finally, in a dramatic show of splendour, rhododendrons radiate through the countryside with their glorious mix of pinks and purples.

Fantastic float fishing.

Spring is, without doubt, my favourite season. Stillwaters awaken with vigour from their slumber and, fortunately for we anglers, this isn't restricted to what happens above the surface. Tench in particular find themselves reinvigorated by the rising temperatures and leave the silt beds that provided a place to hibernate, to head once more toward the margins.

With this exercise comes an urge to feed. Not only to replace fat reserves lost during the colder months, but also to cope with the exertions of spawning that lie ahead. If there is ever a time to target this species it arrives with spring, and the rural county of Oxfordshire calls me time and time again, when it's the season to target *Tinca tinca*. Obviously, the tench grow to specimen proportions here but the friendships formed in the area make it equally attractive as I make my annual pilgrimage.

Roy Parsons is a man who doesn't tolerate fools gladly and he runs the famous Linear Fisheries with a firm but fair attitude. Ably assisted by Chris, Colin, Basil and John, Roy provides the chance for a day-ticket angler to catch both tench and carp of monstrous proportions. Over the years, I have lost count of the number of magazine features I have created around the fishery, and with Linear's help, they usually go to plan.
The steep, marginal slopes around the gravel pits provide perfect ambush points from which to snare a tench, its pursuit further enhanced by the possibility of using a float. Oxfordshire is, to my mind, the spiritual home of lift method fishing with the likes of Stone and Drennan plundering the clear, pea-shingled margins in the 1970s and 80s. Another character who was equally as prolific during this period was John Everard; a man who to this day practises the art to great effect. Fortunately, for me, two of these anglers, Peter Drennan and John, have become personal friends, enabling me to enjoy an apprenticeship in a tactic that is as enigmatic as it is effective.

Firstly, a stout float rod is required and unsurprisingly with my contacts, I use the Drennan Tench Float. Its sweet action and powerful backbone is capable of taming the biggest of tench, and it has the bonus of having enough strength to deal with the odd rogue carp that is an occupational hazard in the county's waters. For me, a centrepin enhances the pleasure of the method still further, and this is loaded with 7lb Double Strength. I know many people shy away from this product, but if you follow two golden rules then unforeseen breakages will not be an issue. Firstly, only use a palomar knot with this material, and always fish it directly through to the hook. This maximises the elasticity of both the line and the rod. Monofilament gains much of its strength by an ability to stretch and the shorter this area is, the greater the reduction. Tie six inches of pre-stretched line to a couple of swivels, and it will break far more easily between these fixed points than, say, over 20 feet. Only with braid is its strength unaffected, so the terminal tackle I use for tench fishing reflects this.

First, an insert crystal waggler is slipped on to the line with a length of silicone tubing that acts as a way to fix it in place rather than the standard shot approach. Should the float then snag in a weed bed, it will pull free without damage to the mono. The length of the waggler is also important to avoid being dragged under by wave movement and undertow. The general rule of thumb is that the stronger the wind, the longer the float.

With lift method fishing, fancy shotting patterns are replaced with a single anchor weight and, once again, everything is done to avoid line damage. By using a micro ring with a loop of braid passed through it, the X2 or X3 swan shot can be pinched on to this material instead. A tiny bead comes next, which then pushes up against two float stops, creating the start of the hooklength.

Spring's here.

Method par excellence.

This can be made as long or as short as required simply by sliding the rubber widgets up and down the line. Last, but not least, comes the hook and this is matched to the bait selected. All that is then left to do is to set the outfit at the correct depth. I like to adjust this to a float length over-depth, and then by slowly winding while the rod stays steady on a couple of rests, the tension created cocks and settles the float with the tip just showing. What has been created is akin to a coiled spring waiting to explode at the faintest of touches; the manifestation being either a rising float or one that is simply dragged under. This is a supreme method for spring tench, although, as always, location is vital to achieve results.

The best item of tackle any angler possesses is his eyes, and dawn normally brings with it paintbrush tails smashing against the surface. Bubbles breaking free of the water are also a dead giveaway, with a frothy residue left on show. Insect hatches should never be ignored, especially the emergence of damsel flies which traditionally herald the prime time for float fishing. Wind also has a huge impact at this time of year because it congregates the natural resources into a confined area. Weed growth starts, too, and despite the difficulty of fishing over this substrate, it doesn't prevent tench from enjoying its rich larder. Here, the method par excellence is the humble garden rake, well, two, in fact, that have been wired back-to-back and connected to a long length of rope. By cutting a narrow channel through the vegetation, the hookbait can be positioned on a clean bottom and sit within an inviting maelstrom of sediment, rich in food. I generally do this the evening before a planned trip, although the disturbance acts as an attraction and fish will arrive to investigate within minutes, let alone hours.

Finally, we come to exactly where to place the hookbait in the swim. Make an incorrect choice here and you could still fail, despite all the planning. At the bottom of the marginal slope silt and debris collect, allowing filter feeding to occur. This, I have found, is notoriously difficult to catch over. Once a fish starts to sift through the lake bed, an angler's bait is soon ignored in preference for natural food. Instead, I look to cast three-quarters of the way down the slope, where there is still plenty of water over the quarry's head but the bottom is made up of clean gravel. This then creates a situation where baits are being picked up individually, causing errors to occur far more regularly. With all types of angling, correct bait placement can play a huge part in catching and sometimes a foot can make a difference. So let's return to Linear Fisheries. A double-figure tench on the float was always a special goal of mine and one that was achievable on the complex, with the methods described.

A glint of sun.

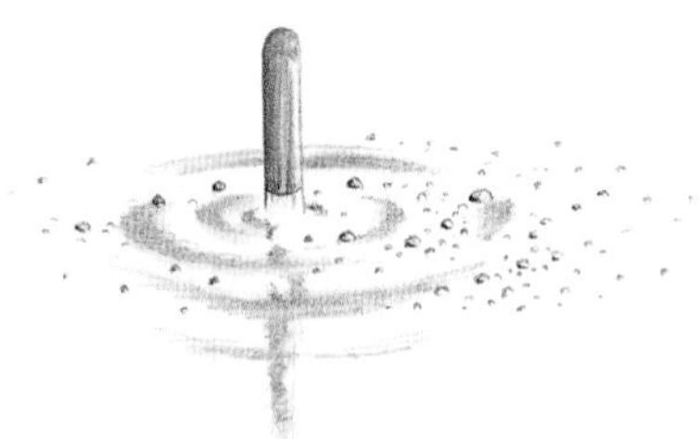

Smith's Pool provided both Evy (John Everard) and I with our first stop of the day. As we walked along the works bank loaded with tackle, it was noticeable that a drop in temperature had occurred since the previous couple of weeks. A gentle south-westerly had now been replaced with a firm north-easterly that cut an unseasonal chill through the air. Fortunately, an area of the lake was sheltered from this cold wind, leaving a bay in its lee, flat calm and bathed in sunlight. We felt sure the fish would prefer this warmth, even if it did go against convention, as it really was bitter. A little hempseed and maggot was introduced down the marginal shelf in two spots while both of us began to assemble our tackle.

Float fishing was to be the order of the day, fished, of course, lift method style. For a hookbait I impaled a single Mini Meaty Fish Bite on the size 12 hook, its oily residue coating my fingertips before dropping on to the lake's surface and causing a slick to form.

I hoped that this would provide something very visual and pungent among the particles, for the tench to home in on should a shoal discover the feast.

Within minutes of casting out it became obvious that fish were indeed present, as the float dipped and pulled in response to line bites. The tench were moving up the shelf, picking up food as they went, and a mistake, I felt sure, would shortly occur. In May, this species can be extremely foolhardy, unlike its post-spawning persona, and over the next few hours three tench fell foul of the meaty offering, though disappointingly, weighing only in the 4lb to 5lb category.

Evy and I decided a move was required if we wanted to catch a bigger stamp of fish; but where? We were spoilt for choice with the number of gravel pits at our disposal and, for once, rather than trust our own instincts, a phone call to head bailiff, Roy, was in order. I don't think I've ever known a bailiff work so hard. He walks continuously around the numerous pits on the complex, and if Roy didn't know where to find a big tench, no one would! True to form, he came up trumps pointing us in the direction of the Guy Lakes complex, identifying Unity in particular as having the potential we sought. At approximately 12 acres, it was home to a big head of 20lb-plus carp, as well as tench into double figures. Roy even managed to tell us the exact swims to fish – now that's what I call service!

Introducing a little free bait two rod lengths out beside a reed bed, I flicked out my float and sat back to await events. Almost immediately, the surface became filled with bubbles as fish below began rooting for food. Within 10 minutes my swim resembled a jacuzzi, but for some bizarre reason I couldn't buy a bite. John though, had seen it all before and told me this was common on the Oxfordshire pits. His theory was, that by fishing at the bottom of the marginal shelf, the heads of the fish become buried in the collected silt while rooting for food. This, in turn, makes good hookbait presentation very difficult. John recommended that I fished closer in, down the side of the shelf where the bottom was hard and gravelly. No longer could the fish bury their heads and their feeding manner was far more conducive for bites. It was a valuable lesson and one that should never be ignored.

Following his instructions, I moved the float's position to under the rod tip and began feeding around it. Like magic it dipped, then lifted, before I struck and the culprit tried desperately to exact its revenge by testing the tackle and sending the centrepin spinning like a Catherine wheel. Over the next hour, more fish in the 5lb class were to follow until, as before, my float rose in the water, momentarily dithering before falling flat and lifeless. When I struck it felt like I'd hit the proverbial brick wall. That was until the pin nearly exploded as a missile with fins screamed off through the reed beds to my right and out into the depths, with unrelenting surges. Sadly, it was clear this wasn't my target at all, but a carp that, on such fine tackle, I felt I had little chance of beating. During the battle, my Double Strength line entered and left the rings with a grating sound, such was its condition, and to the touch it felt like sandpaper – the direct result of being dragged through numerous reed beds. Somehow, after a lot of praying, it held on and after half-an-hour with my arm and wrist aching, a 21lb carp was finally banked. It was proof, if any were needed, that fishing directly through from the reel to the hook does maximise the tackle strength. After that battle, I hoped that no more carp would gatecrash the tenching because I couldn't have faced another exhausting battle. Instead, pleasingly, a string of tincas continued to fall foul of the tackle, with my swim continuously resembling a witch's cauldron as they fed with gay abandon. They seemed to have lost their minds to the gluttonous urges of spring, while I revelled in the sport.

Ten pounds and more.

Once again, the crystal waggler disappeared from view and for the umpteenth time my strike was met with resistance. This fish immediately felt different. It remained deep; its extra weight accompanied by a heavy, ponderous action that lacked the speed of a carp but retained the strength. Immediately, I felt sure I had hooked what I had been hoping for which caused the adrenalin to course rapidly through my veins. For five minutes, it plodded along the margin refusing to show itself, punishing the tackle with its muscular frame and trying to seek out any weaknesses. Then slowly but surely, I began to gain the upper hand. The rod started to impart its will on the fight and my opponent's bulk rose in the water causing the battle now to take place in the relative safety of the surface layer.

A huge, green flank appeared, glinting in the dappled sunlight, before a vast tail slapped as it once again headed for the bottom in one final act of defiance. Heart in mouth, I tried to regain control of the situation and over the next few minutes was once more placed on the back foot. Again, it rose in the water but this time head first and gasping. The waiting net scooped her up and I stared into the mesh in disbelief. Inside lay a monstrous beast, its gravid condition increasing the strain as I lifted it free of the water and on to the mat. The scales were a formality and merely confirmed what I already knew I had achieved; a double-figure fish on the float. The official result was 10lb 5oz. A weight made up of a thousand emerald scales, a pair of red, teddy-bear eyes, and a set of fins with power to spare. What, I asked as I grinned at the camera, could be better than the sun on my back and two big handfuls of tench?

As I have already touched upon, magazine features are an integral part of my Oxfordshire escapades, and, however enjoyable float fishing is, it cannot always be the basis for them. It would be churlish to complain though, as a big fish, however it's caught, always supplies a moment to remember and, of course, it reinforces the notion that in angling there is always more than one way to skin a cat.

The previous season, a local specimen hunter, Stuart Roper, of Linch Hill roach fame, had indulged in a spot of tenching on the gravel pit called St John's. His reward was four doubles to over 11lb – spectacular in anyone's book and a feat I predictably found hard to ignore - but why, like so many carp lakes, did it contain such huge fish? With a limited stock (I suspect the lake's catfish have devoured a few) and an endless supply of protein-rich food, you have a recipe for a leviathan. This potential is further increased if you also factor in that tench are cute creatures that don't often fall for crude carp rigs. It means they can browse unmolested, creating a perfect scenario for growth - and one I hoped to capitalise on.

In the shallow bay where Stuart had enjoyed his success, I placed my gear down and surveyed the scene. The bank to my left ran some 100 yards away from me, with an inlet water pipe situated halfway up the margin. Straight in front, and out in open water, sat a bar at 15 yards that sloped down from three feet to six feet. These two areas would be the focus of my attention, although I did have one slight reservation. For the bay to fish well it needed to be warm but once again, the English countryside was devoid of sunlight and two days of continuous heavy rain were forecast.

This, I felt, could have prevented the fish from visiting the area and, being a busy venue, other options were limited so I tried to remain positive. I hoped that maybe only the lake's carp population had taken notice of the conditions and left the area. If the tench had then stayed behind, they would become easier to target, unmolested by riotous cyprinids. Getting on with the job in hand, both areas were laced heavily with red maggots, casters, and 3mm Marine Halibut pellets via a spod. If the fish did pass through, I certainly didn't want them leaving.

I always find that the tackle for legering on such waters is something of a compromise. You need to cast adequate distances but still have a rod that allows you to enjoy the fight – and, of course, it needs to be capable of subduing rogue carp. Therefore, I settled for a 2lb test curve model combined with a 12lb fluorocarbon main line. It may have been a little heavy for tench but I was not prepared to snap up and leave a carp with a rig in its mouth. For my terminal tackle, I opted for a Method feeder. Tench in spring are lazy, hungry creatures and if they enter the swim and have a choice between one big mouthful, or sifting through particles, the easy option will be taken.

A float-caught monster.

Maggot muncher.

Hold on!

Last laugh.

Eat my hat.

It's not a carp.

The method mix I used couldn't have been simpler. Boiling water was poured over Marine Halibut pellets and then, 20 minutes later, they became soft enough to bind together. At this stage, I used a little trout pellet powder to create a tackier mix, which would help it stick to the feeder better. Finally, a sprinkling of untreated pellets, hemp, and casters was tossed in to further increase the attraction levels.

With the mix prepared, it was now time to connect the hooklength; this was also made up of 12lb fluorocarbon and kept short. A size 14 Super Specialist Barbel hook sat at the business end, attached using a knotless knot. It was vital that the hook was very strong, otherwise it could snap given its small dimension. The forces applied would not be dampened by the mono's ability to stretch and so the hook would take all the strain. Finally came the bait - three artificial casters, semi-buoyant, critically balancing the rig. With everything now ready, I made the casts to the areas identified, marked my lines with pole elastic and waited for events to unfold.

Unfortunately, the carp hadn't read the script. The blighters quickly picked up on the scent of my banquet and did their very best to get me soaking wet by making me play them in the rain on a regular basis. Obviously, the cooler temperatures hadn't prevented them from visiting the bay after all. Luckily, the hook never failed me once and by the following morning, I had tempted a string of fish.
Sadly, not one exhibited a green flank and on Roy's

arrival I gave him some stick about there being too many carp in residence. No sooner had the words left my mouth than the indicator pulled up tight. "Not another carp," I said, convinced that a mud-sucker was again responsible. Roy, in his matter-of-fact-way just told me to stop moaning. Halfway in, and I asked if I could change my mind. I was now beginning to think it might be a tench after all.

"Do you know what you're doing, Mr Bowler?" came Roy's rebuttal. Sure enough, a huge green flank hit the surface. It was as deep as it was long and I certainly didn't want to make a mistake in a battle that had the added pressure of a certain Mr Parsons and his quick wit in the background. A few further flutters of the heart followed before I could touch my prize. It was, of course, now time for Roy to pull my leg.

The dimensions of the tench were amazing, the depth and width being greater than anything I had seen before. On length alone, it would perhaps have weighed 6lb but this was far bigger than that. Its pellet diet had turned it into the Incredible Hulk. Roy did the honours with the scales and read out 10lb 6oz.

Bloody carp!

Under the stars.

The delights of Oxfordshire sit less than an hour away from my home but another huge complex of gravel pits are even closer to hand. The Cotswold Water Park is positioned at the head of the Thames Valley, and covers some 40 square miles with a mosaic of over 140 lakes that have been created from 50 years of quarrying. Having shifted 100 million-plus tonnes of gravel, if you view a map of this area the land is lost in a swathe of blue. Here, in this vast wetland, nature thrives, from the little ringed plover to the lesser emperor dragonfly. Predictably, fish also find a home here, with tench once again high on my hit list as the month of June arrives. It's a pleasure and pursuit that I share every season with a resident to the area, Steve Rowley.

With a bottle of white wine cooling in the lake's margin and the barbecue's coals helping to sizzle burgers, chops and corn on the cob, life couldn't have been better. Combine that with a spot of angling on a summer's evening and heaven doesn't feel too far away. My companion Steve and I had at last got together for a long overdue trip and it had started in our normal, sedate, and very civilised manner. For the time being, our own greed took precedence over the fish.

Admittedly, our carp rods were out but with the bite alarms turned up to full volume, they could look after themselves while we traded fishing stories and put the world to rights. Tomorrow would see the fishing begin in earnest, when we hoped to become acquainted with the lake's bream and tench population. By bivvying up overnight, a dawn start certainly wouldn't be a chore, as it meant rolling out of bed, literally. My seat box and rod were already in place and Steve had baited two spots over the previous few days with groundbait and pellets that we intended to cast to. So, for now, we could relax, enjoy the evening and watch the sun succumb to the night with a blaze of orange, while we drank far too much wine.

Opening my eyes, I stared across a calm surface that gently steamed away as the horizon began to regather its golden glow. A pair of grebes courted each other while a brood of ducklings were up early with their mum in search of their breakfast. They weren't the only hungry ones it seemed, as a tench porpoised over the groundbait, closely followed by the forked tail of a bream. It was time to get up. As I stretched, a sheet of bubbles erupted in front of me, reinforcing the point that I should forego my bed and get a move on.

Slipping into the water, my bare feet felt its temperature and were pleasantly surprised - it definitely had a warm edge to it, no doubt helping to fuel the appetite of the shoal currently in front of me. It was great to be fishing at dawn in a T-shirt and shorts, with the call of a cuckoo carrying across the lake and banded demoiselles skimming the surface. This was a moment to savour prior to the first cast; a delicious blend of anticipation and excitement. Once my mind becomes focused on catching fish, I tend to miss nature's show so a momentary pause before the fishing began in earnest allowed me to appreciate how lucky I was to be an angler.

Roll out of bed.

Social success.

Pressing the feeder into the groundbait, I prepared to make the first cast. The required distance was reached and the rod tip plunged beneath the surface to sink the line and aid bite detection. I had selected a 2oz glass tip to combat the lake's undertow – something that occurs on all but the smallest of venues. It's interesting to note that it doesn't always coincide with the wind direction and should be factored in during swim selection, as natural food items will be carried along on this current. A spin of the reel's handle put the faintest of curves into the tip and I waited for the first sign. Perched on a seat box, I was not only afforded a grandstand view of the situation, I was also in the perfect position to attack the swim. I had learnt, a long time ago, that copying the way a match angler fishes is far superior to that afforded by a carp style chair. Casting, striking and playing fish is carried out in a much more fluid motion which, in turn, maximises results.

For the task of extracting big fish from this weedy water, a heavy feeder rod was combined with a stout 8lb line. This would also help to overcome the rigours of throwing out a large feeder, while I hoped a 4lb hooklength to a 14 hook would tame any fish tempted.

Given the surface disturbance, it didn't take long for the first sign to arrive. A slow deliberate pull on the tip provided the indication but this was no bite - instead it was caused by a liner. I took this as my cue to reel in and shorten the cast by five yards. Picking fish out of the shoal around its edge, rather than in the centre, would mean I could preserve the longevity of the sport I hoped to enjoy. A series of tiny knocks kept me alert but I find constant striking is something to be avoided; today, it was a case of sitting on my hands and waiting for the handle to spin.

As the first tench crashed on the surface in indignation, the 13 foot of carbon hooped over in delight and I knew that my tactical selection had been vindicated, if not by results, just by pure enjoyment afforded by the method employed. Let's face it, a battery of bite alarms and bolt rigs do remove a little of the fun. A large bream next, falling off at the net, made me reconsider momentarily, but this was followed by a run of moderate slabs and chunky tench to over 8lb, all testing the fragile but balanced outfit to the full. As each fight drew to a close, the water boiled and strands of dislodged Canadian pond weed hit the surface before I turned them for the final time and wielded the net. I was addicted. As quickly as I caught, all I wanted to do was recast again!

The next bite was one even a blind man couldn't have missed and contact immediately put me on the back foot. The battle then turned into a game of hide-and-seek, with every weed bed, however sparse, being used as cover and my line slicing through the vegetation. Trying not to panic, I teased the fish out of each one with the rod fully compressed. This caused the mono to act like a cheese wire, severing the strands that held it captive. With her energy spent, the fish submitted to the inevitable and surrendered herself to the surface. She was clearly still in a gravid condition and with this extra weight my scales read out a whopping 9lb 3oz. She was a tench to be proud of on any method but particularly pleasing on a quiver tip. That wasn't the end of it, either. Another specimen of 9lb 2oz also granted me an audience. It had been pleasure fishing at its very best, set against the backdrop of one of the country's finest and largest aquatic environments.

Oxfordshire and Gloucestershire provide more challenges than even a dozen lifetimes would fail to exploit, so when spring casts its spell across the countryside you can be sure where to find me.

Well done, Dad.

Camera: Canon EOS 300D - Shutter Speed: 1/60 sec - F-Stop: f/4.0 - ISO: 100 - Location: Upper Bristol Avon

CHAPTER 09

TALE OF TWO AVONS

Gently, the shoal sways to and fro, its silver complexion glinting as it rides the river's flow. Ever vigilant, the smallest of tremors, be it from a cormorant or a heavy-footed angler, will be enough to see its form evaporate but for now it offers one of the natural world's greatest wonders – a congregation of big roach. After years of decimation, our rivers no longer support many such colonies and the final few continue to fall foul of predation and pollution, so being a river roach angler is akin to being a ghost hunter.

Those fortunate souls who have felt the pulse of a specimen through a taut line as it spins in the flow will know what a struggle it is to give up the hunt; no matter how poor the odds. Like a drug, the addiction needs to be fed and just because the high is harder to find every year, it doesn't mean a roach junkie won't continue to try to get a fix. These are mostly men in their 50s and 60s, who had the good fortune to fish for the species when it was a viable proposition. Unfortunately, my generation and younger have never had that luxury, so just like the fish itself, river roach anglers are a dying breed. Have no doubt that catching a specimen over 2lb is far from an easy task, and if you are to achieve this goal, the search will be a long and arduous one.

Growing up in Bedfordshire offered almost no hope of such a prize, so it was with some good fortune that later in life my adopted home county of Wiltshire, and its neighbour Hampshire, provided me with at least a chance. With both the Bristol and Hampshire Avon at my disposal, they did hold fish to the size I required, albeit still thin on the ground. For an angler used to rivers that hardly ever flowed, the baptism was one of fire and was further exacerbated by my succumbing to the idyllic notion that the West's waterways were paved with silver. The truth is though, that even on these rivers just finding a roach is trial enough, so after a little suffering I soon put this requirement at the forefront of any attempt.

My first stroke of luck in this department was due to the kindness of Pete Reading. He duly obtained a syndicate ticket for me, for a stretch of the Hampshire Avon just upstream of Burgate; the water was controlled at the time by legendary roach angler, Gerry Swanton. At least I knew that however scarce the population, there would be some in residence and that was a good starting place. This then led to my first big Hampshire Avon roach of 2lbs 9oz. A fish, I have to admit, that hung itself on to a maggot feeder rig; the skill level I applied in its downfall was minimal to say the least. The most important thing achieved, was that the spell had been broken and while I was never going to catch vast numbers of specimens, they were no longer impossible. The tactics used on the river also fell into place over the first few years. I couldn't claim to be any kind of expert but I did practise the necessary art of bread fishing until I reached a moderate level of competence. Trust me, fishing this bait in fast flows beneath a float requires an apprenticeship and with each passing season it is one that has fewer and fewer disciples. In time, I fear, it will cease to be passed down the generations altogether.

A tinge of colour to the river's complexion is absolutely essential to achieve success with bread. Find the venue with only a couple of feet visibility, and you're on to a winner with this doughy offering. The tackle I use is particularly suited for England's fast lowland rivers and is based around a 15-foot float rod. This additional length allows me to stay in control of the bait throughout the duration of the trot, something that is vital to achieve natural presentation. This length of carbon is then coupled with either a fixed spool reel capable of an immaculate line lay to ensure a smooth trot, or the more aesthetically pleasing centrepin.

To my mind, the pin should only be employed when fishing at close proximity, for example under the rod tip, and in this scenario a free-running drum, checked occasionally by the angler's index finger, will provide sublime presentation. However, it's vital that once you venture out into the river you don't become a slave to this method because all control will be lost.

Following tradition.

As I'm targeting specimen-sized fish in strong flows, my main line of choice is 3lb or 4lb, which is always treated with line floatant to keep control and stop the bait being dragged off a straight course. When employing top and bottom floats you do not want the line to sink and by keeping it ultra-buoyant, you will mend any bows formed with greater ease.

Float selection, as already hinted at, is a range of traditional English classics like loafers and Avons, both of which provide a buoyant body and a bulbous tip. These will ride through the fast flows encountered during the winter months far better than slimline varieties like sticks, which simply get swamped by the river's power. What I'm trying to achieve is complete control over the bait and therefore models with large shotting capacities are preferred. The last thing you want is your lump of bread jumping around as it passes through a shoal of roach, and the extra weight prevents this. Generally, I bulk shot at three-quarters depth, combined with two or three droppers. Once again, these should be on the heavy side and no smaller than a No 4, otherwise such a buoyant bait will simply waft around in an unnatural manner. I would go so far as to say that the best bread fishermen I know angle in a very crude manner, with floats resembling more those of a pike fisherman than a roach angler!

In recent years, a handy addition has been the micro swivel to replace the second dropper shot. This prevents line twist and tangles caused during the retrieve. Last, but certainly not least, comes the hooklength and this is a pre-stretched line in the 2lb to 3lb category. A spade end knot then attaches a size 12 to 16 hook dependent on the dimension of flake selected. The model chosen has to have a large gape to make a better connection when using big baits.

How you attach your bread will have a huge impact on your strikes-to-fish-hooked ratio, so it is not a case of just squeezing it on. The type of bread to select for hookbaits is a long-life loaf, as the preservatives found in this product will give you a nice tacky piece of flake. Firstly, I take a lump the size of a fingernail and squeeze it down the shank, then twist the trapped hook around so that the point is protruding. Do not press too hard or mould your flake; just a light connection between hook and bread is needed. If it is still connected when I reel in, then I know I have applied too much pressure. A roach wants a very fluffy expanded piece of flake, which wafts tantalizingly.

The groundbait used to entice the roach to feed is also crucial and needs to be prepared with care. A standard loaf should be used now and this must be allowed to dry out a little by leaving exposed overnight. It should then be placed in a liquidizer to produce a fine crumb that contains no lumps or crust. If necessary, I use a riddle to remove any larger particles and throw them away. This will make up 75 per cent of the finished mix, the other 25 per cent being brown crumb. By adding this material, the groundbait will gain binding properties, as well as weight, which is vital to get it through the fast flow and on to the bottom. It's here where I want the tangerine-sized ball to break up and send its milky food items downstream in a cloud. Therefore, I add water slowly to ensure the correct consistency is achieved. As a general rule of thumb, I then feed the swim every dozen casts and continue to do so for an hour, by which time, if no bites are forthcoming, I will move swims. The old adage of 'little and often' is very apt in this scenario and is one of the golden rules of float fishing. In extreme flows,

Show time.

I sometimes include aquarium gravel up to a 10 per cent ratio because this adds additional weight to the mix and gets it to the bottom.

Mobility, as I've just mentioned, is key to bread fishing and I only ever fish with a small rucksack, bait apron, and a landing net. Specimen roach will not be spread out evenly in a river and by fishing half-a-dozen swims in a day, I will have a far greater chance of meeting up with them. Prime time is the final hour of daylight, so I always ensure that I continue fishing right into darkness, knowing that bread has an uncanny knack of tempting the very biggest fish as the sun sets.

Still, I have to admit that however much I try to learn about these fickle creatures they have a habit of staying one step ahead of me. Remember, they have not grown large on angler's feed and do not need to eat my bait, which presents a very difficult puzzle to solve. If there weren't enough already, another problem with tempting Hampshire Avon roach is the size of the shoals, which are often made up of less than a dozen big fish. Unhelpfully, these are accompanied by swarms of dace and smaller roach, too. The chances of you catching your target with these odds are greatly diminished because, once the swim is disturbed by even a tiddler, the wise old monsters simply melt away. I have witnessed this on many occasions, with none more relevant than a winter trip to the spire-filled horizon near Salisbury.

The old boathouse cast its shadow across the side streams and confluence with the main river. In such shade, weed life had never taken a grip, leaving the gravel below crisp and clean; a perfect area for roach to gather prior to spawning. Not only was the bottom suitable but the structure above also provided shelter from the dreaded cormorant. All that was left to hassle them was a silly jack pike that held station a few yards below, but this was no match for a wild old sage of the Avon.

As if this wasn't enough, a further comfort blanket was in situ in the form of two rowing boats and a canoe that swayed gently from side to side, pivoting on the rope that held them in place. It was only when the hulls swung to their furthest axes that Pandora's box was left ajar and the silhouettes could momentarily be seen. Roach of such proportions that would make any man dizzy with excitement lived under the saturated timber. As the door cranked open once again, I came under their spell and I could only hope that this time a similar fate didn't befall me as on the previous trip, when I had failed miserably.

It was quite clear that the specimens were still present but likewise their dace bodyguards were also close at hand and it was these that had previously proved to be my downfall. By hooking one of them, alarm had spread through the shoal, scuppering my chances. Maybe, today, the entire congregation could be made to back out of the boathouse, giving me a chance to stalk the fish I desired. A trickle of feed upstream saw the shoal become agitated but once they realised that the disturbance was being created by food, their wariness subsided and the occasional particle began to be taken. Twenty minutes of this and the big roach started to drift across the current, away from the sanctuary of their green canoe and into open water, albeit still under the boathouse. Unlike the dace though, they didn't hold station here, taking mere mouthfuls before heading back to their base and away from my grasp. What could hold them a little longer? Hemp seed? This pungent particle, I hoped, would stay in the swim longer, and therefore occupy the roach, but once again, my chosen quarry weren't prepared to play ball. If I couldn't get them to remain in this position, there was absolutely no chance of pulling the shoal out into daylight. I needed to find another way to skin the cat!

Boathouse bounty.

What had occurred during feeding was a definite divide in the shoal. The lesser fish had readily accepted the crumb and sat immediately downstream of the feed,

A perfect plan.

while the monsters, as I have already said, were less willing recipients and sat on the other side of the stream. Could this split of sizes be the answer to the quandary I faced?

Back at the van, I grabbed a set of chest waders and the outfit I intended to use. Rods of 15 feet in length may be well the tools of choice in the main river, but here something much shorter was required. A soft, splice-tipped model of only 13 feet was combined with fine line to a small buoyant float and a size 14 hook and I was ready to implement the plan! So slipping into the river five yards above the boathouse, I waded out to mid-flow and peered downstream under its roof and into the darkness. All the time I had been completing this procedure, a trickle of groundbait was being fed down the inside line to keep the interest going. For once, I was going to ignore the rulebook and fish away from my free offerings. I knew the situation wasn't perfect but at least the odds of a successful outcome had been increased - or so I hoped.

On the first trot down, the water continued to do its best to defeat me, this time in the shape of a shoal of gudgeon that blocked the entrance to the boathouse, grabbing at the hookbait until it had been robbed. On the second run down, and now with a bigger lump of flake on, I ignored the first attack as the float continually bobbed from the attention of small fish, only relenting as it entered the canopy's shadow. I just had to hope that the bait was still intact.

Kissing against the canoe, the bulbous orange tip followed its contours, reaching the three-quarters point before dragging under. Without time to make any assessment, I swept back the rod and forced it to yield into a delightful semi-circle. The thump that followed told its own story. I would love to describe the battle with a big roach as enjoyable but to be honest I find it terrifying. With soft mouths coupled with strong flows, disaster is never far away. Every lunge tested my heart until at last the landing net put an end to the torment. At 2lb 3oz, I had proved that where there's a will there's a way, no matter how cruel the river can be. Imagine though, what chance you have of catching when you can't see the fish; a scenario played out 99 per cent of the time?

Avon angling.

Usually, my roach fishing is confined to the winter months but sometimes the lure of a set of silver scales gets the better of me and I have to forego the pursuit of traditional summer species for a riverside jaunt. This season brings its own problems, making catching my target far from a foregone conclusion.

Wandering down across the meadow it was hard to believe that high summer had arrived across England. The sky-blue canvas was interspersed with clouds the colour of ink, a legacy of the recent climate of heavy showers. The strong breeze scudded their shadows across the grass and wild flowers, until finally hitting the Avon, momentarily removing its sparkle. While I didn't relish their monsoon-like properties I knew the low light levels would find favour with the roach. My destination today was a large sweeping bend that saw the gravel bottom fall away to form a large hole and it was inside this bowl that I hoped the redfins would be situated. Alas, I knew these wouldn't be the only residents, because hordes of hungry dace, a shoal of chub, and for good measure a rogue carp lived there, too! I concluded that my hookbait of sweetcorn would confound the dace but the rest of the residents could all be an issue by coveting the juicy kernel. At least the swim was a large one, which I hoped would tolerate any disturbance.

A feeder rod was to provide the backbone of my approach and this was combined with a fixed spool reel and 5lb mono. The terminal tackle involved was not complex. A running paternoster and feeder with a long, 3lb tail, culminated in a size 14 hook to which a single piece of corn could be hooked. To add attraction, the feeder's cargo was a mixture of small pellets and hemp seed. My plan for success didn't rely on bamboozlement, just good, old-fashioned watercraft and, I have to admit, a large degree of luck! So with a sideways flick of the rod, the game of cat-and-mouse began and the feeder descended to the bottom of the Avon. The 3oz glass quiver tip tensioned under its pulse. All I could do in the situation I faced was hope that bites wouldn't materialise from the array of other fish present, allowing the roach to remain undisturbed until the hemp seed proved too tempting for even this most cunning of creatures. Any rustles on the tip caused by desperate dace would be ignored and only a positive pull would see a reaction from me. Well, that was the plan anyway

As expected, the dace did try to tempt me into striking until eventually they became bored, but it was the persistent line bites that concerned me most. The perpetrators could easily devour the corn and I would have no way of knowing until it was too late. A few minutes later, the inevitable came to pass and my rod tip arched over in an alarming fashion. Immediately, it was obvious no roach could exert such force and to make matters worse, the carp to which I was connected did its very best to trash the swim. With each lunge came an equal measure of pleasure and pain for this angler until eventually, a double-figure mirror lay inside the net. My only chance now would be to show some patience, as the water needed to regain its tranquillity before a roach risked a return, let alone a feed. Unfortunately, the chub that then followed would have tested even a saint and with each one, the plan was put back by hours. I was helpless, but at least the odds were slowly falling in my favour. The crucial time would come in the final quarter of daylight, I told myself.

Nothing had troubled me for over an hour and, as the sun began to turn from yellow to orange, the river's trout were treated to a fly hatch that caused a series of explosions on the surface. It had me half wishing I had packed the fly tackle.

The worm had turned.

Sweetcorn silver.

I needed to remain focused on the slender white tip, though, because this period, I knew, was my best chance. So leaning over slightly, I put myself on red alert, and I was duly rewarded by a series of abrupt, but solid movements on the rod tip. Instinctively, I struck and held my breath but had it been successful? And, more importantly, what was on the other end?

A jag, jag, jag sensation resonated back to me in roach Morse code. The roller-coaster ride was about to begin and when each boil hit the surface, my heart skipped a beat. Desperately, I strained for a glimpse; somehow believing that seeing its proportions would settle the nerves. Of course, as a silver flank presented itself I felt worse, convinced that the hook hold was loosening all the time. Twice, I tried to end the event prematurely with my landing net and indeed, I nearly did, only not with the conclusion wanted. I needed to regain composure. A big fish was at stake so I told myself to stop being so stupid! Up she came again under steady pressure and at last, it was time to see who would win the duel.

'Come on, please, please, please,' were the words I spoke out loud until the roach passed over the landing net's frame and relief washed over me. Inside sat 2lb 6oz of the Avon's finest treasure.

So far, I have spoken exclusively of my adventures on the more famous Hampshire Avon but it has been the Bristol version that has supplied me with roach fishing that I never thought was possible in the modern era. Hundreds of 1lb-plus fish, with dozens over the magic 2lb barrier, within multiple hauls of big fish, have occurred on numerous occasions. At face value, this would present the river as an amazing venue but when I reveal that these specimens have been tempted from only four swims along a very short stretch, it puts it into an altogether different light. Protected from cormorants and pike, this unique scenario is not typical of the Bristol Avon and because the shoals are at times made up of 50 fish or more, their capture is relatively straightforward - especially when I started to wield one of the deadliest, but most under-used methods; the pole. So please remember not to believe everything you read, as facts and figures can be manipulated to give a picture that's far from the truth.

A matchman's method.

Cralusso captures.

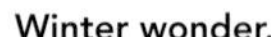
Winter wonder.

Previous experience had supplied me with the river's topography so the first task of this particular trip was to introduce some free feed that could work its magic while I tackled up. A traditional approach would be mashed or liquidised bread but I had no intention of following the specimen hunter's guide book. An equal measure of black roach groundbait and leam were poured into a bucket through a riddle and the larger particles disposed of. The leam would work on three levels; reduce the feed content of the mix, add weight to ensure it landed in the correct position in a rising river and finally, break up quickly once in situ.

To add to the groundbait's potency, instead of straight river water being stirred in at this stage, I mixed it first with a dose of geranium oil. By adding it to the water, rather than sprinkling it over the feed, I could be assured that it had been evenly distributed. Stirring the solution vigorously into the groundbait, I began to bind it into balls, leaving only the task of introducing a few attractive particles. Red pinkie, hemp seed and casters would give an irresistible banquet to each and every tangerine-sized offering of groundbait, and for once, I was going to dispense with the little-and-often approach and instead lay down a carpet of attraction that amounted to six balls in the initial bombardment. I only intended to top it up if the sport tailed off during the session. To the uninitiated, this can look like madness but for whatever reason, the tactic always finds favour with roach and to ensure pinpoint accuracy and reduce disturbance I opted to cup the feed in on my chosen line of 10 metres. Next, it was time to assemble the terminal tackle.

A static bait was required and at first glance in such strong flows a float would seem a ridiculous choice, but a Cralusso flat float has the ability to make the impossible possible. While retaining all the sensitivity of a float's bite detection, it allows the bait, in this case a single red maggot, to be presented as if I was legering. The float's fluted body manages to make easy work of riding through the flow and by choosing the correct size to match the conditions, the hooklength is stabilised on the bottom. An olivette positioned at three-quarters depth keeps the line running straight down from the float's stem and should it not be heavy enough to achieve this, the tip will no longer sit vertically, telling you to put a larger one on. Then it's a simple case of plumbing-up accurately so it sits three to four inches over-depth. Adding to this section of line two No 8 or No 6 shot, dependent on conditions, ensures the hookbait stays firmly fixed to the bottom. Lastly, I then add a No 1 shot to the rig just below the olivette. This does, in fact, sink the float on a slack line but given the flow's force, the Cralusso is pushed back to the surface, meaning a roach only has to breathe on it for it to sink again. It may sound complicated but given a little practice it's very easy to master and on this occasion I was ready to fish within ten minutes.

Dropping the maggot directly over the groundbait, I allowed the tension on the line to force the float into position. I knew that time wasn't going to be an issue, providing I had made the correct calls up to this point and, in fact, my confidence in the method was so great that if 15 minutes had passed without a bite I would have been surprised.

With the stained river forcing itself around the float tip, a 'V' had been cut into the surface, while the rounded body below wobbled slightly under the strain. Release was to come soon as the hookbait entered a roach's mouth. The tip duly disappeared without question and the grooved surface smoothed out. I struck in response, to be rewarded with a throbbing sensation through the pole, and the stretched elastic told me everything I needed to know. The method had proved its worth once again.

Sapping energy, the yellow bungee sought to control my quarry while it remained intent on pulling the hook free of its mouth. With a fin and scale-perfect complexion it had no intention of falling into my grasp and charged fearfully around the swim. Alas for the roach, this was to no avail and she, plus another four specimens all over 2lb, failed to avoid the landing net during a two-hour period.

Amazing fishing in the modern era but it's important once again that these fish are put into context. The Bristol Avon contains very few big roach; they just all happen to live in one area and the myths perpetrated by some are simply a figment of over-exuberant imaginations. That said, if you take it for what it is, you could be transported back to a time when roach proliferated in our rivers and for that insight I will be forever grateful. To catch one 2lb roach is special, and I'm grateful to my local waterway to have been afforded so much more in an era when such roach hauls would seem impossible.

Amazing!

A time for roach.

I felt no rush to be by the river at dawn; in fact, it was closer to lunchtime when I arrived. I knew the impending cloud cover would find favour with my quarry and to wet a line before would only have meant wasted hours. Roach can be tricky adversaries but combine March with mild water temperatures and you will never have a better recipe for success. The urge to spawn is not far away and the natural food larder is nearly bare so for once, the angler has the upper hand and I hoped to exploit this weakness.

I would have liked to see more water in the river, and perhaps a drop of colour, but to complain would have been churlish. I knew that a large shoal had gathered on the stretch but I didn't know exactly where. As I slowly walked the bank, I hoped for a sign, maybe a roll of a silver flank or a swirl sub-surface. Unfortunately, none were forthcoming so instead I decided to rely on watercraft, or luck, as it's better known in my case. So without being totally sure that I had selected correctly, I made my pitch just upstream of a series of overhanging trees on the far bank, guessing that the deeper water here, combined with cover, gave the shoal an ideal home. Next, it was time to decide on the approach I should use.

Given the low water conditions, red maggots held sway over bread. Likewise, my tackle needed to match the river I faced. Should I begin with the float or the tip? No self-respecting big fish would tolerate the disturbance of a float over its head and without coloured water to mask its presence, this tactic seemed unworkable. So instead, a legering outfit was selected and a fine tip section connected. This was vital for the technique to work and the half-ounce test curve provided exactly what I was looking for. Combined with a 4lb main line and a very fine hooklength to a size 18 hook, it gave me a sound position to begin fishing from. I was faced with one final question - whether to use a swimfeeder or swan shot? I erred once again on the side of caution, as a single shot would not only carry my bait to the chosen spot but also hold station there with the minimum of disturbance in the sedate flow.

Before I made any cast though, a little more preparation was required. I felt I had to introduce a little loose feed to gain the roach's confidence, so a catapult full of grubs was fired in every few minutes to meet their needs. Only when I could envisage the maggots being eaten did I, at last, break the river's surface for the first time. The little pull that there was grabbed hold of the large bow I had purposely paid out and tensioned the tip. This procedure was vital to maximise the bite-to-fish-hooked ratio, as a straight line between the tip and shot would only lead to more missed bites. This is because the resistance is increased and with a species like roach, even the minimum amount of pressure leaves the angler with a crushed maggot and no fish.

Settled into my pitch, I continued feeding the occasional catapult full of grubs and tried to guess what the shoal would be doing. I hoped the switch had been flicked, with half-a-dozen silver flanks twisting and turning as they chased the free food before their companions could get a look in. If I had read the situation correctly, it would be these eager mouths that would be the catalyst of a feeding frenzy. Competition is a wonderful aid to anglers that turns shy biting fish into fools.

With each maggot taken, the inevitable drew closer. At first, a tethered bait was easy to spot and dismiss, but as panic began to descend, so it became more appealing. Its somewhat unnatural presentation was no longer an issue and tipping down, a tail waved in the flow while the owner's mouth nudged against the gravel sucking in the food parcel I had snared with a hook. Like an electric current along the line, the sensation hit the carbon within a split second, forcing it to momentarily tap before steadily drawing downwards. My response was predictable and measured, given the fine hooklength in use. A strike hit the mark and resulted in the unlucky recipient spinning away in dismay. The key now was to draw it away from its companions as quickly as possible in an attempt to keep them calm and still feeding.

Back in time.

Zig-zagging upstream, the line cut through the water like a cheese wire and the fight told me it was indeed from my intended target. Splashing on the surface, a fish of such beauty presented itself in a condition that was faultless. At 2lb 4oz, it provided the perfect end to the session. No man could ever leave the river disappointed with such a fish, but unbeknown to me so much more lay ahead and dreams became reality. Maybe they wanted to give me a good send-off given it was the final day of the season, knowing they would be safe from my endeavours soon, but whatever the reason, it seemed that for one afternoon caution was no longer one of their characteristics and feeding was the only concern.

One two-pounder, as I have just said, is great, and two provides a Red Letter Day. Three, though, is amazing and four unbelievable; but what about seven up to 2lb 6oz in as many casts? It seemed impossible in an era when such sport has been destroyed by cormorants and for this day only, I was transported back to the 1960s.

Camera: Canon EOS 5D - Shutter Speed: 1/40 sec - F-Stop: f/4.0 - ISO: 2000 - Location: Giddea Hall

CHAPTER 10

GARDEN OF ENGLAND

A holiday in Kent with an uncle willing to take his 12-year-old nephew on an overnight fishing trip to a gravel pit near Canterbury, gave me my first introduction to the angling delights of the area. The memory of a night curled up in a sleeping bag under the shelter of a tiny brolly, in a monsoon, with forked lightning striking the pit, remains vivid in my mind. Then, as dawn arrived and the storm blew itself out, the surface of a flat calm, serene lake was fractured once again by the crash of a carp.

X marks the spot.

I watched enthralled as a flank of deep purple rose from the water like Excalibur, until only its tail remained connected to home. As the ripples washed toward me, I was transfixed by a creature that was far bigger than anything I could ever imagine catching.

The trip had certainly been an adventure but as dawn progressed it became a lifelong memory because a momentous happening had taken place, and I'd caught my very first tench. Although precise details of the capture have faded with time, I can still close my eyes and see both hands filled with emerald scales. Unlike any other fish I had caught before, the tench, with its smooth skin and muscular body, seemed almost magical. For 25 years, this cherished memory remained my only experience of the fishing in the county, until Chris Logsdon, of Mid-Kent Fisheries, invited me to sample the delights of Pan Lake on the Milton Complex.

Pan Lake was one of the first waters that Chris managed to obtain for the club, back in 1991, and it was obvious that he was very proud of it. If the pictures in the glossy brochure were anything to go by, I could understand why. After the lake was dug out in the early 1970s, Mother Nature had been doing her best to reclaim the land, and now, among the county's apple, pear, plum and quince orchards, sat another delight; a thriving ecosystem, fuelled by water, that accommodated a wide variety of life from grasshoppers to swallows.

Below the 16 acres of Pan Lake's surface, it was equally as spectacular. Living in the depths were 40lb carp, 30lb pike and double-figure tench, which were the reason for my journey. Passing through the gates, I was greeted by a pretty, reed-fringed lake with an array of mature trees breaking up the skyline and adding to the venue's character. The scent of wild flowers filled the air and the surrounding pastures, complete with grazing sheep, added to its serenity.

Chris had arranged for two of the local tench experts, Owen Jones and Paul Harrison, to be on hand to help show me the ropes. They had a large keepnet sunk in the margins, and I was intrigued. I asked them how their day had gone so they pulled the net out of the water slowly, until two very big tench were revealed, sitting in the folds of the mesh. They were both over 9lbs, the better one being 9lb 12oz, and Owen and Paul told me that they had caught a further ten fish, the majority of which weighed over 6lbs. What surprised me most was that they said this was a typical day, and far from the Red Letter category where I would have placed it; and the fish weren't heavily spawn-bound. Suddenly my interest levels rose and I double-checked with Chris that this was indeed normal fishing; something he confirmed with a knowing nod and a smile. It was time to get the rods out.

With a mild south-westerly blowing across the lake, I decided to pitch up one swim down from Paul and Owen in the windward corner. I reasoned that the congregation of natural food would prove attractive to my quarry and my generous guides also pointed out the favoured hotspot, which was a gravel bar at about 60 yards. In the past, Paul had managed fish to 11lbs from here. This was getting better all the time!

With three maggot feeder rods in position, I baited liberally with casters, maggots and hemp, plus a topping of Paul and Owen's special Pan Lake groundbait mixture. Then, with the work over, all that was left to do was sit, wait, and soak up the atmosphere.

Get ready.

Fish on.

According to my companions, the tench were very much morning feeders, the peak time being between 8am and midday, so I wasn't the least bit surprised when night fell and the bobbins remained stationary. Dawn would bring with it a fresh start. Anyway, for now, a bottle of red wine and a curry was shared with the lads and it was nice to forge new friendships based on a mutual passion for angling. Sleep brought dreams of big, fat, green tincas and hopes for the day ahead.

I forced my weary self from the comfort of my sleeping bag before the sun had time to kiss the horizon. I was feeling a little fragile but this was no time for slacking; there was work to do. I needed to top up the swim with a few fresh maggots via the spod and to replenish the feeders. In my experience, tench love a little disturbance and a pre-dawn spodding session seems to get them on the move to help prove the old saying, 'An early bird always catches the worm.'

Pulling up the low chair next to the rods, I put the kettle on and surveyed the scene, using my binoculars, looking for tell-tale signs of tench fizzers. Thick weed surrounded the bar I was fishing and I felt sure that the silt from which it grew would show any tench movements, especially if they nuzzled head first into the sediment looking for breakfast. Just as the kettle boiled, a huge frothing cauldron hit the surface, sparkling in the early dawn rays. Surely, I concluded, it was now only a matter of time before the bobbins flew, but when the alarm did eventually scream, it still made me jump. Lifting the rod, I felt that satisfying thump and the line cut through the surface film. Almost immediately, the free-swimming sensation was replaced by a grating one as the fish hit weed; Canadian pond to be exact. This provided a tangled foil for the tench's getaway and my rod sprung back lifeless. 'Damn!' I mumbled, or words to that effect, as I retrieved the feeder, skipping it across the lake back to me. I had obviously underestimated the weed's density, so I decided to rectify the situation by upping the strength of the hooklength and that of the hook itself.

Thanks, Owen.

Happy with the amendments, I resettled. Fortunately, it wasn't long before they were put to the test; but could they cope? The answer was a definite 'yes' and a gorgeous 8lb fish hit the net. As the sun's intensity slowly grew, Paul and Owen got in on the action and another nine-pounder was banked between them. The action for me also warmed up, with a stream of fish that kept me, and my rods, really busy. The average size was tremendous, perhaps only equalled in my experience by Sywell Reservoir, but the bonus here on the Pan was that there was a more realistic chance of a double-figure fish. By the time midday arrived I was pleased that the action had relented somewhat, such was its frenetic nature. It was time, too, for Paul and Owen to leave but with 20 fish between them, six being over 8lb, I was sure they needed a rest!

I decided to stay on for a second day when I hoped to enjoy the sun and a few more fish. Unfortunately, Kent could provide the sport but not the weather and after enduring a night from hell, when the heavens opened in a familiar manner to that of my childhood introduction to fishing in this wonderful county, I decided to quit while I was still ahead. With 17 fish to 8lb 13oz, I was made up and the long journey home was worth every mile.

The success of the trip also guaranteed my return the following spring when the tench still held their spawn, so I headed back in May, only this time with Hugh Miles, for company. Where better, I thought, to tempt a double-figure fish for our Catching The Impossible series and, with a cricket score of tench to 10lb 7oz, it more than

A cricket score.

lived up to expectations. It was around this period that I began to use a tactic that was to prove its worth for catching big carp and tench, time and time again.

I had never been happy with the results I had managed to achieve with standard bolt rigs, because, compared to carp, tench are far trickier to lure on such tactics, so I reassessed the situation and began to explore the possibilities of a short hooklength and feeder set-up.

Previously, I had encountered hook malfunctions when trying to lure big fish on small patterns, when combined with the pressure added by very short hooklengths. There had been a dearth of suitable hooks; in fact, I didn't feel fully confident in any of the current models. Fortunately, in collaboration with Peter Drennan, we designed the Super Specialist Barbel hook, which even in a size 14 was capable of landing huge fish. So now, I set about constructing my ultimate tench rig.

A size 14 hook was tied to three inches of 12lb X-Line, using a knotless knot, with the tag end left uncut. To this, using a needle, I threaded on three artificial casters, which were fixed in place by pushing the tag through the eye of the hook before blobbing the mono with a lighter. The fake casters supplied just enough weight to sink the hook while leaving it sitting at an acute angle ready to snag up in the fish's mouth. The other end of the fluorocarbon was then tied to a size 9 uni swivel. During the early days, this was then pushed inside a Drennan oval feeder that had been bastardised to fish inline and afford a bolt effect, but Peter eventually took pity on me and produced a range of purpose-built models that removed the need for DIY!

In my opinion, the feeder is far better than a lead and a PVA bag option. Once tape is applied to the holes in the feeder, the flow of maggots into the swim can be a gradual process, which is something that is especially beneficial where small fish exist, because they can quickly devour the contents of a dissolved PVA bag. I used 12lb fluorocarbon as a main line, and when matched with a 2lb test curve rod, it balanced out the set-up, enabling big tench and carp to be landed with very few failures. In fact, even to this day, all my feeder fishing for tench revolves around this method.

Garden of England.

My next visit to Kent came the following spring and Owen was once again to be my companion, although Pan wasn't to be the destination this time. I fancied a change because limiting myself to one water when numerous others are available is not my style. A fresh challenge always gets the adrenaline flowing, so we chose the Handle Lake, which is also situated on the Milton Complex. Not only is it home to giant tench, but the possibility of a big bream added to the attraction. Owen told me that even though the average size was smaller, both species grew to double figures and that was good enough for me. Handle Lake it was, then!

Owen arrived a day earlier than me and pitched himself midway down the pit, which was long and narrow. As it was no more that 80 yards wide, he hoped to pick up passing fish from both directions, but the wind had other plans. From the moment I greeted him, I knew where I wanted to be and that was at the end receiving all the wind; the longest walk from the car park, as usual. For the first time in weeks, a southerly had picked up and as I watched the surface I could see all manner of fly life, trapped in the film, heading down the lake. Sure enough, as we surveyed the bay, one tench after another slapped their paintbrush tails as they frolicked in the waves. Owen and I both knew it; location is the key to all angling and it was here that we should fish. Unfortunately for my companion, it would mean packing everything up. "You've only been here five minutes, and you've got me working already!" he sighed.

Our two swims were, as already indicated, at the far end of the lake, mine being where water turned to reeds, creating a bay. By casting out with a marker, I established that the silty bottom at 60 yards rose two feet and gave way to gravel. It was at this meeting point that I decided to present the bait.

Unlike most tench and bream anglers, I rarely favour a groundbait attack and rely on particles, using a spod. For this trip, I had something special for the tench in the form of 20 pints of dead maggots. All winter I had been saving any spare bait for just such an occasion, freezing it in bags to keep it fresh. Providing I took them to the lake frozen and then fed immediately, I could create a hotspot par excellence. With a few casters, Frenzied Hempseed and Marine Halibut pellets mixed in, I began the laborious, hour-long spodding workout.

With bream a possibility, I swapped the maggot feeder for a large method ball, fished over the particles. The theory was that the fish will always take the easy option and groundbait gives exactly that. Then came the hookbait, as always three fake casters fished on a D rig to a size 14 hook. With all the hard work completed, it was time for the fish to come to dinner, while I waited, enjoying the countryside in the Garden of England. An orchard on the far bank painted a blossom-filled picture for me, with the calling of young lambs providing the backing track. I didn't have too much time for sightseeing though, as my indicator slammed against the butt.

"It's good to be back!" I announced as I struck. A swirl, a flip and a head shake was followed by a tinca rolling under the rod tip, my soft carbon blank soaking up the pressure. This is a vital characteristic because, when using a hooklength of only a few inches, a softer rod will help avoid breakages. For this fish there would be no lucky break though, as I once again made contact with a Kent tench. Sport remained steady and by dusk, Owen and I had troubled the scoreboard on numerous occasions. With tench unlikely during darkness, I swapped over to two grains of fake corn in the hope of a nocturnal species and, sure enough, just before dawn arrived, my hope turned to fact as a 25lb mirror carp rolled into the net.

Come day two, I carpeted my swim with another three pints of maggots as an invitation for breakfast, and it's one the tench found hard to ignore. Owen's fish had been less social but as the sun began to climb, he too received a regular supply of runs. There were no monsters for either of us but seven-pounders can never be called small. Unfortunately, Owen's session was drawing to a close as work called, but that didn't stop him from helping himself to a few more. In the end though, time ran out and we shook hands promising our next trip together wouldn't be a year away. Did Handle Lake have anything left in store for me?

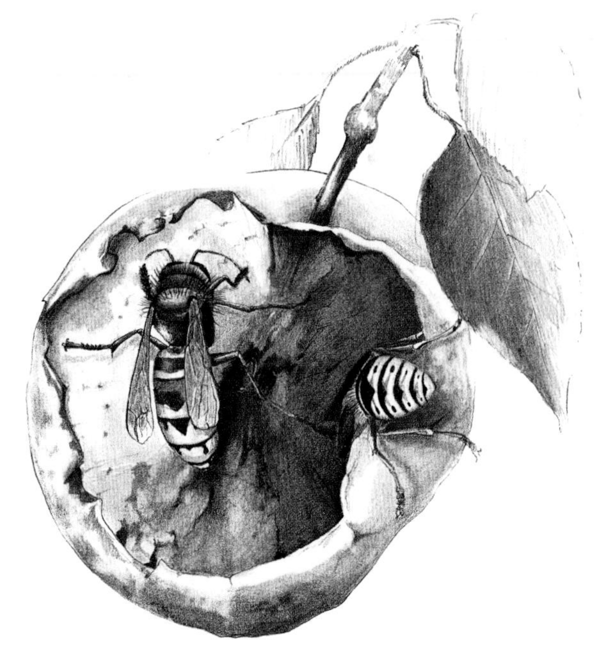

Keeping busy.

Having the time to establish a feeding zone can be very beneficial with tench and so it proved as I slipped into day three and left the real world far behind. The tench came thick and fast and I was barely able to keep three rods in the water. It can be hard work fishing the Method at times like this, because regular casting is vital to achieve maximum results. Unlike most species, tench find the commotion to be attractive and I take advantage of this by spodding periodically over feeding fish.

With tench to 9lb 1oz, I had once again been shown a great time by Kent. Yet again I'd taken a big tally of fish and that, coupled with the great company, had me pulling out of the car park on the long drive home wishing Kent was a bit closer. The complex owed me nothing, although I still harboured hopes that one spring a true goliath would fall foul of my rods.

The tench season is always a race against time for the specimen hunter. During the year there is a small window of opportunity when the tench will feed readily, despite an ever-growing, spawn-heavy waistline and this period gives the angler the chance of a personal best. Of course, purists will say that a gravid tench isn't one that should be counted or, perhaps, even angled for, but the fact remains that this is the time to catch the biggest of the species. It would, I believe, be impossible to catch a British record outside this period and with the vast majority of stillwaters now open, my own serious tenching is confined to the months of May and June. During this time, every season, I try to target venues capable of giving me that giant, even if my choices border on being repetitive. Oxfordshire is always a draw but I continued to find it impossible to ignore the Garden of England, where it was not just the fruit growing plump and large. If I timed it right, a tench big enough to dream about would be ripe and ready to be picked.

Wiltshire to Kent is a long journey but the thought of three days' angling was enough to keep me smiling. The Milton Complex had always been incredibly kind, providing huge catches every previous session. In fact, I would go as far as to say that it is the best tench water I have ever fished. On many venues, the specimens within never amount to very many and repeat captures are regular but here, the quantity of tench weighing over 8lb is staggering, with the chances high of a ten-pounder. To put it simply, I was going back to tench Nirvana!

Unfortunately, my arrival didn't coincide with the sun and despite being mid-afternoon the sky was more akin to dusk. The cloud hung low and black, laden with rain as it scuttled in from the Channel, just waiting to deposit its contents over me. As I stared out from the van's windscreen, the wind whipped across the surface directly into the car park, so at least I had a good vantage point. This point was proven almost immediately when a big green flank rolled between the waves no more than 30 yards out. A promising sign, but when two magpies landed in the swim straight afterwards I was convinced.

Shepherd's delight.

Ridiculous really, but I'm superstitious about these birds and at times get fed up saying 'good morning' to them so as not to put the mockers on a fishing trip. Quite rightly, my companion Owen was not so convinced and on his arrival he demanded that we walk along the windward bank to investigate further, but with no other signs, I made a beeline for the first swim. Happily, it was also closest to the car park and meant I could ready my equipment directly out of the back of my van.

It was rare for me now to bivvy up while tenching because I find the hindrance of a barrow load of tackle costly in a fish-catching sense. Night fishing is next to useless, so by using the van as a base I can be highly mobile during the day, moving every two or three hours until I locate the tench. To complement such an approach, there's no point in filling up swims with balls of groundbait. What is needed is a quick fix; a way of targeting individual fish and progress on from there if results are forthcoming. The little-and-often tactic, using large feeders, was the correct one in this instance. Maggots make up the bulk of the feed, along with a little groundbait, which I use to keep them dry instead of maize flour. This not only infuses the grubs with an aroma, but also introduces a second attraction from the feeder.

When I peeled off the lid from the maggot bucket, the smell was pungent and rich. After spending 24 hours laced in both Source groundbait and liquid, they were ready to be cast out. A quick feel around with a lead

Launching into Larkfield.

had revealed that the spot the tench had rolled on was clear and gravelly, but surrounded by Canadian pondweed. That was good enough for me and three feeders, filled with their tasty cargo, were soon landing in the zone. That was it; I was fishing with a minimum amount of fuss or disturbance.

Meanwhile, Owen was working on an altogether more traditional approach. He called upon the help of marker floats and balls of groundbait, a tactic that had always been successful for him. His swim was prepared for the length of the session ahead, mine in a more hit-and-run style. It would be interesting to see which method would prove more successful this time round.

At least I could seek refuge from the elements while Owen toiled away erecting what appeared to be a circus tent. He then began filling it with more tackle than I have ever seen anyone bring with them. Mind you, I wasn't sneering when a fried sausage sandwich was offered, along with the promise of a full English! 'What's that noise?' I thought, as the brain took a while to kick into gear. Then it dawned on me - it was my bite alarm!

Struggling to put a waterproof coat on, I stumbled down the steps and grabbed hold of the rod while still trying to get my arm in the sleeve. In trying to do two jobs at once I ended up not doing either very well, but eventually, I found the arm hole and could concentrate on the fish. Fortunately, its movements had been unspectacular, lurching from one weed bed to another in a bid to find sanctuary. Luckily, the leaf stems were still sparse and no match for my 12lb line which scythed through them with ease, releasing the tench from their grasp.

I slowly gained line until the deeper margin offered a place for the fish to bore downwards and apply maximum pressure on the hook hold. I was briefly forced to yield some line until the pressure on the rod tip dissipated and I could again crank the tench to the surface. It was only now that I realised what was on the other end; a monster, thickset and deep with spawn. Panic had no time to kick in because by now the net had secured her for me. There was no doubt it was a personal best, but how big? She went 11lb 8oz, a huge body awash with shades of yellows and greens. As I savoured the moment, my happiness contrasted starkly with the gloom of the day.

Surely, the lake couldn't give me any more, but it did. In fact, six tench over 9lb came my way in the next 24 hours until the wind swung round and tempted the shoal away from me. I took this as my cue to bid farewell to three marvellous Kent tench for another year. While I made the journey home, it was now Owen's turn to take centre stage. Another cricket score is probably the best description of his catch, including a giant of 10lb 6oz.

Today, when I close my eyes and daydream of tench it's not just boyhood memories that fill my mind; at Mid Kent Fisheries I have found special friends and special fish.

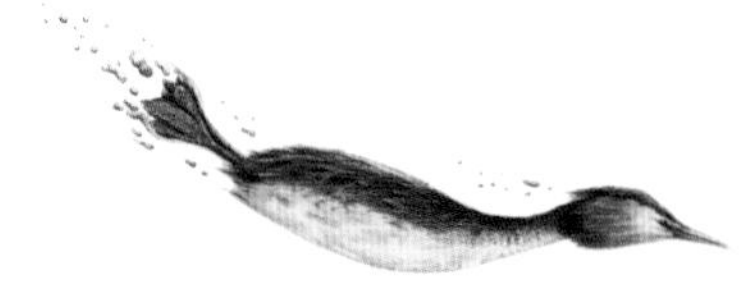

Tench-tastic.

Camera: Canon EOS 5D - Shutter Speed: 1/160 sec - F-Stop: f/5.6 - ISO: 100 - Location: Cotswold Water Park

CHAPTER 11

SPRING SLABS

Let me be honest here, and say that bream fishing doesn't really suit my style of angling or mindset. I'm far too impatient for the long haul required to tempt specimens consistently, and the consensus among experts, of day three being the point at which you start catching, fills me with horror. I want results straight away and a blank night has me looking for a move, rather than settling down with a good book to wait my turn.

Then, once you have finally bored them into feeding, the minimal fighting qualities have you believing that you're dragging in a weed bed rather than a fish! Okay, I am writing this a little tongue-in-cheek but the fact remains; we have a personality clash that needs addressing before I can commence a trip after what is undoubtedly a magnificent creature. Therefore, I always look for a backup when selecting a venue, and this comes in the form of carp, a species that happily cohabits the same waterways. Thus, when the bream are making their minds up to begin feeding, good old cypry will keep me entertained and prevent my itchy feet from dragging me all round the venue. This combination of species may not work for everyone, but it suits my 'Jack of all trades' style and some of my fondest memories have been as a result of this approach.

Brogborough Pit in Bedfordshire stands at an impressive 220 acres and is one of the largest venues in the chain of waters that cut through the heart of the county. Originally created to service the needs of the brick industry, it stood stark and bare against the surrounding pastoral land. Like an open wound, it needed a plaster and, as always seems the case, Mother Nature was on hand to nurse it better. Once vegetation had taken a grip, wildlife found it a welcoming place, with bitterns hiding out in the vast banks of reeds that filled the margins. Common darter dragonflies and brimstone butterflies arrived to represent insect life, which in turn saw a colony of common lizards getting a foothold, basking on rocks warmed by the early morning sun; and, of course, life was equally active below the surface, with rudd, bream, pike and carp thriving in the fertile environment. Alas, the rudd and the pike's heyday didn't last long. The arrival of cormorants massacred one species, while robbing a food source from another. There was still plenty left to grab the attention of local specimen hunters, though, and towards the end of the last century, I purchased a syndicate ticket and began my own exploration.

Drifting across the open expanse, I was afforded a grandstand view of the pit from my boat. Through the clear water, huge banks of weed could be observed but what really struck me on that first reconnaissance trip were the contours. Like an egg carton, gravel beds rose steeply from the bottom and were too numerous to be counted. Then giant bars bisected the water giving the impression of underwater roads that the creators of Spaghetti Junction would be proud of. You could easily have been forgiven for being confused - and I was - but I love these types of venues, so excitement was the overriding feeling as I began my angling. This led to an incredible amount of effort on my behalf. With bream being a nocturnal animal, it was obvious that I needed to be fishing at night, but work and social life didn't allow for enough time on the bank so I had to partake in midweek adventures.

On the face of it this doesn't seem too bad, but imagine dragging your tackle and a dinghy down the bank on a wet evening, pumping up the vessel before sailing, fully-loaded, across the pit, all before staying up all night catching bream! Then you have to pack up at 5.30am and retrace your steps to the car before dashing home for a quick shower and getting to work for 7.30am! No wonder I was a pretty useless employee during the bream season.

On one occasion, this effort even led to a trip to the hospital. After completing the tortuous task of packing up, I reached the car feeling well and truly knackered but also with incredible stomach and back pains. During the journey home, these sensations worsened and by the time I got in the front door, I felt like John Hurt in Alien and it seemed like something was trying to rip itself out of me. I was panicking by now and thought I may have needed to relieve myself but the loo did nothing and by the time I dialled 999, I had already collapsed on the floor. I was convinced that I had caught my last bream, as pain tore through my torso and death seemed quite a good option.

A doctor answered my emergency call and immediately, I was told to roll over as each buttock was stabbed with syringes full of painkillers and muscle relaxant. That was, I can say, one of the most pleasurable experiences of my life because the discomfort began to fade away immediately, leaving me rather pale but still alive! The prognosis was kidney stones, and let me tell those who have been fortunate enough to avoid them, that on a pain level this is the male version of giving birth! I could only thank God that it hadn't happened when I was in the boat, not that it was going to put me off, because a few days later I was back on the bank.

The tactics I employed for bream stemmed from my carp fishing experiences on the surrounding chain of pits, like Elstow. Large quantities of particles and pellets were introduced, along with mini boilies. Traditionally, groundbait was, and still is, the favoured bream angler's approach but I saw no reason to follow suit. Rather than heaps of bait, the swim received a nice, even coat over the bottom. This seemed far more satisfactory, as forcing a shoal to graze always creates more opportunities for a mistake. Generally, I would have tried to achieve this using a spod, but Brogborough allowed the luxury of a boat and this assured perfect presentation, especially as the water was crystal clear. By looking through a bucket with a glass bottom I could guarantee everything below was in order, even the placement of rigs. These were uncomplicated affairs; 12lb main line was connected to six feet of lead core and a 3oz weight. The hooklength was a supple braid connected to a size 8 hook, holding two mini boilies. I felt it represented more than enough guile and strength to land any bream, and also the carp which lived in the pit.

Retro.

The previous week had been very hot, and even though it was only late June it felt like the dog days of summer already. Everything on the pit had ground to a halt, the fish were sheltering from the heat, and they'd lost their appetite. The bream were no different, and despite two nights' angling I had yet to see any sign of life, even at dawn, when not a breath of wind ruffled the huge expanse.

Knackered!

Springtime.

As far as the eye could see...

The area I had selected to fish seemed perfect, with a gravel mound rising off the bottom some 70 yards out, creating a mini plateau in six feet of water. Surrounding this area, weed filled the lake giving, I hoped, an obvious dinner table for the fish to feed on. Sometimes though, you are not going to catch whatever you do when conditions conspire against you, so by the time the sun had risen free of the horizon I had given up hope. Fortunately, in this Mediterranean climate, I had decided to adopt their mindset and skip work for the day, allowing for a leisurely pack up before heading off for a spot of floater fishing nearby.

Pulling out the bivvy pegs and filling the rucksack meant moving around the swim, so when a single bleep on the alarm sounded I thought nothing of it, convinced that I had knocked the rod. The shrill which followed 10 seconds later though, had me jumping out of my skin and making a grab for the blank as line poured through its rings. Before an arc could be formed in the carbon, I knew that this was no bream and the immediate need to back-wind only confirmed this. As the line veered off the hump and into the weed, I felt it plink off the strands of Canadian but thankfully, it didn't became entwined in the stems.

The fish felt heavy, with no head shaking, just a solid force doing its very best to find a weak link. I cannot explain why, but I knew then that I had the biggest carp in the lake tethered to my rig. In a pit with hundreds of other fish in residence, it seemed a bold claim to make but that didn't matter; a sixth sense or whatever you want to call it had me convinced. If I had been using lighter tackle I would never have got the chance to find out if my premonition was right but by keeping the fish on the move it wasn't long, given the circumstances, that the main line began to cut through the margin's surface.

As it passed under the rod tip, I caught my first glimpse of what was at stake and I wasn't disappointed. A long, copper flank and a submarine-type snout powered by a giant tail swept past, adorned with rows of golden sovereign scales, giving the creature an ornate appearance. Better still, it was indeed the jewel of the lake and its biggest carp. I would have laughed out loud if it hadn't been for the fact that I was suddenly giving out line as the fish surged down the marginal slope in a bid to test the tackle a little further. With each lunge and every boil on the surface, I prayed for it to stay on, knowing full well that catching one of Bedfordshire's best-looking carp was at stake. How I love and hate those final moments of a battle, when my mind fills with a heady cocktail of excitement and terror. While I wished my quarry would just come into the net, I also revelled in another special moment that I knew would become etched in my mind forever; and so it was that my net swallowed up the beast of Brogborough.

With a back big enough to put a saddle on and a rounded head making it look angry, it was an impressive creature indeed, and when I gazed at its heavily scaled flank its beauty was unquestionable. The last time I had seen this magnificent monster was in an Angling Times story, with the legendary Alan Wilson the lucky captor. Little did I know then, that I would be next to take the strain for the camera. At 35lb 4oz, it confirmed my premonition.

The sunny, breathless day now seemed perfect as I cradled the carp in my arms and waded out into the pit. I had only had him on loan for a couple of minutes, and it was time to return him to the lake, his rightful owner. Released from my grasp, the cool water reignited the carp's energy and called him back into the depths. I had come to catch bream but there were none special enough to make me swap this moment, leaving me to question once again if I was cut out for this bream fishing lark!

Jewel of the lake.

Treble top.

My desire to catch double-figure slabs was fulfilled when I banked fish just short of 13lb, over two seasons, before it was time to move on. The possibility of catching something much bigger seemed remote alongside the urge I had to seek out new adventures. With so much to explore and even more to learn it was time for Brogborough to become a happy memory. Catching more bream was not a priority, as the barbel bug had well and truly bitten, although come spring the following year when the rivers had closed and I found myself at a loose end, bream would be at their heaviest weight, pre-spawning. I just had to find a venue capable of giving me a new personal best.

Within the CEMEX Angling (then known as RMC) portfolio, the gravel pits in and around the M25 had reached maturity. No longer scars on the landscape after heavy mineral extraction, these aquatic oases had become top class fisheries for specimen carp. Such was, and still is, the clamour to catch this species that many other types of fish slip under the radar, even if they grow to equally impressive proportions. This suited me fine, especially with rumours of large bream emanating from the Kingsmead Complex. Two pits, separated by a narrow channel with a net strung across it, make up the venue, although it was the first water known as Number One which drew my attention. Rumours of fish to 17lb were common from the carp anglers and while I was sceptical of this, a good head of doubles was definitely in residence. The time had come to dust down the bream tackle once again.

During my reconnaissance visit, two areas known as the Heli Pad and the aptly named Bream Swim provided me with the best chance for a bite during the spring months, as this is where they congregated to spawn. So I was pleased to find the Bream Swim free when I arrived with tackle and bait for the first time. Unlike Brogborough, a boat couldn't be used so I was back to spodding. My philosophy of not using a bed of groundbait hadn't changed, and I kept to a bombardment of pellet that had been soaked in tuna and sunflower oil. The days of sweet feed like molasses have long since gone, replaced instead by fishmeals and their incredible pulling power. I had, however, altered my terminal tackle, now capitalising on a method mix. I figured this single ball of feed among the pellets would appear as an easy meal and draw attention to the hookbait quickly. Rather than use a feeder, I opted for a sea watch lead, its polo shape able to grab the scalded pellets perfectly. Above this sat a helicopter set-up, with a scaled-down stiff rig attached to a swivel rotating around the leadcore, and a popped-up mini boilie as the hookbait. Given that all the carp anglers present were using the same bait, it seemed logical to do likewise as the bream must have switched on to them.

Contemplating Kingsmead.

Noisy neighbours.

A few exploratory casts revealed a series of clear bars among weed beds and these provided the ideal ambush points. The most important rule to remember when trying to locate bream is their dislike of vegetation. Being a shoal fish, confined areas unsettle the group and prevent the shoaling instinct from occurring, so it was no surprise when I chose to fish the cleanest and most open expanse of lake available to me.

All three rods were concentrated in this open area, as was the free feed, because the last thing I wanted was to split the shoal with the way I fed. It was important though, to make sure all the hookbaits were cast to the edge of the pellets and closest to me, thus eliminating any main lines running through the feeding zone and potentially spooking the bream as they gorged. With the traps set and the wind pushing in toward me, everything seemed perfect, especially when a forked tail presented itself in the waves, confirming why the pitch I had chosen was called the Bream Swim. This wasn't an immediate prelude for a bite, which I guess was due to the bright sky, but at least the area had been scouted in preparation for a night-time feed. Or so I hoped.

As the skyline began to lose its colour and definition, the middle indicator slammed against the blank and grabbed my attention. No bream could be responsible for this; it was the first of many carp that fell during my time at Kingsmead. It pleased me, because it proved that the pellets had been placed in a suitable spot, and if the carp were willing to feed, so too would a shoal of dustbin lids. With even greater confidence, I settled down for the night and for the first time experienced the full impact of the Heathrow flight path. Noisy is an understatement. The tranquillity was shattered every five minutes by a Jumbo skimming the treetops and when Concorde took to the skies, the earth actually shook. For a while, it came as a shock but I soon became conditioned to it, although I can't say I would want to live in the area! I'm pleased to say that aeroplanes weren't the only reason for a disturbed sleep that night, as the line pulled tight before dropping back twice. Each was met with a strike and a dead weight on the end before winching in the proverbial carrier bag. It wasn't plastic, though, but bronze scales that greeted the landing net and I certainly didn't make any derogatory remarks about their size and shape. Weighing 12lb 10oz and 13lb 2oz it seemed that the rumours were true and specimens were in residence.

Over the next couple of months it was rare not to catch at least one double every night, and sometimes many more, although they always remained in the 10lb to 13lb category and with my catch rate I had expected a bigger fish to appear. Were any present? The answer to this question came on a wet May night when clouds hung heavy in the sky and were seemingly within touching distance. With rain bouncing off the bivvy and filling the stream that runs behind the Heli Pad swim I received a bite that had me rushing to pull on my boots. The alarm's urgency made it a frantic exercise despite the prospect of getting wet.

Another double.

Only now could my head torch end the uncertainty, and instead of a suspected leathery flank, I was greeted by the shape of a big bream. Its jet black fins added trim to scales full of coppers, yellows and browns. The length was certainly more than any bream that had come before it, plus the width across its back dwarfed even a 13lb fish. I filled the weigh sling, hooked it on the scales and hoisted, making the dial spin to 14lb 15oz for a new personal best. This time the roles were reversed; there wasn't a carp in Kingsmead I would have swapped it for. The story doesn't end here, though. Once again, a big carp did provide a memorable moment in the campaign, and while it couldn't match the bream, it did remain indelibly etched on the memory.

This time the strike didn't connect with a dead weight that was happy to be dragged in, and while line wasn't pulled off the reel, its kiting motion had me questioning what species was responsible.

This mindset continued for the entire battle until the relentless dives under the rod tip convinced me that a carp was the culprit. Half-a-dozen times I tried to end the fight, each attempt failing as tail slaps rocked the surface, sending ripples in against the bank. I had no option but to let the rod slowly subdue the energy and to remain patient. With zero moonlight I had no visual confirmation of my opponent and this remained the case until, at last, I managed to end the tussle.

The carp had proved a nuisance on the venue, especially with a fresh stocking of young, greedy mirrors having taken place. These could ransack the swim, quickly scaring off the gentle bream. When I then received a take in the bay which sat to the right of the Heli Pad, and a wake formed on the surface, I cursed my luck; and even more so when it managed to tangle itself around a scaffold pole. Swearing at the fish, I tried to free it by pulling in every direction but it was to no avail. It was stuck fast. I was left with no choice but to strip down to my underpants and wade out in a bid to untangle it which, I can assure you, was not a pretty sight!

Eventually, after much shivering and many deep breaths, I reached the pole and grabbed hold of the leadcore. I pulled it gently, only to feel a force respond in kind which confirmed that the culprit was still on; bloody thing.

It's not a carp!

Over the moon.

Carefully, I unwound the leader until I could feel the weight rising and then suddenly, I came face to face with a monster! Rather than the suspected double, a huge golden head stared at me, a head that belonged to one of the two 30lb-plus commons that inhabited the lake and the main prize for the carp anglers. Time to take things a little more seriously, I thought.

I still remained snagged, only this time to a piece of wire protruding from the pole. The only way of releasing the tackle was to push the rod and reel underwater and pass the whole lot through the obstruction. Simple enough if I wasn't chest deep in freezing water with such a prize at stake! The common must have sympathised with my situation and amazingly, remained calm and allowed me to lead it to safety. With the line free, I then dragged myself to the bank like a drowned rat and began to play the fish in a more civilized fashion.

Once again, there was little appetite for a battle on my opponent's behalf and even on bream rods it remained subdued all the way to the bank and into the safety of my landing net. The pesky thing had scared all the bream off, I jokingly told my carp angling colleagues, as I posed for the camera with a 32lb brute of a common!

Writing a weekly column for Angling Times doesn't lend itself to campaign fishing. Chasing huge bream, like my quests for all other species, has to find a slot in this hectic agenda, but most springs I find time for at least one trip after specimen slabs and with three days at my disposal I once again called on the CEMEX portfolio.

At Westhampnett Pit, near Chichester, there had been reports of carp anglers catching fish to 17lb so it was hard to ignore the chance to investigate this particular venue. With the prospect of such specimens, I could turn a blind eye to its location, right next to the A27. Indeed, one complete bank of swims would not require a torch at any time of the night due to the number of street lamps in position. Fortunately, a tip-off from the head bailiff, Matt Cloud, found me pushing my barrow along the opposite bank to a swim which sat on the end of a peninsular. From here, I had a vast expanse of open water at my disposal which was perfect for the bream because it gave them plenty of unhindered movement. So, I erected the bivvy on the spit, choosing it as the place to make my stand. It would be bream or bust here for the next three days.

Plumbing revealed a pretty constant topography at 11 feet deep, occasionally featuring a small amount of weed growth. There was nothing then to 'hang my hat on' so I decided instead to make my own feature at 70 yards with a big bed of bait. For me, the base ingredient in any bream mix has to be halibut pellets, therefore a bag of both 3mm and 6mm were combined with a kilo of 6mm Source pellets. Then came a kilo of 10mm fishmeal boilies, followed by two cans of sweetcorn; one standard and one

Kingsmead king.

strawberry flavoured. Last, but not least, came two attractors; a bottle of oyster sauce which coated the pellets in a rich pungent aroma, and a couple of handfuls of sea salt flakes. With a bucketful of bait ready to enter the swim, a bout of spodding would normally be in order, but I could save on the hard work because bait boats were allowed and this time the Micro Cat could take the strain.

Tackle then needed to be set up, with the outfit revolving around a 2lb test curve rod and 12lb fluorocarbon main line. The terminal end implemented a Method feeder and a short hooklength supporting two 10mm boilies. To fish this rig correctly, it was vital that the groundbait mix used to mould around the feeder was suitable.

Road to reward.

To my mind, an adequate specimen method mix isn't available, with all the products aimed at carp puddle fishing. Here, the groundbait needs to break down immediately, whereas a specimen approach requires the same process to occur over a much longer time span. Hence, I chose to combine a boilie base mix and trout pellet powder on a 50/50 basis to achieve a nice, tacky, long-lasting mix.

It was close to dusk before I felt satisfied that I was fishing as best as I could and while I prepared dinner, the man-made lights replaced nature's illumination. In the distance, a huge bank of cloud was heading in off the sea and as it hit land, rumbles of thunder momentarily drowned the constant drone of cars. The weatherman had predicted a stormy, rain-sodden night and by the time I climbed inside the sleeping bag, the nylon roof above my head was the only thing preventing me from getting a soaking. Safely snuggled down, though, sleep soon arrived, until a constant warble from the alarm woke me.

Stumbling out into the darkness, I struggled to focus before a dazzling light lit up everything before me. The electrical storm held station over the pit and then, maybe unwisely, I chose to pick up 12 feet of carbon. Conscious of not becoming a conductor and frying myself, I held the rod low to the water, only lifting it at the final moment to ease my prize into the net. There, inside the mesh, lay 13lb 3oz of bream, giving me a great start and maybe, more importantly, settling my mind in the swim selection stakes.

The remainder of the night passed quietly on the catching front, which was a good thing given the storm. With two more nights left, though, it would be interesting to see if the shoal now moved in en masse and prevented me from becoming bored with my lack of movement.

The adage 'be careful what you wish for' would be apt at this point because by the early hours of the final night, I was seriously contemplating reeling in the rods to get some sleep, especially as a rogue carp had just run me ragged, and this on top of a huge amount of bream, including four more doubles. By marking the distance of my baited spot on the line with pole elastic and placing it in the spool clip, I had managed to continue fishing accurately throughout darkness, which, no doubt, increased the catch rate. Spurred on by the thought of the next fish being a monster, I set about moulding the groundbait around the feeder and re-baiting the hook while ignoring my eyelids' request to shut. Maybe this bream fishing lark wasn't as sedate as I was led to believe. Tired and slimy, I eventually decided that enough was enough. Beaten by a shoal of bream - who'd have thought it?

Beaten by bream.

Camera: Canon Nikon D3 - Shutter Speed: 1/80 sec - F-Stop: f/8.0 - ISO: 100 - Location: Woburn Safari Park

CHAPTER 12

FISHING WITH FRANK

Angling is full of characters and over the years, I have been fortunate enough to meet and share a day on the bank with many of them, but no collaboration has been as successful as the one I have forged with Frank Warwick. This affable northerner has assisted me in achieving more than one Red Letter Day and his bankside banter and colourful tales have really made fishing with him a highlight in my angling career.

Pop-up prize.

It seems a long time ago now when we first became acquainted on CEMEX Angling's Kingsmead Lake. The fluoro boilie boom was in full swing and I'd arranged a trip for my Angling Times column with its inventor – yes, you've guessed it, Mr Warwick. He didn't disappoint an eager angling journalist wanting a new story...plus a big fish!

I was already fishing in a swim called the 'Heli Pad' when Frank arrived, greeting me with a hearty handshake before immediately engaging in angling chitchat as if we had been friends for years. I could understand why he had risen to prominence in the carp world, not just for his captures but also for his showman-like style, which made the man a very interesting individual. It was a point reinforced when he began to cast his rods out. Compressing the carbon to a far greater degree than I would ever be capable of, each lead sailed out toward the horizon, accompanied by his trademark hi-viz pop-up. It was while casting the fourth and final rod, though, that the true fireworks began. As I sheltered under a brolly, the air filled with a noise akin to the cracking of a whip, and immediately I jumped up to investigate. Poking my head round the bivvy, I saw my companion holding a broken reel with blood over his hand. "Not to worry," came his chirpy response, "last time I did this, I broke my finger!"

It seemed as if the inertia created by such a vicious casting movement had re-engaged the bail arm of the reel, causing it to smash apart. I knew straight away that this session was going to be interesting, especially as he seemed to have quite enjoyed the whole saga. 'A larger than life character' has to be the best way to describe Frank.

His laid-back persona can fool you into thinking that he isn't taking things seriously, but nothing could be further from the truth. Working at his own pace and remaining unflustered allows him to come to the correct conclusions quicker than most, a point I began to understand shortly after the trip began, when his indicator rose steadily and his first fish of the trip slipped up. It may have been a 10lb 12oz bream and not a carp, but it demonstrated that he didn't wear the blinkers that come with a lot of carpers because, refreshingly, he enjoyed every capture no matter what species. This trait, in my experience, is common to the best anglers. An open mind allows for a greater understanding of the aquatic world and ultimately that helps with the pursuit of their chosen species. For example, I'm a much better carp angler now I have experienced a wide and diverse range of fishing situations than I ever was when I only pursued carp, and that's because I am capable of thinking outside the box. I digress; back to the story.

With his rod back out in the expanse of Kingsmead's open water, it wasn't long before what he had intentionally come to catch was chugging up and down

Refreshing attitude.

along the horizon, before succumbing to the pressure of Frank's sturdy rod. At 28lb 14oz, it was a good fish for Kingsmead at the time and provided full justification for a method I had previously seen as a gimmick. Another bream of 11lb also came his way, while I troubled the scoreboard as well with a carp and bream. The newspaper feature had been a success but much more importantly, a friendship had been made that would lead to so many more adventures.

Situated in 3,000 acres of deer park, Woburn Abbey has been the home of the Dukes of Bedford for nearly 400 years. Among the estate's glorious variety of countryside is a chain of lakes, famous in angling terms for being the birthplace of UK catfish and zander fishing. Alas, the lakes in question had been closed to anglers for many years and so the stories of the leviathans it held turned into myths, safely guarded within the estate walls, protected not only by gamekeepers but also the lions and tigers of the safari park. The question was, what did still swim in its sculpted lakes?

Fortunately for me, the perk of being an angling journalist is access to some off-limits venues, so without hesitation, I agreed to accompany photographer Mick Rouse on a journey into the unknown. Pulling up outside the estate office, I was greeted by my fishing partner for the next two days - Frank. He, too, had accepted the invitation to trial the lakes' potential and like two overgrown school kids we chatted excitedly, imagining what was in store for us while we waited for the head gamekeeper to arrive.

Drawing alongside in his Land Rover, at last he arrived and immediately indicated for us to follow him along the track that wound its way through the estate. Soon, we were pulling up next to a large, locked gate, which we hoped would open up to a piscatorial paradise. Down the path we followed in convoy, catching the first tantalising glimpse of the lake on our left-hand side.

A vast array of trees lined the bankside, providing a backdrop of ancient woodland made up of oak, beech, and ash, interspersed by azaleas and rhododendrons which added a splash of colour, their petals resplendent in spring. On the far side, open grassland was filled with grazing deer including rare pere davids, while pheasants strutted about, pecking at the soil in hope of a meal. A church sat just beyond the ground's walls, intensifying the beauty of the landscape, its weathered stonework and ancient gravestones adding a little gravitas to the greenery. We travelled the full length of the lake before pulling up at the dam wall. As we stepped out of the van, eight acres of water lay before us, with an island sitting 50 yards out that housed a huge Japanese pagoda. The estate's history felt tangible to us all.

I don't know whose face had the biggest grin, Frank's, or mine, but I do know we were both extremely excited. We fought to control our smiles but we were already drunk on the atmosphere. Our guide explained that details of the lake's stocking were a little hazy but he was adamant it held large carp, pike and catfish and with this perfect pitch of the water's potential, the gamekeeper wished us luck and left us alone to explore. It was time for a stroll around the margins and, we hoped, a chance to gain a glimpse of our quarry.

In the lion's den.

Halfway up the lake, a bed of reeds extended into the water, and through our Polaroids, the early-forming maroon leaves of a lily bed could be seen. Suddenly, like a ghost, a large armour-plated common drifted into my vision. Momentarily, we eyeballed each other before the shock of a strange encounter and the survival instinct kicked in, sending her fleeing for the sanctuary of deeper water. That was the sign we needed. With fish present, and the centre of the lake giving us an optimum vantage point, the areas either side of the reed bed would provide Frank and I with an ideal starting point. To call them swims would perhaps be a disservice, as I am sure the lush grass had never supplied accommodation to a brolly, bedchair and four rods before. I chose the right-hand side, which offered the pagoda island in front of me, while Frank settled for an area sheltered by a large overhanging tree.

I started to plumb around the water in front of me, and soon opted for the margins of both my bank and the island. These spots were weed-free, as well as supplying a depth variation. Bait for these areas was to be a combination of hemp and crushed tigers with a sprinkling of 15mm tiger nut boilies. With the high attraction level supplied, I felt sure the concoction would tempt the taste buds of these virgin carp.

After the traps had been set, there was little else to do but to sit back, put the kettle on and wait for events to unfold. How exciting would that first run be? Would we even get a run? These and a thousand more fishy quandaries filled our minds as the hours ticked slowly by, eased by copious cups of tea and coffee.

Darkness fell across the lake to the roar of lions and the chatter of chimps, and I headed for the comfort of my bag.

Sleep wouldn't come easily as my mind raced, still full of excitement and expectation.

Beep! The blue LED on the buzzer illuminated my rods. Beeeeeeeeep! I was away. Desperately, I scrabbled for my boots, momentarily contemplating charging across the wet ground without them, the shrill of the alarm turning me into a madman. Panic over, at last I picked up the rod and tightened the clutch. The carp, far out in the lake, kicked in response. A huge swirl appeared on the surface sending ripples against pagoda island.
"Oh no you don't!" I muttered, applying maximum pressure to prevent the fish from kiting around the back of the obstruction. What a fantastic feeling it was, connected to an unseen, untouched beast, while ancient trees silhouetted the sky and a church spire lay on a canvas of stardust. For the next five minutes, my knees knocked as the adrenaline levels rose until a vortex appeared under the rod tip. A huge white flank rolled on the surface and I heard the carp gulp its first taste of air, always a sign that the battle is nearly won. Arm outstretched and trembling, I guided her into the safety of the net. Yes! She was mine; but what now lay wrapped in the mesh?

Securing the net, I dived back under the brolly to grab my torch. The moment of truth had come. Its light first hit a large leathery flank with a few scattered scales. Its frame was round and deep, typical of the Italian strain. Most importantly, I had my prize safe to enjoy, and at 32lb 6oz, it was more than I could have dreamed of in such a theatre. With the fish comfortably sacked in the margins, I sat up waiting for daybreak hoping that Frank

Woburn wonder.

had also sampled the intoxicating liquor of success. Peering around his bivvy in the half-light, I scanned the water and yes, there too sat a sack. Frank recalled his own events and although a large fish had been lost, a gorgeous, chestnut-flanked fish of 18lb 12ozs had succumbed to his tactics.

It had been a trip to remember but I remain convinced to this day that I landed the biggest inhabitant. Why? Well, as we left I enquired what the derelict cable car that traversed the lake was for.

"Oh, that was for the sea lion attraction which used to be here," muttered the keeper. Somehow I couldn't imagine much surviving in that environment, so perhaps on this occasion, beauty really was only skin deep.

Innovative.

Carp catcher.

Larger than life.

Over the years, I have come to call on Frank many times for my media requirements and when I started an angling DVD company, his was the first name on the list to film. Catch? Of course he did, with a new personal best, but I think our greatest ever success came in April 2004 for, once again, an Angling Times feature.

Frimley is home to some of the most gorgeous-looking carp in the country and with Pit 3 providing unequalled quantities of big commons, it was a trip I was eagerly anticipating. Arriving mid-afternoon, I pushed my barrow down to the gate and took in my first glimpse of the water. Fifteen acres stared back at me, still wearing the stark complexion of early spring. With a north-westerly blowing down the lake, the bottom half looked appealing, its surface ruffled by the blow. A long bar sat proud of the water in this area and with waves lapping against it, my mind was made up – this was to be the area that I would investigate. The only issue to decide was whether I would fish the side of the bar or the front. Cue a mobile phone call from Ian 'Chilly' Chillcott, who was stationed on the other side of the lake, fishing to the same bar from a swim called the 'Double Boards'. Chilly kindly offered me the advice that carp had been jumping along the front of the bar in an area called 'The Noddies' and, in his humble opinion, my interests would best be served setting up there.

Initially, I succumbed to this suggestion, pushing my barrow back down the path until a nagging doubt crept into my mind. Did Chilly really want to assist or was he making sure that my bait stayed well out of his way? You see, the 'Stick Swim', which covered the side of the feature, would ensure any fish travelling down on the wind had to cross my path first, a place better suited to the task of catching, I felt. Again, the barrow was pushed along the path, this time to the area above Chilly. Meanwhile, my friend opposite watched on and a series of amusing text messages began to be traded.

First came 'what are you doing?' Next, 'don't you want my advice?' When I replied that it would all be okay, providing I didn't get pestered by that stupid common he'd been after for years, I then got 'If you do, I will kill you!' There was nothing malicious in any of it, of course, just a bit of bankside banter, but the die had been cast and some prophetic words spoken. Now it was time to begin the quest.

Soon my marker float was sailing out toward the exposed bar revealing clear gravel. My plan was to stagger the three hookbaits at varying depths where the substrate sank away into the main body of the lake. Maggots were to supply the thrust of my attack, fishing half a dozen grubs directly onto a strong size 11 hook while littering the swim with 20 spodfuls of free offerings. Nothing complicated, just a need for accurate casting and faith that it's not always big baits that catch big fish. With the work over, it was time to sit back and await events – but where was Frank?

Following a quick ring on his mobile, I discovered that he had just endured a day from hell – lost credit cards, moving home and now a blown-out tyre would have seen a lesser man cry off, but not Frank!

Light my fire.

The only problem was that it was now 5pm and he still had a four-hour journey to make. There was absolutely no chance of him being here before nightfall and with the venue producing the majority of fish at night, I didn't hold out much chance for him when he got here because the cloak of darkness would prevent him from assessing the lake.

At 9pm, he arrived, surprisingly cheerful after the day that he'd had. Now Frank is like the Inspector Gadget of the angling world, always producing a new fantastic rig or having a piece of tackle up his sleeve, but above all else, he's a catcher of carp and if he's got a line in the water, he's in with a chance. Swim choice would be difficult in the pitch black, even for Frank - or so I thought. Unzipping his bag, he produced something in the shape of a mini telescope and putting it to his eye, he began to scan the water.

"Oh, there's a carp, it just rolled," said Frank.
"Don't be daft, it's night time," came my reply. Passing the device over he ordered me to take a look. Blimey, it was daylight again! I couldn't believe it. Trust Frank; he had an image intensifier, SAS-style! Fishing in the darkness was not, after all, going to be a problem. Choosing to fish the swim to my left, and at the back of the bar that Chilly had recommended, his baits were eventually in place by 11pm. Half a night was better than nothing was the typically positive way that Frank looked at the situation. For a while, we chewed the fat but with a hectic day catching up on both of us, we soon wilted and headed for our bivvies.

Dreams were never to come though, as no sooner had I got into my sleeping bag than the buzzer screamed. Scrabbling around, I got my boots on and ran to the rod. On lifting it, I was surprised to feel no resistance and couldn't quite work out what was happening. As I wound down, eventually I felt some pressure and found that the fish had kited to my left while heading toward me, and was now on the near side of the bar. Out of the gloom, Frank appeared in the swim after hearing the commotion.

"Feels like a bream," were my first words to him. By the light sensation on the rod tip I was absolutely convinced it was a small fish. As I guided it gently towards us, Frank readied the net and at this point a huge vortex appeared on the surface, followed by a little panic from my end of the rod as the fish dived down the marginal slope.

Perhaps it was a carp after all, but I still wasn't convinced of its size. For the next five minutes, it

Red Letter Day.

hugged the marginal shelf, never really going anywhere, but always staying deep, resolute in its unwillingness to say hello. Eventually, the pressure began to take its toll and a huge gleaming flank hit the surface.

"It's a common," said Frank, and before I knew it, he had it sitting in the bottom of my landing net. In the light of the head torch, a monster of epic proportions stared back at us - but exactly how big didn't become apparent until we lifted her free of the water. Like a breeze block covered in golden scales, she lay quietly on the mat, shell-shocked like us, with the events. Placing her gently in the sling, we hoisted her up – 39lb 4oz of common carp, read the scales. I was blown away. I also realised that it was Chilly's target fish and the one he had warned me not to catch! The biggest fish in the lake within hours; how jammy was that?

With the fish safely sacked, Frank said that if I had the common he would have the 30lb-plus fully-scaled monster that inhabited the pit. As I crawled back into my bag, I told him to call me when he had it and drifted off to sleep with a huge smile. Two hours later the phone rang – it was Frank.
"Sorry to wake you, mate, but I have a big, fully-scaled carp in my net. Can you come and weigh it with me?" he said.

This was incredible! There in front of me was a beautiful creature, just as he described. The scales read 31lb 2oz, a new record weight for that fish. It really was a surreal moment. Someone upstairs had obviously taken a liking to us on this crazy night. As you can imagine, sleep was difficult and by daybreak, we were both excited to feast our eyes upon two of the lake's jewels again. Before this, there was one final, cruel task to complete and that was to inform Chilly of events. The opening moments of the conversation revealed that he'd only received liners during the night and I teased the situation by first revealing Frank's success before ensuring he was sitting down.
"You know that stupid old common...?" was all I needed to say for the hammer to fall. Despite the wind being taken out of his sails, he behaved like a true gentleman and insisted on coming round to witness the great fish and to shake my hand.

Frank went first, posing for pictures with one of, if not the, best-looking carp I have ever seen. Then it was my turn to lift the monster. What an awesome creature and I looked rather pathetic, straining to lift her to pose for the camera! She was a burnished gold bar, etched with a thousand scales and one of the country's finest carp. It provided a fitting end to one of the best angling nights I've ever experienced. I am also glad to report that Chilly's time did come with the great fish and nothing pleased me more than ringing to congratulate him. Just reward for one of angling's good guys.

Fishing with Frank never disappoints. I hope the years to come bring many more adventures with one of the sport's many larger-than-life characters. True friendships always stay strong, while memories of captures fade.

Frank's forecast.

Camera: Canon EOS 40D - Shutter Speed: 1/200 sec - F-Stop: f/5.6 - ISO: 400 - Location: Hungerford

CHAPTER 13

KENNET CAPERS

Bubbling up from the swallow headspring on the Marlborough Downs, this chalk watercourse is no more than a trickle, but long before it becomes a tributary of the Thames, it will announce itself as the River Kennet, flowing through miles of enigmatic countryside and becoming home to side streams, sluices, and specimen fish.

Mind's eye.

Under the drifts of water crowfoot, dreams can be made, for here, grayling, roach, dace and pike, to name a few, enjoy one of lowland England's finest waterways, and if angling means more than just catching, then the environment doesn't disappoint. Cock reed buntings call boldly from the tops of territorial bushes, and the splendid arigon dragonfly buzzes over the water meadows. I hope now you can begin to understand why I love my visits to the Kennet.

Dave, the river keeper, has always laughed at my pike fishing prowess, or lack of it, and it became a standing joke that whoever accompanied me on a jaunt to his beat would be the one who lured a big old Esox while I blanked. So obviously, when I arrived with the deadly duo of Terry Lampard and Tim Norman, the curse looked set to continue.

"There's no point in you bringing your rod," were Dave's first words before he let out a huge, bellowing laugh which saw his belly wobble and face redden. It wasn't hard to argue with him, either. The day had already begun badly; reversing off your drive and crushing your wife's car is not the best way to start a fishing trip. This news, over a cuppa, only served to amuse the keeper still further and neither Terry nor Tim exactly offered a shoulder to cry on. It looked for all the world as if the joke was on me for the day. Still, I couldn't think of a better place for it to happen, amid such stunning landscape.

Dave's river is a slice of paradise sculpted over the decades deep in the south of England, where it flows over and through sparkling weirs and pools. Just to walk its banks is a privilege and time spent in the fishing hut chewing the fat and drinking tea is always special. The lure, though, for those afflicted with the fishing bug always wins in the end and permission to wet a line in such a place is tantamount to angling heaven. With Dave promising to meet us back at the hut for lunch and round two of the mickey-taking, we began our stroll downstream, allowing the water's therapeutic properties to begin to turn a bad day into a good one.

Every sense was catered for, from the rustle of fallen leaves and the pulse of the sluice gates to the buzzard that rose high above as it searched out the meadows for a mouse, vole, or rabbit. Even the touch of the wooden bridge, damp and clammy with lichen, seemed somehow inviting, telling its own story, and conveying history. Our late arrival, coupled with tea and a chat, had seen the sun rise higher than a pike fisherman would normally desire but we were in no hurry. The heavy frost of the previous night had been sent into retreat, clinging on only in the shade of the tallest trees, so the picture painted in front of us was therefore nearly perfect, save for the need to add three small splashes of colour in the shape of our floats that each supported a livebait. All was set for the main attraction to arrive but she failed to materialise - initially at least.

Good old Dave.

A splash of colour.

To be successful when river piking, mobility is a vital ingredient, as a lazy angler who sits in one pitch for the day will rarely outscore those who are prepared to walk. Subsequently, a single rod is all that is required. With only ten minutes in each spot, searching every likely-looking ambush point is the key and carrying a huge amount of tackle has no place in this quest. Instead, a small shoulder bag is all that is needed. My net also assists my wanderings; it's a salmon model that can be slung over the back and forgotten about until required. A chair can also be left at home but to help with kneeling I wear a pair of neoprene thigh waders, which keep me dry.

Following this golden rule, we allowed our fishy offerings to explore the river's every nook and cranny, where the water deviated from its natural course allowing the flow to abate and a slack to form.

The darkness of a bridge strut and the confusion of a weir pool were also tried but our opponent was conspicuous by its absence. Occasionally, a big brown trout would eye up each offering before thinking better of it, while the agitated nature of the float kept us on edge as we anticipated a bite at any moment. Sometimes it's too easy to say that angling adds up to more than the sum of its parts when words of beauty are used to offset a lack of action, but I'd defy any man not to enjoy himself in the company of two mates in such a setting.

The confidence of knowing what you're doing is right, comes with experience. Too many people swap a winning method when there is no need, convinced that the tactic being used is no longer effective. Tim and Terry, though, are too long in the tooth for such thoughts, and without the slightest hint of questioning our method we continued on our journey, certain that the right time would come – but whose time?

Disengaging the bail arm, I allowed the dace's weight to pull braid from the spool as it fell on to the water with a splash. Such a commotion always alerts a pike, its senses finely attuned to a free lunch. My eyes were still trained on the silver flank of the dace when, within an instant, it faded in the presence of a huge shadow. The next vision was fleeting but one that every angler lives for, to be recounted around a crackling fire in a comfy pub. An enormous creamy, white belly and polka dot flank devoured the space where my bait had been sitting before vanishing into the depths.

It would have been easy to believe it was nothing more than my imagination had it not been for the float following in close pursuit, marking the path of the beast. A serious case of trembling hands afflicted me as I just stared into the river, but fortunately instinct kicked in with a drill carried out hundreds of times. With the clutch checked, the reel handle spun until I felt a weight on the rod tip before sweeping back the carbon. In response, a huge head-shake resonated up the braid and I was released from my hypnotic state. By now Tim and Terry had arrived alongside me but given the screaming clutch, whatever was below didn't want to meet them! The first surge then relented but what came next confirmed that something substantial had come out to play.

As the pike headed back upstream, the rod transmitted a dead weight and the braid strained as it tried to cope with the pressure applied. This spelled out everything we needed to know. Tim continued the running commentary but only odd words were heard. 'Bloody hell', 'broad back', and 'get it Terry' was all I remembered. Fortunately, two grinning faces soon held

Last laugh.

a bulging landing net and together we hoisted it ashore and explored its contents. With a huge humped back and eyes to match, the pike looked every bit as impressive as its size dictated. We all then had a guess at what the scales would reveal and the instrument itself settled for 26lb 14oz. A bad start to the day had just got a whole lot better! She was ours for a few short moments and then it was time to say farewell. A final pat on the head and a thank you was followed by a whoosh of the tail.

Marching back to the fish hut, Dave's booming laugh greeted the news. A bacon and egg lunch to celebrate followed, and four friends relaxed with another angling tale safely stored away.

Having not fished CEMEX's Burghfield stretch for a few years, I decided to call Neil Wayte, a man who knew the river here very well. He may look a little scary but if the truth be known, Neil is a gentle giant and is always willing to help out and offer advice. Typically, my telephone call soon changed from a list of questions to arranging a time to meet, as he kindly volunteered to take time out and guide me along the river, personally.

From the off it certainly seemed to have potential, especially given the proximity of a café. A full English is the finest way to begin any adventure and while we tucked in, Neil listed a catalogue of big fish, which certainly made the day even more tempting. A barbel over 14lb is a very big fish and Burghfield contained more than one. So, with full stomachs, we made our way down the riverbank trading banter and generally putting the world to rights. The debate stopped, though, as we arrived at our destination. Here, the Kennet changed from a canalised shadow of a river into a dynamic weir pool, as rich, chalk-filtered Wiltshire water spewed out in front of us. The boundary for big barbel had been reached and here was a place where dreams could be made.

Our first task was to wander up and down the bank assessing each swim as we went, but to be honest, everywhere screamed 'fish'. The river played host to endless bends and creases but Neil was adamant that the most prolific swims contained an element of cover to them. With the stretch holding very little weed, these areas gave the barbel a feeling of safety.

Weir pool magic.

So heeding this advice, we opted for a series of rafts and introduced a few dropper-loads of pellets and hempseed in an attempt to lure our opponent from its lair and on to our hooks. For bait we both chose a halibut pellet, combined with terminal tackle which was pinned to the deck to avoid detection. Neil and I knew full well that a line cutting through the water would spell certain failure, as pressured fish do not take kindly to such mistakes.

Slowly though, despite this attention to detail, the day slipped away and, save for the odd small chub, all remained quiet. It seemed as if we had found the river in a mood; was it the low water, high pressure or perhaps something altogether more simple, our lack of ability? The fact remained that when it came time to reel in, we had failed to trouble the scoreboard. Licking our wounds, we headed for home but a head torch grabbed our attention; its owner, by coincidence, was a former pupil of Neil's guiding service. Overjoyed, the man recounted his tale of the barbel he had just slipped back, all 16lb of it. After offering congratulations we continued on our journey, while I quipped: "At least it proves you're not a completely rubbish guide!" Neil's reply was, of course, that perhaps it was down to his present company's failings and not his! Trading insults was all well and good but we had blanked so we decided that round two would commence the following afternoon. We were down but not out.

A new day brought fresh hope and, with both of us encamped in different swims, the barbel surely couldn't

Showing me the way.

ignore us again. Well, alas they could, as once again my rod failed to bend in anger. Neil needed to save the day and when a huge grin emerged from his beard, I couldn't help but laugh.

"I thought the guide was meant to catch me a fish," I declared.
"He was, but you were making such a mess of it that I had to help out," came the retort and with a 13lb 4oz barbel in his grasp, I didn't have a leg to stand on. A shake of the hands brought a hard but enjoyable session to a close. I wasn't for giving up on capturing my own specimen, though, so I bided my time, waiting for a return match.

Angling is all about personal challenges and goals, which is what makes this sport so special. I love to set myself aims for forthcoming months and these spur me on, adding to the capture when, or if, I achieve it. Sometimes it's not about a big fish either, but perhaps a method or a venue that I want to conquer. So for now it was a Kennet barbel, and a big one at that.

Tension builds.

At last.

Over the years, I had been lucky enough to bank specimens of 14lb or more from five different rivers and a sixth was proving to be very tempting. The obvious place to look at was Burghfield, but unfortunately, as you have read, the barbel and I had yet to become friends. In my experience, investing time and doing the groundwork always pays dividends and even if the previous trips had not yielded a fish to yours truly, it did see Neil arm me with plenty of information on the barbels' location. This, I hoped, would prove invaluable on my return and shorten the route to success.

My diary was solid over the next few weeks with filming commitments, so an imminent return did not appear likely. Fortunately, a bank of rain and low cloud cover scuppered the plans and suddenly, I was left with a spare day. The conditions may not have been to the camera's liking but they absolutely screamed fish!
Being an angling jack-of-all-trades, I am usually left in a quandary about what to do, but today would see no such dilemma; I had a score to settle with a certain river. I marched through the drizzle along the towpath before the Kennet began to resemble a river once again. I think that it's these canalised sections that upset the balance of the venue for me and sends my mind out of kilter. They do appear very alien.
'At least,' I told myself, 'that CEMEX section was proper flowing water.'
And indeed it was every bit as splendid as my last visit, despite the now grey overcoat.

The swim I hoped to fish from was the very same one I had blanked in but with a huge snag in situ I knew full well that the barbel would be in residence. Luckily, given that it was a busy stretch, I found the peg vacant so I promptly claimed the spot for myself. Instead of reaching for the dropper I decided on a much more cautious approach, with free offerings only being introduced via PVA bags. Such venues can be difficult to read with regard to bait requirements because the previous angler may well have chucked in a bucket of pellets, so the last thing you want is to put a load more in. Unfortunately, it is impossible to know this and to my mind if everyone fed a little less, we would all catch more. In damp conditions, though, I do have a litmus test for the swim I intend to fish; footprints.

For me, the best possible sign is none, as in all probability it was vacant the day before. Now you can understand why I was suitably impressed with unmolested ground.

On a river the size of the Kennet, I normally fish with a single rod but on previous advice I decided on two areas, one upstream and one downstream, both of which would receive an identical attack. A 15mm Meaty Marine boilie was accompanied by a bag of 6mm halibut pellets and, of course, the obligatory bolt rig. My hooklength was a 12lb coated braid, but given the suspicious nature of the residents, I peeled back the last five inches to expose its fine core. For a belt and braces approach, I then pinned it all to the deck with a back lead. Today, though, I hoped the fish would be a little less paranoid because the overnight rain had definitely tinged the water and increased the flow. Perfect, especially given the long dry spell that had preceded it.

Given the obstacles present, tackle needed to be robust, so 12lb mono and a 2lb test curve rod appeared in order and with both outfits at last ready, I deposited the rigs in the desired position and sat back to wait. Being only lunchtime and with the prime catching time of dusk some hours away, I could well have been sitting down a while but for some reason it felt different today. In fact, I was so confident that I felt giving up angling on the Kennet altogether would be the best option if I failed! Sometimes you just know the fish will feed and sure enough, as the half-hour mark arrived the upstream rod was wrenched round with gusto. No matter how much I expect it, such ferocity always takes me by surprise and my heart skipped a beat as I made a grab for the rod. A suitably savage fight ensued and culminated in an eight-pounder safely banked.

Although pleasing in itself, I was equally as excited by the fact that it showed that the barbel were 'on' and feeding. Indeed, that capture was just the beginning. I went on to catch numbers two, three, and four, including a 10-pounder. Then came an 11lb fish followed by numbers six, seven, and eight – this one being a big '12'! Number nine followed shortly afterwards and, to coin a phrase, this was barbel fishing from the top drawer. Greed now played its part I'm afraid, as I knew with each capture the odds would shorten on catching the aimed-for 14-pounder. On this occasion, I would not be leaving the venue early.

Twenty minutes later, the tip folded over and I commenced the most brutal of battles. Neither of us was willing to give an inch because to do so would spell certain defeat for either party. It was now down to a game of chicken and I'm glad to say that the barbel blinked first, but only just! As it powered upstream I could feel its full weight and when the flank rolled in front of me, my suspicions were confirmed; this was the one I wanted. Into my net she rolled and I let out a huge sigh, as there before me sat my goal - all 14lb 5oz of it. I thought a phone call was in order to thank Neil!

Six over 14lbs.

The beauty of the Kennet is in the variety of species on offer. Whatever the conditions, something is willing to feed, even when winter has gripped the countryside and robbed all colour from a frostbitten vista.

It's not uncommon during the colder months for me to commence an angling trip in pursuit of tiny fish like gudgeon and chublets. Strange, you may think, for an angler who spends most of his time chasing specimen fish, but there is a method in my madness as since time immemorial, anglers have practised the art of livebaiting for predators knowing of its deadly effectiveness. In a different era, a roach sent out with a Gazette bung, or a minnow removed from a trap made with a lemonade bottle and then suspended under a perch bobber, was considered the norm and the tactic has been passed down the generations from father to son without issue. Until recently, that is. There is within angling a 'PC' brigade that love nothing better than to write a letter to the magazines condemning a method that is perfectly legal. Most seem to ignore our heritage and misunderstand the potential knock-on effect of eliminating its use. I have no intention here of defending the tactic, and I want to state that I don't wear sandals with white socks and eat tofu, but I do enjoy livebaiting and see nothing wrong with it. So, with a dozen tiny fish which I had cropped from an overpopulated weir pool I moved a few yards downstream to a swim where I knew the occupants would relish sampling the fruits of my labour.

Situated along an otherwise barren stretch of river were two bushes whose foliage had, over the years, made contact with the water, creating an area that captured a range of debris during every flood. It made for a perfect home. Nestled within this maze of underwater timber sat a shoal of striped bullies. Their aim in life was simple; to ambush as many unfortunate fish as possible to satisfy their ravenous appetites. As an angler, knowing this was obviously beneficial to my chances of success, as a little fish dangled in front of their noses would prove mighty tempting, especially now dusk, prime-time for a feeding frenzy, was a mere two hours away.

The bait and location part of the puzzle, I felt sure, had been completed correctly; all that was left to put in place now was the tackle selection. An old favourite, the Drennan Tench Float rod would provide the backbone, while a reel loaded with 6lb line, I hoped, would be strong enough to extract my adversaries from their lair. Given the speed of flow in and around the swim, the logical place to position my fish would be in the slack created by the two bushes, but even here the water moved with purpose and measured no more than a couple of feet wide. Generally, I will opt for a paternoster rig with the tiniest float possible but the conditions this time demanded something a little cruder. The paternoster would stay in place, as a free-roving bait had no chance of staying in position long enough to be spotted, but the float needed alteration to a larger four swan loafer. Fortunately, despite being untidy, my tackle box contained the required implement so I could set about constructing the rig.

First, the float was slipped on the main line, fixed with two float rubbers before the boom section was created. Like my tackle box, that is an ice cream container, I see no reason for fancy contraptions, opting first for an overhand loop in the main line. To this, a short hooklength of 7lb fluorocarbon and a size 6 hook was connected in a loop-to-loop fashion, while the main line tag end was used to attach the holding weight, in this case a series of swan shot. I was left with a simple but deadly outfit, although I knew it would be rendered useless until I carried out the final, vital procedure correctly – plumbing.

To fish a livebait and paternoster rig to its full potential, a pinpoint check on the depth is vital. What needs to be achieved is the loafer cocking with exactly half its body protruding from the water.

Ambush time.

Lucky livebait.

Now under tension, when the fish moves downwards the float's buoyancy comes into play and tells on its movement, forcing it back to the original position. Of course, the livebait continues to repeat this procedure time and time again, drawing attention to itself. Fish the float over-depth and with too much slack, and the safety of the bottom can be reached, while too little and the float becomes submerged, rendering bite indication impossible.

With the plotting and planning complete, it was time to start angling and maybe prosper from the couple of hours of preparation time I had invested. Satisfyingly, I watched the rig land in the desired spot first cast with three splashes (one for the shot, one for the float and one for the fish) indicating no tangles. By placing only a single rod rest into the ground, I then could keep the rod tip high meaning no line was grabbed by the flow. Throbbing and pulsing, the loafer float was full of energy and this served to keep me on the edge of my seat as occasionally, the gudgeon would rest before surging downwards, convincing me that I wasn't the only one keeping an eye on proceedings. Sure enough, the hunch was to prove correct when only minutes later the float's tip was smacked against the surface in a single, savage motion. The perch had struck; now I only had to wait for it to move off with its prey.

The strike was delayed a further five seconds as the hook was transferred from one mouth to another. This was to be a scenario that replayed itself over and over again in the last hours of daylight, with both of us taking turns to win. My reward was a photo and the perch's, a slipped hook hold. An empty livebait bucket and darkness drew a conclusion to an adventure that had allowed me to enjoy the harvest of Mother Nature in the most exciting way possible. The result was eight perch to over 3lb. So, in celebration, I headed off to the keeper's cottage for the warmth of an open fire, a dram of whisky and a toast to tradition.

If I were ever forced to pick one species to target on this river, there would be no contest. The sight of silver flashing over fast shallow gravel runs becomes less frequent every year and one I cherish more with each passing season. Imagine what life must be like when every beak and jaw has you right at the top of the sushi menu and even if you're lucky enough to survive such trials, then man will do his best to trash your home. You see, the life of a dace is a precarious one and avoiding cormorants, pike, and pollution is a day-to-day trial, but they do manage to find some respite in the narrow reed-fringed carriers.

To many, this freshwater herring does little to spark any interest but in its life of a decade or so it will truly need Lady Luck on its side to become a specimen. Indeed, by then it would have as much right as any fish to be called 'special'. A dace over the 1lb mark is probably more rare than a 40lb carp and certainly more difficult to catch than a double-figure barbel. These proportions are normally only reached by the hen fish during late February and early March when, plump with spawn, they grow by three to four ounces. So, when I left home one November day, I did so without the slightest ambition of such a specimen. The bottom line is that I'm a sucker for bites, especially when I can see the fish taking the bait, and for me, an afternoon wandering over water meadows and peering into chalk-filtered pools still decorated with a weed green trim is heaven. Big fish are just a bonus in such environments; to be there is always enough.

With numerous weirs, side streams, bridges, sluices, and bends to explore I had no idea where my legs would take me but with a little poking and prodding, I hoped to find a few fish. Although the river was as radiant as ever, the sky did its best to change my mood and in the gathering gloom came rain that was persistent and heavy. Walking upstream, I pulled my hood up and shrugged my shoulders. Even if the heavens wanted to chuck buckets of water over me, it wasn't going to kill me or put me off.

As I picked my way along the river, the droplets of water disturbed the surface and prevented me from spotting anything, so perhaps, I thought, a side-stream would give me a better view. I branched off to the left, took a reed-lined offshoot that had a little more cover and began catching glimpses of the gravel bottom no more than three feet down. Seemingly perfect swims were devoid of life, testament to the shortage of silver fish in the upper reaches. Mind you, they could easily be missed, with roach and dace being masters at melting into the background. When the fish are tucked up under fallen stems, it can be very easy to walk past an entire shoal.

As I peered over a bed of foliage, I could see that the water in front of me suddenly plunged away into a deeper pool and, staring intently, I tried to pick out the bottom by focussing on the light gravel bed. There, hugging the stones were a dozen shadows; not clear but definitely in residence. Almost barbel-like, a flank twisted momentarily, revealing a bright silver overcoat of a dace. Now, such a fish is never going to look massive but I knew from experience that it was a monster. I put my tackle down gently, and now felt confident to begin fishing, but only after I'd regained a little composure from witnessing such a sight.

Any moment.

Surprises in the side stream.

With such shy fish, I resisted the temptation to use a float rod and instead opted for the tip. My fine-tipped quiver would be perfect when combined with the lightest top section that culminated in a 0.5oz test curve tip. Using an 11-foot rod meant that I could easily reach over the reeds and its soft action would, I hoped, prevent the dace from feeling any resistance. Double Strength line of 4lb was then threaded through the rings with a paternoster rig slipped on at the business end. Here, most people use knots to create such a rig but these do not compare well against using float stops as the conduit for carrying the tag end. The line is not weakened and the length of tail can be adjusted with ease. To begin with on this trip I settled for three feet, ending in a 1.14lb bottom to a size 18 hook with two red maggots. Balancing your leger rig on a river is every bit as important as it is with a float. It needs to 'fish' and by this, I mean carry just enough shot to hold bottom, occasionally shuffling across the gravel, and to achieve this you may need to use a combination of different shots and not just an SSG.

With an AAA and a BB working perfectly, it was time to introduce a little feed. Over the next five minutes I kept up a constant stream of grubs heading downstream and hoped this would be enough to kick-start a feeding reaction which, given the darting shadows within the pool, appeared to have the desired reaction. Impaling two maggots onto the hook, I then made my first cast. Instead of the typical seat and rod rest approach I decided to hold the rod, as by standing I could keep the line free of the near bank reeds, plus my reactions would be quicker than those of the dace.

Allowing a bow of line to form, I prevented direct resistance and readied myself for action, and before I had time to re-feed the swim from my bait pouch, the tip tapped once before steadily pulling round. A strike made contact but the force was light and almost immediately, a 6oz dace spun on the surface. Not big, but I still felt confident that the fish I'd previously seen was somewhat larger. A repeat of the process ended in a similar result, as an identical-looking fish headed into my landing net. Keeping up your feeding rhythm is vital even while catching, so again, another dozen grubs headed downstream. Unfortunately, this free lunch had attracted an unwelcome visitor, which grabbed at my hookbait and became snared, doing its best to wreak havoc before the rogue trout launched into mid-air, smashing not only the surface but my hooklength, too. Ripples radiated from the splash, sending every living thing beneath the surface heading for cover. It would be a while before I could expect another chance.

Still the feeding had to continue. With rain falling once more, I stood heron-like with a motionless rod in my hand, and maybe half an hour passed until out of the blue, the soft tip buckled under pressure. A sideways strike hit a solid resistance and I waited for a roach to boil on the surface due to the bend in the carbon. Sure enough, a silver flank did appear in front of me but not the one I suspected; instead an enormous dace boiled and suddenly the whole fight took on a more serious outlook. I did not want to lose this fish but with only a 1lb 14oz bottom, every piece of weed and reed would prove fatal and, boy, did I know it!

True to form, she did her best to bore under my feet. Letting go of the reel, I held the rod at full length to avert the impending danger. My heart was in my mouth as I made a desperate scoop for the dace and it was with huge relief that she sank into the green mesh. I lifted her and took my first close look. Immediately, I knew that it was over 1lb, which was amazing really, given the time of year. Even without a pigeon chest, the length and width indicated a sizeable expanse that was adorned with mother-of-pearl scales. My own scales span round to a fraction over 1lb 3oz before settling exactly on the ounce.

This dace was a monster at any time but without spawn it was incredible and a potential record-breaker. Placing her back in the stream, I wished her well and hoped that she would continue to remain safe from every beak and jaw. The Kennet is certainly a special place.

Mother-of-pearl.

Camera: Canon EOS 5D - Shutter Speed: 1/200 sec - F-Stop: f/7.1 - ISO: 100 - Location: Dorset estate lake.

CHAPTER 14

LIGHTNING STRIKES TWICE

Fate doesn't always have to be cruel and a journey beginning with apparent failure can end in jubilation. A three o'clock alarm call dragged me from my warm bed, my wife, Jo, being less than pleased about being woken up. Effort plays a large part in success, though, and I knew that arriving on the water at dawn would make all the difference, even if it meant being in the doghouse for a while. This is the time to locate tench, so it makes swim choice simple.

Bubblers.

Arrive an hour after dawn and you have to rely on guesswork, so for the sake of losing a couple of hours' sleep you gain a golden opportunity to spot paintbrush tails slapping against a millpond surface, or streams of fizzing bubbles erupting against the pads.

Dawn arrived with a stroke of pink tracing across the horizon just as I pushed open the gate and loaded my barrow before starting to push it around the lake, pausing every so often to look for a sign. Two hundred yards along the bank I was greeted by a real Mr Crabtree scene; rolling fish and plenty of frothy, white bubbles in and around the weed beds. 'That will do for me', I thought as my barrow came to a grinding halt. I was confident in my assessment as well as excited by the prospects that lay ahead, as the gravel pit in question had only recently produced Darren Ward's record at 15lb 3ozs.

In an attempt to capitalise on the potential that faced me, two rods were quickly prepared with 12lb line, bolt rigs and fake caster hookbaits, finished off with PVA bags packed with casters. This tackle may seem a little over the top but the pit was riddled with snags, from tree trunks to metal poles, and to give a fish line at any time in the fight would result in losses. Factor in the carp population, and using lesser tackle would not only have invited failure, it also would have been irresponsible.

Both rods were cast to a gap between two islands 20 yards out from the bank, and on to a gravel bar that had been, and still was, the scene for much of the disturbance. There was no need today to plumb around or check that the bottom was clear as I knew the swim well; a benefit of getting to know the venue over the previous season. Twelve spodfuls of red maggots then sailed out to the same area to lay down an appetiser to tempt the tench into making a mistake. Now all that was left to do was to put the kettle on and continue to watch the sun rise in the sky, sending darkness into retreat and alerting my quarry that breakfast time wouldn't last forever. A perfect dawn, and a perfect time to angle when the only company is the call of the cuckoo and the shriek of a bite alarm, which on this occasion came three times with the best fish weighing just over 8lbs.

Far away from the world, it was easy to forget humanity, until my tranquillity was broken by the mobile phone. It was Adrian Eves, a guy who I'd become friendly with after spending time in his company on this very pit. I think it was fair to say that Adrian had struggled, at least by his high standards, with a poor last six months and he needed a confidence boost. With these tench feeding heavily, a trip down seemed the obvious choice, so arrangements were made to fish the night with me and by five o'clock in the afternoon when he arrived, I'd had another three fish, a point obviously not missed by him as he set up next door to me. 'Poacher!' was the jovial banter, but in fairness I would have done exactly the same and he knew it! His bait was positioned up the side of my right-hand island with the aid of his bait boat, and he threatened to put his spare rod out under the cover of darkness in the middle of my swim. At this juncture, I told him I would sink his boat if it came any closer! Not that I was overly concerned as he had put the same effort into catching the record and I've always believed in destiny.

With all our rods out we settled down to put on the kettle again and continue the banter, which grew when we were joined by two other friends, namely Ben Hamilton and Terry Hearn, who were also fishing the pit at the same time but for carp. The climax of the evening's events was me losing a carp, but with the sun out and good company it was still a fine way to spend a few hours. Unfortunately, time stops for no man and dusk drifted into night so at about 11pm we all headed for the warmth of our sleeping bags to dream of big fish.

My eyes opened slowly to see Adrian standing over me with a cup of coffee and telling me it was four o'clock in the morning. Now, Evesy has never brought me a drink at dawn and immediately, I smelled a rat.
"What are you up to?" were my first words of the morning.
Looking sheepish, the reply came "Oh, I had a fish a little while ago," as if it was no big deal. "How big"
"Oh, 11-7."
"11lbs 7ozs!" I yelled. "You jammy bugger!"

I spent the next couple of minutes calling him a poacher but to be honest I was made up for him. Adrian had spent numerous days on the pit last season with me for very little reward and finally the pit had paid him back.

I clambered out of my bag, we headed off to his swim and on unzipping the tube I was blown away. The fish didn't have an ounce of spawn in it and would have been a genuine 11, even in winter. I had seen tench to 12 ½lbs but this was a much bigger fish; a true Goliath. I gave Adrian a hearty handshake and went off to wake Tel from his slumber to help with pictures. Obviously, I would have loved to have caught the fish myself, but I find that I'm equally as excited by being involved with the big fish scene, especially the capture of a monster and I was not sure who was more thrilled, me and Tel, or Adrian, as we took the photos.

Sensing that the time had come to leave the lake, as in all probability I had just witnessed the record fish spawned out, I began to mull over my next option. Serious thinking wasn't required, though, as my phone signalled a text bringing with it the answer.

Jammy bugger!

Night shift.

Ian Welch, boss of RMC Angling at the time, had been fishing a venue under his jurisdiction that we had both earmarked the previous summer as having great potential for monster crucians. In fact, it was where Adrian Eves had caught a record-beating fish, so there was a degree of karma to the situation. After this capture, though, the stock had been removed and placed in the nearby Summer Pit, it being, I guess, a better commercial option. Despite this process, not every fish was rehoused and during an overnight session the previous year, rolling crucians had been spotted and even though we failed to catch, a return was certainly earmarked the following spring and Ian confirmed this by his text stating that he had tempted four 4lb crucians over the last month. Understandably and immediately, I tried to regain permission to visit the venue, hoping that I, too, could join in the gold rush. Happily, access was granted providing that Ian accompanied me, and a date was set to change my attentions from tench to crucians.

The name now used to describe the pit is Little Moulsham, but on my arrival I knew it only as Eversley and after following directions I began to push my barrow across the football pitch, which then led me to a narrow path and my first glimpse. Typical of the pits in the Yateley area, it had matured nicely with its ten acres broken in the middle by two heavily wooded islands. As I pushed on down the track, such was the vegetation filling the canopy and removing the sunlight that it had a claustrophobic feel, until a clearing appeared in which sat Ian, already set up in

the only real open swim available. I guessed it was the place where he had enjoyed his success, and from information gleaned from Adrian, this was the bank to target. Its marginal shelf was closer to the edge as well as being deeper which meant that the fish could enjoy the full cover of overhanging trees, unlike any other part of the pit. Unfortunately, Ian reported that no action had been forthcoming but this didn't put me off, especially as there were plenty of virgin areas to explore and with crucians' tendency to be territorial I could easily land on a pod, providing, of course, that I was happy to set up in the undergrowth.

Assessing a successful angler's approach is also a key component in piecing the jigsaw puzzle together and I was interested to see Ian's tactics as he swung his rig out into the water. The trip the previous summer had made both of us realise that float fishing all night for a limited stock of fish was both punishing and unproductive, so it came as no surprise when a bolt rig sat at the core of his set-up. If memory serves me correctly, a cage feeder, coated braid hooklength and fake, popped-up corn were the components and while I agreed with the bolt rig approach, I felt that something a little more subtle was called for; not that it had been detrimental to Ian's catch rate.

A Kamasan Black Cap feeder full of red maggots sat on the end of 6lb main line, which was semi-fixed by a float stop. A short, three-inch, 7lb micro braid hooklength and size 12 hook made up the business end, which supported a tiny grain of maize critically balanced with yellow foam. Finally, a dynamite stick made up of liquidised bread, micro pellets and crushed hemp completed the approach. Laying it in the margin, I watched as the PVA melted leaving a tantalising bed of bait that was so light, a fickle crucian would have had great difficulty in avoiding being hooked, or so I hoped.

Super-confident in the approach, I retraced my steps 20 yards back up the bank to where the overhanging trees parted, leaving a small but fishable gap. Under the canopy, it was difficult to wield a 12-foot rod, but on lowering a lead gently into the margins, I liked what I found; a clear, gravelly slope falling away into six feet of water and flanked by Canadian on both sides, supplying the perfect habitat. In fact, it seemed to me that I would be fishing in their home, rather than on a patrol route that the more open swim provided. Happy with this assessment, I positioned two rigs halfway down the slope and dusted the area with a minimal amount of casters, hemp, and pellet. I hoped it would be enough to attract the crucians but not the tench whose unruly behaviour would, I felt, lead to too much disturbance.

Darkness brought with it a relief that I had indeed avoided the tench but what about the golden dinner plates; had they begun to move like the bats now did above the surface? Ten-thirty brought the answer, as my alarm broke the silence that had enveloped the valley. Rushing towards the rod, I had to control the strike so as not to become tangled in the branches and was relieved to make a clean connection. The fish below responded by making a circular motion while trying to bore into a nearby weed bed. Unfamiliar with a large crucian's fight, I was confused by this tactic and had no idea what to expect when the silhouette of a rounded head popped to the surface and I took my best guess on where to place the landing net. Only when the mesh was shipped back to my feet did the torch let me in on the secret; a big crucian was the prize. Weighing an impressive 4lbs, its attractiveness didn't quite match up, being dull in complexion and with a slight deformity to its mouth. On the plus side, it had character with its long years etched over every scale and only an ungrateful angler would judge such a book by its cover. I had, after all, caught what I had come for; an enormous specimen with relatively little effort when compared with the spring tench campaign. Content, I made the crucian safe for the night, re-baited the rod and jumped back into bed with a smile on my face.

What should have been a peaceful sleep was anything but as the bobbins continually twitched, setting off the alarms without a proper bite manifesting itself. A group of crucians were visiting the swim, of that I had no doubt, but why I couldn't catch one was a question I had, I'm afraid, no answer to. Well past midnight, I finally gave up thinking and fell asleep, only to receive a startling 4 o'clock alarm call. Why does a fish tearing off after its mistake create so much panic in a grown man? Well, it always does for me and it certainly did that night as I dived out of bed forgetting to put either my glasses or boots on!

Still considerably less than fully aware, I stood ankle deep in water, the temperature of which was an indicator as to how warm recent days had been, while the rod performed a copycat of the previous battle. Autopilot had now kicked in and despite my semi-blindness I remained in control. Well, that was until I came to wield the landing net again. Dangerously, I poked and prodded, ultimately taking my best guess, which I could only confirm had been successful when I pulled it back toward me. Talk about bad angling; this was certainly a time when I needed Lady Luck on my side.

A crucian was definitely inside the net but I struggled to assess its size, given my visual predicament, so propping the net frame up I rushed to get my glasses and only then did I realise the magnitude of the situation; a fish of gigantic proportions stared back at me. It was a classic shape, rotund with its high back and rounded mouth set off against a buttery yellow flank. All my Christmases had come at once! The scales also had a present for me, reading 4lb 9oz 9 drams and another record, completing a magical four-year period for me when I really could do no wrong in the specimen angling stakes, giving me two British records as well as the biggest barbel, perch and crucian braces ever. Effort and luck are a deadly combination and as I slipped the monster back into her home that morning, I struggled to see how angling could get any better. Of course, this was wrong as a journey through the piscatorial world holds a never-ending stream of adventures.

Lightning strikes twice.

Picture postcard.

Where do you go crucian fishing after reaching its pinnacle? Surely, nowhere could match Eversley? Well, of course, if size is the only indicator of success then my career would be over, although I did return to visit the pit's monsters for 'Catching the Impossible', such was its unique specimen status, but I have always prized the taming of new waters so the desire to catch these magnificent fish never left me. The only problem with crucians is finding a water that hasn't had its gene pool tainted by hybridisation.

Coveted as an ornamental fish, I believe the crucian's origins in this country are probably through this route rather than an indigenous status and therefore a corruption of its genetics has occurred over centuries. Who's to say a crucian we call genuine today is not a bastardisation of the original species, but its transition has been completed over hundreds of years with subtle alterations to the DNA? One thing's for sure; I have debated this complex subject without a satisfactory answer many times.

Peter Rolfe is one such philosopher who has a vast knowledge on the subject and his counsel has the added benefit of having been conducted on the banks of his wonderful Wiltshire ponds. A world away from Eversley, the lily-fringed, shallow waters engage a crucian angler like no other and in the murky water with its silty bottom, lunch is always served, demonstrated by an endless stream of frothing bubbles. I may have been responsible for inflicting the abomination of a bolt rig on the crucian world, but I'm not soulless. Here, a float swaying in the vortex of fin-wash gives salvation for the sins committed, and size, I can genuinely say, is of no concern, as fishing cannot always be judged by pounds and ounces. Kicking the Eversley habit completely, though, is not easy and when another species of carp was thrown into the mix a few years later, the temptation to return became overwhelming.

Wrong.

Right.

Returning to a scene of a triumph is always a dangerous thing to do. Somehow, everything seems to be an anti-climax and sport fails to live up to expectations. This was at the forefront of my mind as I returned to the home of one of my most treasured memories, conscious of not pushing my luck or friendship too much. Carp, once again, were on the agenda but another subspecies this time, that I hoped would take centre stage – a mullet-shaped creature with flanks of golden scales. It was, of course, the grass carp and with fish to over 30lbs present, I might be able to bank my first ever specimen.

Birdsong filled the air as I walked along the path and then down under a shroud of trees, with fond memories flooding back. For the majority of the time, nature was free of man's intrusion on the lake but today was to be different. Over the intervening years since my last visit, small saplings had become heavy with vegetation, giving an even greater feeling of claustrophobia to the lake. It was at its densest where I had caught my record, but more importantly, once again it provided the only combination of a sharp drop-off along the margins with the cover of protruding trees. If anywhere could house a crucian it would still be here, I surmised. The question was, though, did they still exist?

Even a few years ago, they had looked old with thinning backs and craggy features. A whisper on the grapevine had told me that one four-pounder had been banked that spring, so at the very least a remnant of the population still hung on. It was sad to think that once they were gone, the finest crucian water in the country

A scene of triumph.

would be just a memory, as reproduction had appeared unsuccessful. Then, save for a few anglers, no one would mourn their passing - a situation, I'm certain, that wouldn't exist if this were the last bastion of a bird or a butterfly! However, this wasn't the time for maudlin thoughts. I had an adventure to look forward to, and with the margins identified as my crucian hotspot, I raked the bottom half a dozen times to release the trapped natural larder.

It was now time to think about the grass carp that would occupy the attentions of two of my rods. Directly in front of me, some 60 yards out, was the main island and to the left of this I could see a small section of another one. Between the two ran a narrow channel, so this seemed to me like an ideal ambush point for one rod. The distance was approximately 100 yards and the textbook indicates a particle approach for grass carp, so I felt it prudent to call on the services of my bait boat for pinpoint accuracy. I could surround a popped-up tiger nut hookbait with a liberal coating of hemp, maize, groats and pellets.

With the first decision taken care of, I took time to ponder the second rod's placement. To the right of the main island a prominent bar ran out into the lake with the depth gradually increasing over it. Here, where it reached four feet, seemed a suitable spot, confirmed in a spectacular way as a carp surfaced exactly where I had chosen. I certainly didn't need a second invitation to drop a popped-up tiger nut boilie on the bar, and surround it with 100 similarly flavoured companions. Everything was in place and it was time, as always, to put the kettle on and wait for nightfall.

A flock of Canada geese flew in across the tree-lined horizon to join me for the evening, while a jay bounded through the air intent on finishing its chores before the sun sank away. I had little to do except relax and watch the whirligig beetles send themselves dizzy as they circled where my lines cut into the water. I wanted to catch both species, that was for sure, but given a choice, a grass carp sat a little higher on the 'wanted' list. I just hoped that I had got the tactics right, having no experience and only the guidance of other anglers to call on. The key words that always seemed to be mentioned during these enquiries were 'tiger nut', so with this well and truly covered, I had no reason to think that the tactics employed wouldn't fool one if it came across my traps.

It was the time when a torch was first needed, as twilight merged with nightfall, that an alarm called for attention but with my mind being on the grass carp, it was ironic that the crucian rod was the one taken. A small piece of maize had been devoured but what had eaten it? Well, I was about to find out. Its weight ruled out a crucian immediately and put tench at the top of the suspect list. Occasionally, it would surge off, but there were few dramas as the surface was broken and a head appeared. Under the canopy, it was impossible to see anything but a silhouette, so given what I had witnessed, reaching for the pan landing net by my side was an understandable mistake to make. The moment my opponent touched it, all hell broke loose as something much longer than any tench exploded and veered away at a rate of knots. Amazing - a grass carp on the wrong rod!

When the second chance to net it came around, I had wisely swapped to a carp version and on this attempt I became the proud captor of a 21lb 8ozs specimen. It did indeed look like a mullet crossed with a chub. Grass carp are vulnerable creatures, so I hurried to complete the bankside proceedings before returning her back home. It may have come to the wrong rod but I wore a smile as I climbed into my sleeping bag and thanked the lake for continuing to show favour to me.

Clean up.

A time to dream.

Dreams had yet to arrive before the balanced tiger nut rod came alive with the indicator falling like a stone as it dropped back toward me. Of course, it couldn't do this unassisted, but my strike met with little resistance as whatever the culprit was kited hard left. Frantically winding the reel eventually reconnected me to it, but once again, the response from the fish was far from aggressive and only on one occasion was there a need to give line. Nothing in the prelude had prepared me for the final act, though. Up she came into the moonlight, still unimpressive until her body hit the air and then I realised I had Moby Dick on the end! Four feet of fish wallowed in front of me and rapidly I plunged the net under its torso. Only now with the mesh wrapped round its flanks did it want to fight. Waves of water were thrown up over me, as its tactic for escape now seemed to be to wash me away in a tidal wave. Drenched from head to toe, I refused to let my grasp weaken on the handle until at last it realised the only option was a visit to the unhooking mat!

I knew immediately on lifting her that she was something special but how special was only told by the sales reading 37lbs and 2ozs. It was a monster that took my breath away, clad in enormous golden scales that spread out down the body of an Exocet missile. If the first grassie sent me to bed with a smile, this one made me look like a Cheshire cat. One of my target species had certainly arrived with a bang, but what about the crucians? Did the remainder of the night hold any more battles with leviathans?

Exocet missile.

After landing the beast, I was a very happy man indeed, if a little sodden from the fish's escapades. I couldn't ask for any more of the night but at the same time I felt extremely confident about the rod positioned in the margin, with crucians in mind. The swim itself under the canopy of trees had, over the years, seen a huge amount of leaves fall into the water. Fishing over such matter, I knew, would be problematic, and aid the carp in escaping from my rig. With a soft, moveable substrate, their feeding behaviour would be vastly different to that over gravel where they couldn't bury their heads up to the gills. Luckily, experience had taught me this, so with a rake the previous evening, I had cleaned the bottom back to its original clear and shiny condition. A couple of handfuls of mixed particles, 3mm halibut pellets and casters then littered the area as an invitation to enter the newly polished swim. Then, all I had to do was drop a hookbait down under the rod tip into this zone. The rig I used was the same as the one I had created on my first ever visit to the water some years before. With a single exception, the feeder had been replaced with a 1½oz inline lead as I felt the intervening years may have made the fish suspicious of such a bulky item of tackle.

Under the canopy.

The tactic had worked on every other occasion that I had fished the venue, so my level of confidence was high, the only question mark being the extent of the population still left. They looked like the grandmas of the crucian world a few years ago, so could I reasonably expect them to have survived?

As I fell asleep, once again the marginal shelf suddenly came alive as a shadow drifted along the slope paying special attention to avoid the deeper water where the unruly tench lived. Trying to get a meal among them was an impossible affair, being jostled continuously and pushed aggressively out of the way. What this creature was on the hunt for was a more sedate place to snack, close to the bank and under the cover of a tree. Day or night, predators coveted such a delicacy dressed in golden scales and this point wasn't lost on it after years of running the same gauntlet. A need to remain suspicious at all times was paramount unless, as occurred occasionally, a feast was spread out before it undetected by the tench. Tonight, the particles that carpeted the clean gravel proved just too tempting. Slowly, its dinner plate body upturned while one eye still kept a lookout for danger. Two mouthfuls in, its guard began to drop, pecs rotating in glee while its small tail wagged in the same fashion as a dog's at dinnertime. That golden nugget looked good presented on a bed of groundbait, it thought, and with a single suck it was all gone.

In the stillness of early morning, a shrieking alarm is hard to miss and I was beginning a frantic attempt to put my wellies on. A rush for the rod followed and I collared the thief who was trying to steal my maize. The carbon transmitted the fish's struggle to regain freedom but, unlike a tench with its savage whips of the tail, this felt more frantic but less powerful. Instead of surges stripping line from the clutch, the battle was played out in a circle and by now, I knew what was responsible. This only served to raise the stakes still further and with each roll in the gloom, I prayed the hook would hold. Lady Luck had no intention of leaving me tonight and with a final pop to the surface I guided the fish into the net. Immediately, I illuminated the mesh with my head torch and there inside sat an ancient looking crucian of gigantic proportions. Prehistoric in appearance, the once vivid colours had bled into a dull bronze and if a fish could have wrinkles, it would have been covered in them. I half expected to find a walking stick alongside it!

Its beauty may have left it long ago but that didn't lessen its presence to me; in fact, it enhanced it. Holding such a creature was a privilege and when the scales swung round to 4lb and 3ozs the icing was well and truly put on the cake! Placing her gently in a large tube, I reasoned that time to recover would do her no harm while selfishly, I wanted to record the moment in better light. What more could I ask for in a single night?

The lake owed me nothing now; in fact, it never did after the British record, but for some reason it must have liked my face. The crucian rod sounded its alarm again and another fight with now familiar characteristics ensued. In disbelief, I was given another gift in the form of an identical crucian weighing exactly 4lb 3ozs. It, too, was weathered and ancient but as I posed with an incredible brace I could only marvel at them. I had just experienced one of the most successful nights in my angling career and was totally blown away. Eversley will always have a special place in my heart.

Old-age pensioners.

Camera: Canon EOS 300D - Shutter Speed: 1/60 sec - F-Stop: f/5.0 - ISO: 100 - Location: Dorset estate lake

CHAPTER 15

GOING PRO

Never in my wildest dreams did I ever consider the possibility of making a career out of angling. If anything, it was an excuse to get out of work rather than to add to it, which is why if the truth is known, I decided self-employment was more suited to the pursuit of my passion.

A leap of faith.

Even though my job at the time, as a polymer technologist, afforded the luxury of a half-day on Fridays, it just wasn't enough for someone as obsessed as I was, and I needed to come up with a plan. So over a period of a year, I started to advertise in the Yellow Pages offering flat roof and pond-lining services. These were the types of materials that the company I worked for produced and when I was successful at getting a job, I would sub-contract it out, taking my cut of the profits as the middle man. You see, I knew from an early stage that manual labour wasn't for me and if I could create enough work, time spent on the bank would be dramatically increased. I must have done something right because eventually, I was able to shed the shackles of a nine-to-five job, but as the business flourished, sales and book work took its toll on my hoped-for free time and it turned into a proper job. What it did allow, though, was an ability to choose my own hours and that meant I worked during busy weekends on the bank, while mid-week I was free to fish without the struggle to get a good swim. In terms of results, this flexible position was much more important than the amount of hours spent angling, and afforded me some great captures, of that I am sure.

During this period, even if unknowingly, I was taking my first tentative steps toward becoming a professional angler by sending pictures of my captures to the angling press. This, I freely admit, was at first due to a combination of ego and pride, factors that must drive everyone who publicises what they catch, even if some deny it. Why, I have to ask, report anything if it isn't for ego? I strongly suspect these same people are the first at the newsagent's on a Tuesday morning! Whatever my original reasons, the net result was the same – attention; especially after I won the Angler's Mail Specimen Cup and broke the British barbel record.

Writing for a range of monthly magazines came next, and this was a great way of learning what it takes to be an angling journalist who must supply pictures as well as words. This apprenticeship helped me to understand what editors needed, and that wasn't always the biggest fish. A good story or angle was, and still is, far more important and remains at the top of my list of dos and don'ts when creating a feature. Another important skill for a professional to gain and become comfortable with is public speaking, which unfortunately can't be learned in a sedate manner. It's more of a baptism of fire because any failings will be brutally exposed in front of an audience.

It was, then, a stomach-churning moment when I took to the stage on a wet, dreary night in Dunstable to present my first ever slide show. The initial couple of minutes were difficult but as I relaxed a little, the words flowed and I began to make sense. Whether it was the gift of the gab, or just plain bullshit, I'm not sure but everything went well and the audience seemed genuinely to enjoy themselves. In fact, I received a couple more bookings and the 'Bowler Road Show' was well and truly under way. The nerves remain, even years down the line, every time I go on stage and whether it's 10 people or 300, I still get butterflies. Remember, I'm just an angler with no training trying to do my best, but I believe if you speak honestly and with passion, the audience will forgive any lack of style.

On assignment.

Magic moments.

During this period, I was also in the fortunate position of being asked by two companies to become a sponsored angler and promote their products. Bob Church, who has become a dear friend, was the first to invite me to a meeting where he proudly showed off his business. I did, however, sense that its success was solely down to him and given Bob's unquenchable desire to fish, and retirement not too far away, the options to expand with his company would be somewhat limited. Leeda was the other option and after a meeting with the then marketing manager, Nick Young, I was sold that this was the best way to forward my career. Suddenly, I wasn't just being given products; I was being paid, too! So began a happy relationship that lasted a couple of years and taught me a little more about a trade that doesn't always revolve around the riverbank. We even brought out a pair of barbel rods in my name under the Giant brand, which I'm proud to say are great rods even today. I've always stuck to the rule that if it's not good enough for me then I won't promote it and fortunately, every company I have ever worked for has been happy with that philosophy.

Then came an approach from Angling Times, a move that, I guess, was the pivotal moment in me becoming a professional angler. For the first few years of seeking to publicise my captures, I reported them solely to the Angler's Mail and it was the incumbent editor, Tim Knight, then working on the news desk, who dealt with those initial photos. Eventually though, a relationship with Steve Partner at the Times was formed and I swapped my allegiance after I was presented with an opportunity to write regularly in angling's largest magazine under the guise of 'The Specialists' column. This revolved around five well-known specimen hunters, who took turns recounting their experiences over recent weeks. We were expected to supply pictures as well as copy to fill a page in the paper. So on June 21st 2000, my first article, about float fishing for big bream on a large windswept Bedfordshire brick pit, was published and this spelt the start of a new chapter.

With this increased profile, I soon came to be noticed by the most esteemed tackle company in the trade – Drennan. A phone call from Peter Drennan asking to see me was like an audience with the Pope as far as I was concerned, with his legendary status in the sport dating back to the Walker era. From Peter Stone to Ivan Marks and everyone between, he had known them all. He had also built a world famous company that began with making floats in a garage and had grown into a multi-million pound business. Therefore, quite simply, the opportunity to meet him was too good to miss.

A date was made in the diary and I found myself sitting in his Oxfordshire boardroom discussing my future. Did I wish to be sponsored by his company? Of course I did, though I wasn't prepared to break the six months left on my Leeda contract. Typical of the gentleman Peter is, he totally respected that decision and informed me that he was prepared to wait. It was an offer I couldn't refuse. With good personal terms and the backing of a successful company, it made perfect business sense but, more importantly, it felt like a comfortable working environment.
With a warm family atmosphere combined with a brand that stood for top quality and not just hard sales, I felt my career could thrive. Leeda had been good for me but I needed to move on. I made the dreaded phone call to Nick and in his typically pragmatic and understanding way, he took the news well, realising, for want of a better word, that the 'promotion' was too good for me to miss. Kindly, he released me immediately from the contract I had with him, signalling the start of a relationship with the finest businessman in angling, as well as the beginning of a close friendship.

Soon after the Drennan 'stamp of approval', I was to meet with another company who felt that an association could be mutually beneficial. Dynamite Baits, and in particular, Pete Chandler, may not have had the same history as Drennan, but only a fool wouldn't have realised that they were going places. This was a revolutionary firm that saw the advantages of consumer-friendly bait and was about to rewrite the rulebook; I wanted to be part of it. This Pete, though, was a different character to Drennan but remained equally affable and driven by quality. I knew immediately he was a man I could work with and it helped to cement a long-term relationship. As far as I was concerned then, and I feel the same today, I was working with the two best companies in the industry.

My mentor.

By now, The Specialists had been running for a few years and as with any series, fatigue had begun to set in. Writing on a monthly basis can be surprisingly taxing. It forces you to adjust your fishing to suit the variety needed and this can soon become a bind to a specimen hunter who targets individual fish. The column had run its course, with me as the last man standing, but conversely, I had actually enjoyed the process and wanted to carry on. It was decision time for me, and the paper, with Peter Drennan suggesting a meeting in the comfortable surroundings of the famous Le Manoir aux Quat' Saisons in Oxford.

Before I outline the meeting, I have to say that 'a fish out of water' would be the best way of describing the culinary experience for me. I'm sure what we sampled was a series of gastronomic delights but to my uneducated palate, it was simply lost. What, I ask ungratefully, is wrong with a steak and ale pie in a good, old-fashioned pub? Still, Angling Times editor, Richard Lee, seemed to be enjoying himself, which may have had something to do with the very expensive bottles of wine that kept arriving! The offer to write weekly was put on the table but could I make this leap and become a professional angler? I was confident of catching the fish required but would I be able to survive burnout? That question was not such an easy one to answer. Writing a weekly column that involves catching fish constantly is incredibly difficult because the deadlines just never stop coming. Even if the weather is terrible or you feel ill, you're still required to produce the goods. To do it correctly doesn't just require hard work, it needs to be an obsession, and I was left in no doubt that my life would change. Of course, there could only be one answer, and I said yes; but what had I let myself in for?

Richard and Steve had shown faith in my abilities and I wasn't going to fail them, so immediately, I threw myself head first into the challenge. Year one was, I knew, the trial period and without a high standard of material I would be yesterday's man, especially as my work would be judged against the likes of Wilson and Hayes. Catching fish, like I've already said, is the easy part; it's the photos and the relentless need for new ideas that really provides the challenge. The only way to achieve this is to treat every fishing trip as work, with the need for material always outweighing the actual angling.

A mountain to climb.

Perfect partner.

climbed mountains and posed in busy town centres to get these images; most are self-timed I might add, but it's these, not the trophy shots, that convey the essence of angling and are vital to obtain. A good question to ask, though, is 'does all this work detract from the enjoyment, which was the very reason I choose to go angling in the first place?' In my case it's an unequivocal 'no' because I gain as much enjoyment portraying angling to the best of my capabilities as I do catching, so a good picture or story gives me immense pleasure.

For example, take a perch fishing trip when you are coming up to dusk, the peak time to catch. If a fish is caught while there's plenty of light, it's vital that the photos are taken immediately, even if it costs you valuable fishing time when more perch could be banked. A trio of fish pictured in darkness is worse, in magazine content terms, than a single specimen shot in good light. Sometimes prime time may coincide with a blood red sky and a splendid dusk; essentially perfect conditions for a great shot. It may require moving swims to get the right backdrop and many a time I have been running across a field with a rod in one hand and a camera tripod in the other trying to capture the best picture to showcase fishing. I have

By following these principles, my single page soon grew to a double-page spread and ensured a continuation of my rising profile. At this point, I knew that something would have to give, especially as I was still involved in the company outside angling. A choice of pond liners or fishing really was a no-brainer and by leaving it behind, I had the beauty of working on my own. For me, the process of employing people was not something I enjoyed. I am a single-minded and stubborn character, with few man-management skills or a high tolerance level for humanity, so I was born to work alone. Now the only person I needed to consult with was me, and that suited me perfectly. I could begin a life of splendid isolation…or so I thought!

I had met Hugh Miles a few years previously while tench fishing at Sywell Reservoir and then again, when his 'Caught in Time' film hit the shelves. Of course, I was acutely aware that he was the man behind 'A Passion for Angling' but never did I consider the possibility of filming with him. The account of what happened next has been well documented in the book that accompanied the 'Catching the Impossible' series so I won't go over it again here, but the next five years would prove to be some of the most rewarding but also most difficult years of my professional career. Pleasingly, after the punishing process of making nine one-hour films, the Holy Grail and ultimate aim of getting UK fishing back on terrestrial television was achieved when Channel 4 aired our work. It was a very proud moment for all involved and the legacy it leaves will, I hope, encourage people to take part in our wonderful field sport.

Maybe surprisingly to some, the personal gain from working with Hugh Miles isn't to be judged by the further raising of my profile but the gift of being able to portray angling via a new media – television. After serving this apprenticeship, I didn't wish to stop working in this format but wanted, as is normal with me, complete control, so I invested in the required equipment and formed a film company called Aqui Vista. To make a film, though, requires someone behind the camera as well and I knew that if the relationship were to work, it would have to be with someone very compatible. A close friend, Mick Jackson, was the perfect choice because not only did he have an artistic flair, but also an ability to switch off from my incessant talking, so we agreed to be partners and learn together the art of film-making. When our first project, 'Warwick's Way With Carp' came to fruition, I was as proud as I had been with 'Catching the Impossible'. There really is something wonderful in being involved creatively, but if you think making a good angling film is easy, think again, because the old adage 'if it can go wrong it will go wrong' could have been written for the process.

The weather needs to be perfect; dull light, rain and wind all conspire against you and given that these are perfect fish catching conditions, the task is not easy. Conversely, still and sunny days are best for filming, although trying to get a bite in such conditions is an altogether different matter. Similarly, night fishing is virtually 'no go', which is unhelpful to say the least when targeting many species. Due to costs, another hurdle to overcome is the restriction of one camera and this limits the angles possible. By filming from a single fixed point, a very one-dimensional scene is created and to give this more life, a series of painstaking cut-aways are then required. After the scene has been shot live, it is then re-enacted from other angles, which, once blended in the editing stage, bring the moment to life. That is, of course, if you catch in the first place. Fish and scripts don't go together!

Fun times.

Mick's moment.

Next, we move on to the editing stage and stitching a story together really is a time-consuming affair. If you work on the basis of five minutes of film equalling one week's work, you wouldn't be far wrong. This time-span doesn't include the grading, soundtrack, and narration, which all take time. Finally, after months of work, a master copy of the DVD needs to be produced and this is the template for the production run, alongside the artwork. All that is then left to do is to sell it in the hope of a meagre profit that, given the amount of illegal downloads, becomes harder and harder to achieve. Don't think for one moment that a television slot is a way to riches; in fact, you're more likely to have to pay them to get screen time. Of course, the whole process can be shortened and cheapened but after being schooled by Hugh Miles, compromise isn't a word I am willing to accept. So why do it at all? Simply, the joy gained from capturing a magic moment is hugely rewarding, be it a monster fish or a stunning vista. Saving these moments is reward enough, as long as you don't go bankrupt in the process!

Making a living out of portraying angling is no easy task and the reality is that without sponsors it would be impossible. You do not get paid a living wage for your journalistic work so outside support is vital. As already mentioned, Dynamite Baits and Drennan have been incredibly helpful and fortunately, I have only ever felt that my fishing has been enhanced by these associations. This is crucial because I would not promote anything that didn't actually aid an angler. This degree of integrity by both the manufacturer and sponsored angler is vital to maintain, because the buying public are no fools and soon realise when they are being misled. Likewise, a long-term relationship is essential in this process. Continually swapping brands simply does not instil confidence. I can honestly say that I believe I work for the finest in the business and that's a good place to be.

Working with the best only serves to improve oneself and I've been extremely fortunate in serving a relationship with many at the top of their game. As a professional angler, you will go a long way to find a better example than John Wilson, who I have known all my life. A dedication to stay in the public eye and provide good material, be it words or images, is hard for many anglers to achieve continuously for a year, let alone the decades that he has. I have tried to take from him the professionalism to remain focused, alongside the reliability required to appease ever-demanding editors.

Chris Yates is an altogether different character, with a much more laid back approach to life. Few can argue that he's angling's greatest wordsmith and being able to convey one's love for the sport is a gift. While I can never hope to rival his words I have been able, I hope, to develop a style that combines technical advice with an element of passion for what I do. Perhaps the most vivid way of portraying the countryside is by the medium of television, and Hugh Miles and Bernard Cribbins remain peerless when it comes to angling films.

Pub talk.

An extreme level of dedication that borders on insanity has instilled in them a never-say-die attitude, but it's Hugh's ability to locate the scene that needs to be captured that remains the most valuable skill. Every lake or river has a sweet spot where its image should be filmed or photographed; capturing it is easy, finding it in the first place is not.

Another man with the ability to capture the moment is Mick Rouse, Angling Times' chief photographer. Over the years we have worked together he has helped me to gain a better technical understanding of what can be used to produce a more artistic image. A portrait shot of captor and fish is a vital skill to master, and Mick is certainly the man who I would want at the other end of the lens if I had another record fish. Spending the time to understand your camera is a vital component in becoming a professional angler – no pictures, no job.

Staying with Angling Times, the editor, Richard Lee, was the man who gave me my big break and for that I will always be grateful. There is no one better at knowing what the reader wants than him, and he has embraced a bold and modern approach. I've gained much from his single-mindedness and he's unafraid of breaking free of old school thinking, even if it means tipping over the apple cart. Tradition should be preserved if it's good but never for its own sake and pushing the boundaries is essential to keep our sport moving. When talking business, however, Peter Drennan is in a league of his own and his advice is always valued. Any man who can create the empire he has deserves respect but it's the way he handles himself within the trade that I have tried to study most. If the name 'Bowler' can be half as successful as Drennan then I will have gone a long way. His passion for his business and unshakeable confidence in his abilities is to be admired.

As always, the list could go on and on but it wouldn't be complete without mentioning Steve Partner at Angling Times who has worked with me since the beginning. Our careers have grown in unison, with Steve becoming one of angling's best journalists. Forging close relationships is crucial if you are ever going to succeed because, in reality, the people behind the scenes will make or break your career and they are vital to continued success - a point lost on some of angling's more well-known names. For anyone reading this who has a desire to make angling a full-time job I would say, go for it. Remember, the fish you catch will only afford you the opportunity to attempt it, but writing, talking and filming can make it happen. I have always believed the two most important factors in any success combine a healthy obsession with hard work; talent trails in a distant third.

Achieve your goal, though, and you have a wonderful life – a life that affords you a journey through the best that nature can offer and a never-ending adventure. A little hard work for all of that is a small price to pay.

Fishing with legends.

Camera: Canon EOS 40D - Shutter Speed: 1/2700 sec - F-Stop: f/4.0 - ISO: 400 - Location: Chippenham town centre

CHAPTER 16

THREE RIVERS

November 2002 was, I believe, the pinnacle of my barbel-angling career. I was hungry for success, which is a vital ingredient in catching big fish, my enthusiasm was unlimited, with travelling, weather or conditions no boundary to the degree of effort put in. This enthusiasm was also in perfect step with the species' golden era, as river records up and down the country continually tumbled.

The time was right.

Mild, wet winters were combined with an influx of boilies and pellets which supercharged growth rates and, happily, I can say that I made the most of this period, maximising the era's potential to the best of my ability. So when the first real floods of the winter arrived each season, it was no surprise to find me on the riverbank.

A couple of years previously, I had made my move to Wiltshire but with a young son still based in Dunstable, I continued to make the long journey up and down the motorways on a fortnightly basis. Picking him up after school on a Friday then returning to Chippenham before retracing my steps on the Sunday was, and still is, a tiring affair, so quite often a pit stop on my journey home was required to remain sane and this, of course, meant a couple of hours fishing. I knew the area well, so winter would see two species on the shopping list, both residing in the Great Ouse. When the river ran clear, perch were on the agenda, while, as on this particular visit, high-coloured water meant barbel and the chance of meeting a monster.

Arriving at Kickles Farm in the late afternoon, I was surprised not to see any of the other syndicate members' cars, which was unexpected, given the conditions. Not that I was complaining, as angling competition is always a key factor on deciding if you will catch on many venues. With the sky and river full of warm rain, I knew the barbel would be feeding and for once, if I blanked, failure would be solely down to me. Travelling light on this venue was vital if a heart-attack was to be avoided, especially given the length of walk involved and the terrain needing to be covered; mainly thick, heavy mud churned up by the cattle. A small rucksack catered for the bait, scales, and terminal tackle while a single rod, rod rest, and landing net continued the mobile theme. This approach also allowed for plenty of the river to be searched, which was key to catching fish from such a low and nomadic population.

Fighting through the mud and trying not to break my ankle in a rabbit hole, I eventually reached the river where a cattle bridge spanned its width. Here, the river struggled to stay within its banks, the tea-stained water whistling by, dragging along with it all manner of debris, which to the uninitiated would spell a return to the car and an evening watching television. To me it was perfect and better still, the temperature gauge read a positively tropical 53°F. No self-respecting barbel could turn down an invitation to feed. Time to make a choice and turn left or right? Both had potential but with only a handful of fish in two miles of river, a correct decision was vital. I would like to use the word 'instinct' here, but 'a good guess' would be more appropriate as I headed downstream to a sweeping S bend which had a track record in such conditions.

Tackle revolved around a 2lb test curve rod and 15lb line to which a long length of anchor tubing and a safety clip was attached. The creation of a stout

Catching at Kickles.

anchor in such a flow was vital, so for this task a 4oz watch lead was called for, and as an added bonus, its polo-type shape could accommodate boilie paste moulded around it, giving an increased amount of attraction in the swim once in situ. The hook link, as always, was 12 inches of 15lb coated braid combined with the finest floodwater hook ever; a size 6 Drennan Continental. I did alter its form slightly, in-turning the eye with a pair of forceps to increase its potential to snag in the barbel's mouth. An AAA shot also found its way on to the braid directly under the hook's eye and this, once again, was to assist the rig's self-hooking properties. Last, but not least, came a 15mm boilie on a hair, which I hoped would be to my quarry's liking, although conditions and correct choice of location were going to be of far greater importance.

As I lowered the rig right under my feet it confirmed impact with the gravel bottom by sending a resounding 'thump' down the rod, which was closely followed by the Ouse grabbing hold on the main line in an attempt to drag it downstream. I was pleased to see the lead holding firm and I watched as the rod nodded to the rhythm of the Ouse, but would it go on to dance to the tune of a barbel?

Unfortunately not; and as the hour mark passed, I was convinced there were no fish at home. In my experience, when conditions are good it doesn't take very long to catch and therefore I concluded that I needed to move. My initial guess had been wrong but at least I had time to correct my mistake. Retracing my steps, I passed the cattle bridge and headed upstream to the inside of a bend which supplied smooth, turbulence-free water, no matter how high the river's levels rose. These conditions allowed me to present the bait in the middle of the river without fear of it being washed away, and, given the solid drop I received on my first cast, it was a suitable spot to catch a barbel.

By now, darkness had taken a grip on proceedings so an isotope was needed to enable me to keep an eye on the rod which, assisted by the amount of driving I had done over the weekend, throbbed mesmerisingly, causing me to slip into a trance. Momentarily, I marvelled at the psychedelic rainbow created across the sky before I suddenly realised something had grabbed hold of the bait and was trying to wrench my rod from me.

In panic, I made a lunge for the rod's handle, forcing it upwards, which duly met with an opposite response as the carbon hooped over and line was begrudgingly yielded by the clutch.

Heading upstream, my opponent offered a wonderful energy, unbroken by head shaking, and stubbornly dogged, with its strength leaving me in no doubt that a goliath of a barbel had been hooked. Suddenly, I became a God-fearing man as I have many times in my career, offering prayers to the sky in a rather shallow manner. If he was listening he duly obliged as the weight began to lift slowly toward the surface. I couldn't see it but I didn't need to. The barbel's proportions were confirmed as it rolled, the noise resonating up and down the bank. In hindsight, this was probably the best thing, helping me to stay calm and get on with the task of netting it. Making sure its lips kissed the spreader block, I lifted the mesh trapping a huge length of copper scales, while the fish, sapped of strength, lay quietly inside. Doing a jig of delight, I prepared the scene for the obligatory weighing and was delighted to record 16lbs 6ozs of Ouse monster. That evening the drive home didn't seem half as bad as usual.

God-fearing.

Four days later, the rivers of the south of England still heaved under the pressure of floodwater and, if anything, conditions were even better than during my visit to the Ouse. 'If you can't catch barbel with a winter temperature of 54°F then you may as well give up', I told myself as I decided to go fishing again.

I didn't fancy driving much so I decided to remain close to home on the Bristol Avon and I felt a double-figure fish was still a good possibility, if not quite in the league of the Ouse. A home venue also afforded me the benefit of pre-baiting, as the areas within five miles of my house received a regular introduction of freebies throughout each winter season, and this cultivation of the sport certainly paid dividends. Pellets were not yet being introduced in vast quantities and boilies ruled the roost, so having a successful recipe was of paramount importance.

Barbel under the bustle.

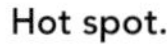

Hot spot.

After a lot of trial and error, I settled on a birdfood mix that was to tempt most of the specimens I caught during this period. Cinnamon essential oil was combined with a very high quality caramel flavour and a liquid sweetener called Betalin, which produced an aroma close to that of Christmas cake. However, the really interesting part was the levels used for my hookbaits, which were incredibly high. Four drops of oil to a single egg may not sound very much until you consider that only one drop was recommended in six eggs for a standard mix! In addition, two mil' of flavour and one of sweetener was combined in this single egg, giving a rather potent liquor which then had birdfood powder added to it. I hoped this texture would allow the flavour to permeate downstream even quicker than a standard boilie, but why was I creating such a bait? Well, my thinking was that in the maelstrom, I wanted to draw attention quickly to the hookbait and drag barbel across the river or upstream to investigate. In reality, it wasn't too far away from the principle now used by carp anglers with their highly successful fluoro boiliess. Likewise, it was my edge and at the time a closely guarded secret, so armed with the sickly-scented sweets I set off for an afternoon on the Bristol Avon.

If memory serves me right, the first few hours were spent pottering around in the woods just outside Chippenham, trying to locate my quarry among the trailing branches and fallen trees. Alas, this proved unsuccessful but I wasn't too concerned as I had a banker swim primed and ready to go when darkness fell. Here, under the glare of streetlights afforded by the town centre, was a large population of quality barbel, a fact missed by all but the locals. An automatic sluice gate controlled the river's flow and prevented the town from flooding. On a 45-minute cycle it would lift, pushing extra water downstream.

It was during this period that the fish really fed in earnest, leaving their homes of overturned shopping trolleys and rampaging up and down the gravel strips. The sluice area itself proved highly popular with the town's kids who lined up on the high wall that skirted it, behind the backdrop of a car park. Many an angler was born within this industrial landscape, although their first barbel was landed on tackle more suited to sea fishing.

Packed with punch.

Taming tackle.

While I spent some time in this area, it was a spot a couple of hundred yards downstream below the flyover bridge that provided a more sedate area (relatively speaking) to angle from. Here, the fast water had created a deep channel down the far bank, providing suitable cover during normal conditions, but it was an area of dry land on my side of the river that grabbed my attention.

Religiously, in the autumn months I would ensure that this sandbank was free of debris in preparation for the floods to come. You see, I knew that in high water, fish would push over to the more sedate strip of water and, of course, in this situation I had an intimate knowledge of their new home. When the river behaved in a spate manner, it would easily have four feet or more of water over it and this always meant a barbel or two falling foul of my bait, providing the weather was mild.

Driving the short journey back into town, I parked up in a small gateway at the side of the main road and hopped over the fence to assess the situation. The heavily stained river had broken its banks here and the sandbank had been swamped in the flood. To fish it properly would mean wearing a set of chest waders as I needed to get out in the water, affording me an angle on the run, thus avoiding the potential hazards of a large tree which sat behind it, and was now also in the river. It was a situation I was used to and with a good knowledge of the land's contours, I felt comfortable wading out to waist height, even in the most ferocious of conditions. Being surrounded by such power while doing battle with a barbel is just so exciting and for that moment alone, coping with the cold is a small price to pay.

Suitably dressed, I pushed out into the Avon before readying myself to make a sideward cast to propel the sea lead and cinnamon boilie out into position. The aim was to land the rig a few yards further out than I really wanted it to and then allow the force of the river to bounce it into position, thus minimising any alarm to the barbel.

Out of control.

This could be achieved in two ways, involving correct lead selection, which if balanced enough would regularly lose its grip in the faster water and gradually move, and/or keeping a taut main line. Without a bow in the line, the flow exerts a higher direct pressure on the tackle and it's possible to work the bait across the river by giving and taking back line. With the greatest care, I then made the cast and forced the bait into position, with the pungent aroma sweeping over the bottom and agitating the fishes' nostrils. Holding the main line between thumb and forefinger, I waited to see if anyone was at home while all around me, debris swept past, swallowed up by an angry river.

Only ten minutes had gone by when a sharp pluck resonated into my fingertips and through my body, alerting me to a barbel testing out the bait. Then seconds later, all the tension on the tackle was lost as the lead's grip slipped, caused by a savage head shake. Following a well-drilled routine a strike was made, driving the hook home, which forced the barbel to try to flee the area. This was not part of the script, though, as a fish allowed to charge around in such conditions will only lead to one thing – a loss.

Given the barbel's tough mouth and my stout line I felt confident in stopping this fish in its tracks, while applying more pressure as I cranked the reel handle. Thoroughly enjoying myself, I took no prisoners and let the rod soak up the thunderous lunges, which given the force I was applying, soon subsided. A fish of 11lbs presented itself on the surface, gasping in frustration at its foolish behaviour before slipping into the net. A good fish and a good start but I instantly wanted more, addicted to that initial connection made and the tremendous battle. Being a prolific river, multiple hits were commonplace and twice I was fortunate enough to catch 9lb, 10lb, 11lb and 12lb fish in successive casts; it was as if they had formed an orderly queue. Tonight was no different as four more barbel, including another double, failed to resist temptation, fuelling my addiction to the full.

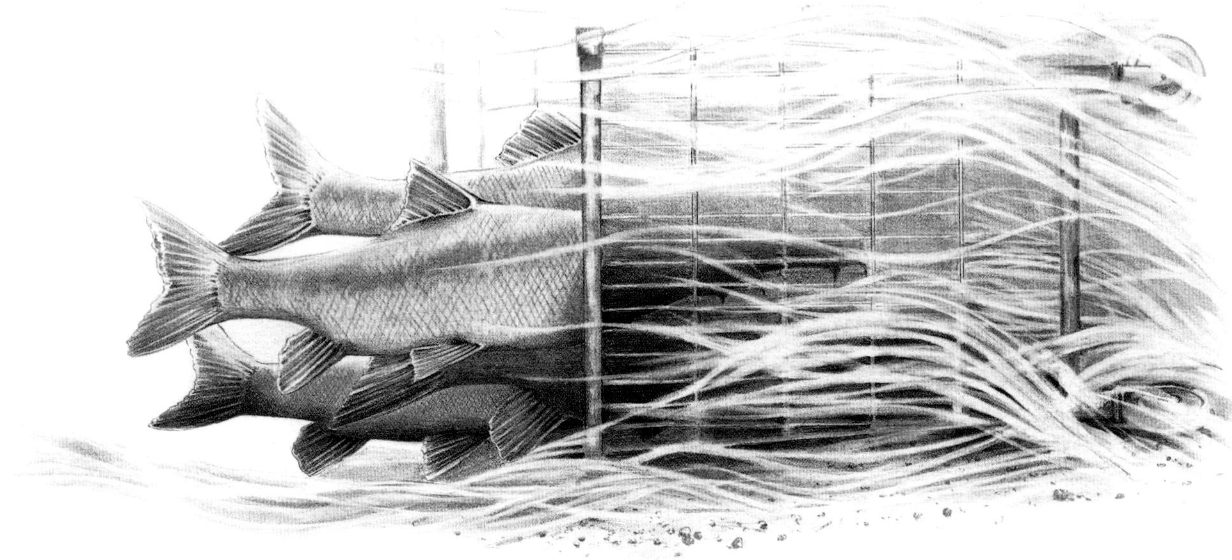

Twenty minutes then passed without any indication although I still felt another chance was on the cards, but maybe what remained of the shoal had slipped back, understandably, a little cautious. The next cast was further out than before and once the rig was forced round on a taut line, I had a bait positioned at the tail end of the swim. Instantly, I got a response as a barbel did its best to drag the tackle downstream, raising the spectre of the danger I faced. By fishing further down, the angle on the tree had been reduced and I faced a real possibility of having the fish wedged behind it. As I wound down for all for all I was worth, a grimace crossed my face in response to the alarming test curve on the rod, which now had its tip plunged under the surface, the blank bent to the proverbial butt in a do-or-die struggle.

Beneath the surface the barbel spun like a Devon Minnow, desperate to avoid a trip to the bank. Confused by the situation, it suddenly sought to yield to the pressure and headed upstream which to me, was a godsend. No longer was the tree an issue; instead discarded rusty bikes and shopping trolleys posed the main problem. I knew this was a big fish but that didn't see me deviate from my swashbuckling style, forcing line back on to the spool when it really didn't want to go. Up she came until in the streetlight I watched as a huge tail sent water flying as it smashed the surface in anger. I knew now was the time to topple the monster by filling its mouth with fresh air, sapping any further will to fight.

When the next chance came, I risked everything and refused to back down, causing the barbel to flip over, exposing its head to the night sky. With the fish's fighting spirit broken, the white underbelly of surrender was waved in my direction and I drew the barbel into calmer waters in readiness to end the contest. Here before me lay something very special and quite possibly the best barbel I have ever caught. It was of proportions I had come to associate with Adams Mill and Kickles Farm but here it was, instead, among the hustle and bustle of Chippenham town centre. With its energy spent, netting the fish was a formality and once it was safely inside the mesh I was afforded an audience with one of the Bristol Avon's finest ever barbel. Fifteen pounds and 2oz was totally unexpected and I stood beside the river in a state of euphoric bliss, knowing full well that barbel fishing couldn't get any better; or could it?

Best ever.

It was just four days later that the barbel bug bit again, and this time the Dorset Stour was on my radar. A few trips to the Throop section of the river during autumn had afforded me a little knowledge so at least when I arrived to see it heavily coloured I wasn't completely blind. Being a very long section of water it was impossible to cover it all in a day so I chose to investigate the deeper, slower end, which ran beside a golf course. After seemingly weeks of high water and south-westerlies, I was working on the theory that most of the fish would have sought respite downstream. A water temperature of 52°F was very welcome and as with the two previous rivers I had I fished, I found it hard to believe that the barbel wouldn't be on the prowl. Two like-minded souls also felt the same with an equal level of confidence and had decided to join me on this venture, namely Chris Holley and Ray Walton. Both men were masters of the traditional method of rolling meat, which would afford us a range of tactics in our pursuit.

Naturally, I had no reason to change from my deadly boilie and bolt rig approach, although I had adapted it slightly to keep up with my colleagues. Mobility is a key component for success and the years spent in Walton's company had reinforced this approach, especially, as I've already explained, that it doesn't take long to catch a fish if you find it in perfect conditions.

We worked the river by leap-frogging each other, poking and prodding every crease and slack. Fishing mid-river was out of the question today given the amount of debris and with the onset of more rain bringing with it a rising level, the Stour was in no mood to make it easy. Sodden, I pulled the hood over my head and continued the quest, only stopping occasionally to wipe my glasses. Somewhere, a barbel nestled behind a reed bed riding out the worst of the storm and if only I could find it, perhaps it would fancy a snack. Well, that's what I told myself in an attempt to remain confident and keep going. Today was turning into a test of willpower. Chris and Ray had also failed to trouble the scoreboard although importantly, Chris had an indication to report. While rolling his luncheon meat down the crease formed between the river and a cattle drink, a solitary knock had occurred which he felt was certainly from a fish. Unfortunately, nothing else was forthcoming and he had moved on. I took note, though, and vowed to investigate later with a different method.

Rain dance.

Today, there seemed no way of prising open the door and I could hardly blame my friends when they decided to head for home. Darkness was close at hand, the rain remained angry, and only a madman would stay on, but I was that man! Quite why I didn't call it a day I don't know, but I still had the cattle drink swim to try and before Ray and Chris had reached their cars, I was making my first cast. At least the slack afforded me a degree of shelter from the torrent, which was still on the rise. A drowned rat was a good description of me as I watched the tip take on a slight bend while the cinnamon flavoured boilie below leached out its flavour.

Life was good on the Stour for this barbel, especially given the perpetual mild winter conditions and an influx of protein-rich, nicely flavoured offerings with which the anglers tried to grab his attention. No longer did bland baits such as hemp and meat excite his senses, and he had become far more refined. So even given the chaos that raged above his head, the sweet, sickly scent aroused the taste buds and made the whiskers twitch. Staying put and riding out the storm was the sensible option but food was calling and his stomach rumbled.

In the flow.

Spectacular Stour.

With a single swish of the tail the sanctuary of the decomposing weed bed was left and the flow momentarily stopped him in his tracks, forcing his pecs to work overtime to provide stability before he could again push toward the source of the smell. Blinded by the conditions, a thorough investigation of the scene wasn't possible although he felt confident in the assessment that nobody would be foolish enough to be fishing in this. With barbules working overtime, the boilie was locked on to and without any further ado, it was engulfed with a single, powerful suck. Like a giant boiled sweet the taste coated the wall of his mouth, justifying the effort taken to reach it, until a hook snagged into the corner of his mouth. Alarmed by the sensation, he behaved as any wild creature would by fleeing as quickly as he could. His folly was my salvation as the situation transmitted itself back to me on the bank.

'I seem to be making a habit of this', I thought, as another big fish did its best to smash the tackle apart. Again, the by now well-worn clutch was left to control the situation while I leaned back and made the barbel work against the carbon. I always felt floodwater fishing was the time to tempt a whacker and I seemed to be proving it in some style. As the barbel headed ponderously upstream, all thought of the effort and discomfort involved during the day simply melted away and it was worth every minute, especially when another giant copper flank hit the surface in front of me.

Following a well-practised ritual, the aim was now to drain the energy from my quarry, forcing lactic acid to suppress the tail's power. On a short line, this would be achieved quickly so the clutch was tightened a fraction and the barbel made to work a little harder as I didn't want to prolong the fight. I remained in full control as the net was prepared and the fish submitted to the inevitable. Even without a torch, the gravity of the prize was obvious as the net frame struggled to cope with what I was trying to drag into it. Although events were somewhat rushed, it did manage and one amazed angler looked down on what lay inside. There rested another monster that defied all the odds of even the luckiest angler. Fourteen pounds and 12ozs was the weight, completing a trio of fish that no man had the right to catch in such a short space of time. Even being forced to wade through waist-deep water in Wellingtons, in a bid to reach my van and return home that night couldn't wipe the smile from my face. The pinnacle of my barbel career had been reached, of that I was sure.

I reached the summit.

Camera: Canon EOS 5D - Shutter Speed: 1/320 sec - F-Stop: f/6.3 - ISO: 100 - Location: Newport Pagnell

CHAPTER 17

HOMESICK

'Making hay while the sun shines,' has never been more apt in my angling life than it was for the Great Ouse. Even though I now had some fantastic new fishing opportunities in the West Country, I found it hard to ignore the generosity of this special river. Barbel beyond comprehension swaying to the rhythm of the streamer weed; chub; thickset and plump, jostling for position, or perch bigger than childhood dreams; it was all on offer so no wonder I was homesick.

Better than ever.

In January 2004, I hit a perch-angling milestone that I never thought would be possible to reach. During Oulton Broad's halcyon days of the early 1960s, perch were thick on the ground but Les Proudfoot's tally of 21 specimens over 4lb was still a very special achievement. In fact, it was a benchmark that most thought would never be equalled. Of course, back then the Ouse wasn't even factored into the equation and crayfish were confined to our native white-clawed variety. Some 40 years later, though, that special number was equalled, with the extremely fortunate angler being me. I can safely say credit for such a marvellous feat doesn't lie with the fisherman in this case, but with the environment which allowed the perch to grow. I was just keen and in the right place at the right time. Indeed, such was the river's dominance, I even smashed through the 4lb fish barrier over 30 times giving me a plethora of perch tales – but which one to tell? A 5lb 4oz monster and personal best takes some beating, although I think a story from the winter of 2003 remains at the very top of the list when, for a while, the angling world went crazy.

Ever since I began working with Peter Drennan, I had recounted tales of perch the size of dinner plates and these must have whetted his appetite because on a mild March afternoon we strolled across the boggy, post-flood fields to do battle with the striped leviathans of the river. With cloud cover filling the sky like a giant duvet, prospects looked good, especially with a combination of rising air and water temperatures. Even given these conditions though, we had been in no rush to arrive; dusk really was the only time we needed a bait in the water. It was a lesson learned from years of experience.

Of course, being the guest, Peter would get first choice of swim and I knew, given the small window of opportunity in which the feeding period would take place, that we had to get it right first time. Calling on the knowledge of recent captures, and a little history, we whittled down the choice of swims to just two and, as already said, Peter had first pick. Without hesitation, the junction where a side-stream and the main Ouse merged was chosen. Here, a wonderful crease to fish along had been created. Combine this with a large set of dead pads and we had all the ingredients for a perfect lair. Indeed, it had been the scene of many of my encounters and without doubt looked very fishy. The only drawback as far as I could see was if the perch had migrated up the stream to spawn and then the far more barren swim left to me would come into its own. I genuinely hoped this wouldn't happen, as I really wanted my guest to catch and come to understand why I raved about the place so much. For now though, it was just a case of biding our time and waiting for the witching hour to arrive.

When I first started perching, worms were the only bait I ever called upon but taking into consideration the pressure, I felt it was time for a change and my tackle reflected this with the use of small livebaits. A 1lb test curve rod was combined with 5lb line and the obligatory loafer float, although now it supported a simple paternoster rig. By forming an overhand loop in the main line at three-quarters depth, I could connect a short hooklength on a loop-to-loop basis with a size 6 hook fixed with a grinner knot. The remaining section of the main line then supported the three swan shot which sat on the bottom.

Livebait.

By carefully adjusting the depth, I could make the loafer sit cocked on the surface with half its body on show. This extra buoyancy above the water allowed me to use a very small single swan shot version, keeping resistance to a minimum and, vitally, the bait working hard. Every time it tried to dive for the river bed the float would drag it back, providing the maximum level of attraction and one that was difficult for the perch to ignore. All that was left was to lip hook the bait and flick it a few yards across to the back end of a tiny raft. Here, among the collection of debris, I hoped there would be a set of beady eyes that coveted the flesh and scales of the roach.

It really did look good, as vibrations pulsed across the surface of a river tinged with green that only days earlier had been stained brown with floodwater. Winter was definitely on the retreat and birdsong celebrated the fact that the east no longer held a grip on the weather. A south-westerly front had softened the atmosphere and if either Peter or I were near perch we couldn't fail to catch, of that I was sure. Another bob of the float confirmed the bait was still working and then it shuddered and lifted a little before vanishing. A giant mouth down below had devoured everything in one go. With my heart pounding, I sought to make this monster answer for its crimes against my livebait and swept the rod back with vigour, pulling the hook into more bone than flesh. How sweet the moment is when you first make contact and the smile on my face confirmed that today was no different. The head-shaking translated

Making history.

into thunderous bounces of the carbon as I tried my best to take control. Despite all my experiences of the past, I remained a nervous wreck, a feeling that only intensified as a set of stripes a tiger would be proud of flapped on the surface; the sight of which dreams, or occasionally nightmares, are made.

'Keep calm and don't panic,' I told myself, as the dives subsided and the landing net came into play. There, finally inside, sat a fish so magnificent no words could ever do it justice. Even by putting a weight on it - 4lb 11oz to be precise - doesn't go close to depicting just how big it was. More than content, I placed her safely in a tube and rushed to tell my friend the news, knowing full well that where there was one, there would be more, and another chance would come.

For a minute, Peter listened patiently to my excited chatter before reporting no action of his own. I knew then that none would be forthcoming and duly offered my swim to him. The fish had migrated and he needed to move. Peter pondered this situation for a moment before declaring that he was content where he was. This wasn't because he thought he had a better chance by continuing to fish the junction but, being the gentleman he is, he wanted to see me catch more. I tried again to change his mind but nothing I could do would sway him. All he would say was 'go and catch something special'. Maybe, from his years of experience, he knew something I didn't; perfect conditions, swim, and tactics were about to collide.

No sooner had my float resettled in the swim than it was savagely removed by an angry fish and its mood didn't get any better as I tried to get my hands on it. A perch of 4lb 7oz joined its brother in the tube and I continued to plunder the river. Five more fish were hooked within the hour, with three of them banked at impressive weights of 4lb 2oz, 4lb 1 oz, and 3lb 10oz. In total, I had four fish over the magic 4lb mark. It was just crazy and I struggled to comprehend the situation as the camera flashed in the darkness of the Buckinghamshire countryside. For once, I was lost for words as I tried to come to terms with the trip of a lifetime.

During my formative years on the Ouse, a 6lb chub was an incredibly big fish for the river but, as with both the perch and the barbel, these fertile grounds soon saw a spreading of the waistline and a feast of specimens. Now, given their new proportions, they were worthy adversaries in their own right, especially toward the back end of the season when their weight reached its peak. With this exciting prospect, I decided to return to the stretch that had seen my love affair with the river begin.

Radwell had been the scene of my first ever barbel and it was time to return. I had been away too long and it would be great to wet a line in a water that I knew as an old friend. Back in those days, it had been full of enough barbel to keep an eager young specimen angler happy for hours on end; but what lived now under the dense canopy of vegetation that had supplied so many big fish? Many anglers had visited the swim since I had left but I hoped she would remember me and treat a familiar acquaintance kindly.

The gate that led me down to the river was jammed with jetsam and it was obvious that recent floods had battered the area. Today though, the Ouse had become a little more subdued, reverting to her intended course and changing complexion from a dirty brown to a splendid greeny-blue. As I followed the path to my intended spot, it was obvious that spring was starting to do battle with winter. The level of birdsong had increased and the temperature meant a reduction in the number of layers I needed to wear.

'Even an idiot could catch today,' I muttered to myself as I looked directly over to the small bay in between a row of overhanging trees that held so many fond memories for me. If I made a cast into the area of slack water where the overgrowth relented slightly, a bite was surely a certainty. I just had to decide if I wanted to catch chub or barbel. Occasionally, experience tells you that a Red Letter Day is close at hand and my confident persona reflected this. The problem was that I couldn't make up my mind which species I wanted to tempt; a crucial factor because chub are far more suspicious of terminal tackle than barbel and require a more subtle approach.

Favourite swim.

Greedily, I wanted both and I didn't want to lose any; time to get my thinking cap on! Maggots were certainly going to be the bait of choice because nothing has the power in winter to turn both species on like they do. A feeder would be used to introduce them, namely the new, at the time, Drennan inline block-ends, and by trapping one on a very supple 12lb clear main line with float stops, I could fish the mono straight through to retain its maximum strength.

I tied on a size 14 barbel hook that was camouflaged by a fake caster pushed up the shank, combined with three real maggots nicked on the bend. The hooklength was kept to a minimum, measuring a short three inches, and on to this, I took the precaution of fixing two No 1 shot to pin it firmly to the bottom. Holding it up proudly, I looked at my rig and knew that now I could catch them both! My cockiness was soon knocked out of me though, as on the first cast I managed to put the contraption up a tree! Nevertheless, a few minutes later the first feeder load was being jettisoned on to the river's bottom. A steady stream of grubs is the key to success with this method so every 15 minutes I followed the same ritual until on the hour mark the switch was flicked.

Brutally, the tip wrenched down and, following the plan I had thought out in case of just such an event, I grabbed the rod, refused to give any line and cranked the reel handle for all I was worth while running up the bank. The battle would be won or lost in seconds from this snaggy swim and given the bulging landing net, it was apparent that I was the victor in round one. Inside, a chub clad in

Chunky chub.

immaculate bronze armour lay on its side, looking as fresh and clean as a chublet. This one though, was somewhat bigger, 6lb 11oz in fact, giving me all I could have wished from the trip immediately.

The fish was safely unhooked and returned and I decided to push my friendship with the Ouse still further by making another cast and, as is the way with her generosity, she obliged. Four more 5lb chub and two barbel kept me busy until in mid-afternoon she put the icing on the cake. As before, I didn't give a single inch, running up the bank like a madman. With each thump on the 12 feet of carbon, my heart jumped into my mouth until the fish began to rise in the water when it very nearly jumped clean out! The chub just got bigger and bigger! A quick, desperate scoop with an outstretched arm saw an end to my panic but how much would she weigh? The needle stopped tumbling round at 7lb 6oz, giving me a new personal best and an enormous smile. My favourite swim on my favourite river had come up trumps once again.

Even after catching the record barbel at Adams Mill, I found it hard to say goodbye, and how could I? Fish beyond dreams drifted across the polished gravel runs, sending shivers of excitement down my spine and then the rod, which lay hidden in the grass, was dragged towards the water as a barbel fled having realised its mistake in picking up my baited hook. No mortal could remain composed or wish to surrender such sport. It had its detractors but these people remained ignorant as to how special the area was to angling. Sure, at times, it could be described as a circus but this was hardly the barbel's fault and the fact remains that the species had never grown to such proportions and in such numbers before. A true marvel of nature and one that should have been celebrated not ridiculed. Summer was in full bloom and the meadows were awash with wild flowers and bumblebees drunk on nectar. The mood was one of heat-induced serenity. Even the cattle sought shade over cud, but to a keen barbel angler, this was no time to rest. The river was clear and that meant a chance to stalk.

Waiting for Kickles to kick.

Strolling to the edge of the high ground that looked over the Ouse, I found a watercourse running on its bare bones and in desperate need of rainfall. On the plus side, however, all sediment had dropped away leaving the system clear and with a lack of flow, every pebble and weed bed could be clearly seen. It was a perfect time to locate my quarry because there was no hiding place at their disposal. I figured that due to angling pressure the barbel would have dropped back from the popular Adams Mill and found themselves on the stretch I was gazing over – Kickles Farm. Being the first year of syndication, the angling pressure had been tempered here, meaning the barbel behaved in a natural manner. Instead of being holed up under snags, even on boiling hot days they would willingly hold station mid-river unconcerned and unmolested.

I continued my wander and began to work downstream, checking each hotspot religiously for a sign, but by the time I reached the cattle bridge I had, unsurprisingly, not seen a thing. Had I called it wrong? Were the fish still on the Mill? The questions entered my head but within another 100 yards they were soon dispelled, as first a shadow, then a glint of copper, forced my eyes to refocus. There, sitting in the flow, were half-a-dozen fish, all of goliath proportions. Even if the barbel world were split over their credibility, I would have challenged any of them to stand where I was and not be overcome with excitement. Some sights stay with you for a lifetime and this was one of those moments. Better still, judging by their movements, they looked more than willing to feed, but before I could progress this train of thought any further, I needed to get my heartbeat down a little and gain a degree of composure.

Failing miserably, I prised open the bait bucket and filled my hand with a mixture of 3mm and 6mm pellets, but where should I place them? During that period I had come to notice that the fish were more willing to feed on top of the weed rather than the pristine gravel and after years of slipping up on the same spots it made sense, even if contrary to the text books. Also, once engaged with this substrate, they would quite literally rip the bottom up in their desire to feed. I had also witnessed a similar mindset on the Bristol Avon and Dorset Stour when known hotspots failed to produce. Likewise, casting a line downstream to feeding fish was to be avoided at all costs, with the prospect of flanking a fish with taut mono a real possibility. Therefore, drawing the barbel to me was the preferred option and I stuck to these principles when I introduced the bait on to an area no more than a couple of feet out from my bank and on to a bottom lightly coated with silk weed. Here, the riverbed gently sloped away on to a more traditional substrate of gravel, with dense reed beds either side. These stems had channelled the Ouse into a narrow path and with the increased flow, the oxygen levels had risen making it a barbel haven. The introduction of pellets agitated them further and it was clear they had a desire to feed.

Trying to remain patient in these situations is probably the hardest challenge because it's so easy to make a rushed cast and ruin a perfect plan. This is, however, easier said than done when barbel the length of a Labrador dog begin to gather and then push their way on to your bait. Without any of the concern or suspicion that you would expect from a wild creature, four leviathans worked as one giant vacuum cleaner, hoovering up the bottom while I lay no more than a few feet away. Given the lack of water over their heads, tiny vortexes were whipped up to the surface adding to the frenzied scene. I knew that the feeding switch had been flicked and what I needed to achieve next was to get a few bigger food items accepted to avoid preoccupation. When I'd done that I felt, and hoped, that hooking a beast would be a formality. Waiting for the swim to clear, I bided my time before flicking in a dozen small balls of paste, their fawn colour standing out like a sore thumb against the dark strands of weed. Would they be eaten? I was about to get my answer as the shadows regrouped and headed back to the dinner table.

With great gusto, a head smashed into the bottom sending up a plume of silt and engulfing a piece of paste. I reasoned that it was time to get the tackle ready and crept quietly towards it. My rod was already prepared with a small inline lead sitting between two float stops on a clear 10lb main line. This arrangement afforded me the ability to fish directly through to a size 10 hook, maximising the mono's strength. All I needed to do was clip on a back lead and impale a 12mm boilie directly on to the hook without a hair-rig in sight. Why? Well, I had by now realised that my quarry could clearly see the metal and any bait lying in its vicinity was to be avoided.

The Traveller.

Fish learn by association and even though what I was doing appeared to be old fashioned, it gave no reason to raise any suspicions. Providing I ensured the point was exposed, the bolt rig would still do its self-hooking task. My only challenge now, was choosing the right moment to lower the rig into the swim without spooking the fish, and given their gluttonous behaviour it could have been a long wait.

Ten minutes later and there was no let up. I was getting decidely trigger-happy, but how could I cast when the lead was sure to smack one of the barbel on the head? Scouring the floor, I found what I was looking for; a small branch that I broke into pieces. Then I began to flick these pieces on to the surface where the feeding orgy was taking place to cause a little disturbance. It was enough to force the barbol to switch their attention momentarily, without over-agitating them and when the river swept each fish back a few yards I took it as my opportunity to lay the trap. First, the main weight landed and then I forced the main line upstream ensuring the back lead kept the mono far from harm's way. The rod was then poked into the vegetation to keep its presence undetected. It was a task completed in double-quick time because the barbel were already upon me again.

I could feel my body tense and mouth dry as I watched the enormous heads grab at the bottom in a crazed manner. My boilie was next in line for the biggest barbel; a fish of epic proportions that was as wide as a breeze block. For a split-second, time stood still as the monster pondered a little, obviously wondering what had caused his sudden toothache. Then reality dawned and he shook his head with thunderous motions in a bid to rid himself of my hook, while swiftly rising. When this failed to release him from his tether, the only option left was to charge from the swim like a bat out of hell, with my rod in tow!

Reacting to this burst of speed, I made a grab for the handle and only caught up with it at the edge of the water. I didn't need to force the rod to compress any further because it was already pushed beyond safe limits, while the clutch uncontrollably gave line. These moments provide great memories but at the time, they are tortuous affairs where the divide between joy and doom hangs in the balance by the thinnest of threads. Today, the pendulum had swung in my favour and even in the obstacle course of underwater obstructions, the beast could find no safe house in which to seek refuge. Waist deep in water, I stared inside the net and then punched the air. The king of the river, and the barbel destined to be Britain's new best, the Traveller, lay tamed. At 17lb 2oz, I had a new personal best. What more could I ever wish for from the Ouse, a place that seemed to provide a constant gold rush. I had my happy ending but could the same be said for the barbel?

Alas, something else other than anglers coveted their golden overcoats and the end was nigh. First, the fish lost their tails and then the majestic monsters were found on the bank with their throats ripped out. Tarka was in town; the result of an idiotic reintroduction programme that gave no thought or consideration for the natural world below the surface. Look down now into the river that made history and the entire population of barbel has gone. No one stood up for them and when I look across the empty gravel runs, I could cry. Angling politicians and bodies hang your collective heads in shame. You weren't there when these fish needed you most, and for those so-called environmentalists who caused this disaster, well, you are beyond my contempt.

Camera: Canon EOS 300D - Shutter Speed: 1/125 sec - F-Stop: f/8.0 - ISO: 100 - Location: Wye Valley

CHAPTER 18

VALLEY OF DREAMS

Plynlimon, high up in the Welsh mountains, is the source of a magical river that surges over broken slate beds and through deep, limestone gorges supplying some of the country's most dramatic and stunning scenery. Straddling the border between England and Wales, its dense, native woodland along the banks still holds sway and the vertical cliff faces offer seclusion to all manner of wildlife.

Natural vista.

Goshawks, dippers, and sand martins revel in this ecosystem, while at ground level all manner of mammals find a home. The polecat, with its secretive and nocturnal ways, stalks the forest floor that in places almost merges with the river, while the fox can be seen as the sun reacquaints itself with the landscape, following the water's course back to his earth.

Man, too, has left landmarks on this stunning natural vista, namely Hay, Ross, Monmouth and Chepstow, like the animals, drawn to a valley full of enchanting beauty. It is my favourite place in the British Isles to cast a line, whether that is lost in the wilds of Wales or closer to its conclusion at the Severn Estuary, the River Wye always has something to offer. Unsurprisingly then, it's the place I choose to renew my association with flowing water at the dawn of a every new season.

I have no desire for fish of monster proportions, just an urge for lovely surroundings, and an empty riverbank that serves my melancholic outlook on social interaction for this special day. Given these parameters, a journey once again over the Severn Bridge and through the valleys was embarked upon on the afternoon prior to the glorious 16th. The upper Wye was the destination and though the coarse fish stocks would diminish somewhat as the river was backtracked to its source, so too would the number of anglers who sought to plunder its rich waters.

Destination point was reached in the shadow of the Black Mountain whose foothills were filled with arable crops as the locals maximised their efforts to extract rewards during these benign months. As I skirted a field of wheat yet to be turned golden by the sun, tractors busied themselves collecting hay while only a few feet above, four red kites had left their thermals to await any prey driven from cover. Merge this scene alongside the boulder-strewn Wye which surged by my feet, and I knew that the choice I had made was a wise one. Here, coarse anglers have rarely wetted a line so stock levels remain something of a mystery. Chub and barbel, I guessed, were my targets, which therefore required a distinctive habitat. The rapids that tumbled over thousands of smooth pebbles could be discounted; what I needed was an area where the Wye's energy was displaced.

For 200 yards the river split into two, parted by an island, and then, as the two forces rejoined, the water suddenly gained depth, which was further enhanced by the scouring process against a fallen tree. If coarse fish were to live anywhere on this stretch, this would surely be the place. Now the plan was to lace the swim with a dozen orange-size balls of trout pellet groundbait filled with 6mm Marine Halibut pellets, to add encouragement for any fish in the vicinity to feed. By leaving them unmolested until the season commenced, natural caution would give way to greed and, in turn, they would fall foul of my hookbait when it arrived; or at least that is what I convinced myself would happen as I headed back to the van for supper and a few hours kip.

I didn't need the 4 o'clock alarm call. The kettle boiled while I watched the sun on the horizon begin to summon

Where better?

all its strength in a bid to illuminate the stunning scenery which spread out in front of me. The vegetation was sodden from morning dew and I was glad of the chest waders' properties while heading river bound. Shards of light penetrating the leafy canopy of the valley caused the mist lacing the water's surface to become visible. Swirling and dancing in the half-light, it seemed to be rejoicing in this short window of opportunity where it was given life before this energy would be removed at daybreak.

Wading through this vista, I was accompanied by a single rod, two rod rests and a bag of bait; this was all that was required for the plan I intended to employ. A stout 1¾lb test curve rod combined with a reel holding 12lb line would, I hoped, cope with everything the river could throw at me. After the previous day's pre-baiting, only a large open-end feeder would be needed to carry any feed into the swim, spiked, of course, with a pellet hair rig two feet away. As I squeezed the groundbait into the cage, I watched as hoards of fry feasted on the waste caused by my eagerness. If the same reaction occurred in the swim, I would be in for a bonanza!

Unclipping the bail arm, I loaded the rod with the feeder's weight before launching the rig over to the far bank. A controlled splash on the surface was followed by a paying of line to create a huge bow, helping the feeder hold station, and heralding the beginning of a new season for me. Now knee-deep in water, I watched the tip nod in unison with the pulse of the river, feeling connected to this rich tapestry of life which was enhanced as all tension fell from the once bowstring-taut monofilament. Carbon swept through the mist cutting it in two before stopping over my shoulder, no longer straight but forced to yield into a semicircle. No angler alive could have failed to be impressed, not by the size of chub, which battled valiantly in the flow, but by the memorable moment in time that the Wye had granted this lucky angler. It was a scene that was to be repeated many, many more times before the morning turned to lunchtime and flotillas of sad souls deluded themselves that a canoe would bring them closer to nature. While they screamed and shouted over a backdrop of thrashing paddles, I left unnoticed, fulfilled, and happy with the opening day adventure that the river had bestowed upon me.

In you come.

My attraction to this place may be somewhat puzzling given my track record with specimens, for here, a double-figure barbel is a very big fish indeed. Size however is relative and any fish caught should be judged by the water from which it came, not on a national scale. Combine this with all the superlatives I have already used to describe this venue and it would take a soulless angler, indeed, to find nothing of value here. A major prize, therefore, is a barbel over 10lbs and one I rather fortunately achieved on my very first visit, which, I'm afraid, didn't prove to be a precursor to more; for that I had to wait another five years.

Unlike their cousins of lowland England, these fish are long, lean, fighting machines without beer guts fuelled by a pellet overload. They are as nature intended which results in supercharged battles should you be lucky enough to hook one. In my experience, it is never their cunning that stops this from being achieved but the vastness of the environment they live in. The population is not spread out evenly throughout the system and dozens of potential swims can prove to be void, only for a huge number of fish to be located in one area. The key to catching is, of course, finding this hotspot. A depth change is without doubt the number one give-away, especially as this rarely occurs in isolation and appears with other alterations to the river. Bends, salmon groynes, rafts, and bridges are all tell-tale signs that the barbel may be at home. Assuming that you find and hook one, your problems have then only just begun, with a boulder-strewn bottom just waiting to devour your tackle. Even in summertime, I use my standard floodwater outfit and avoid the use of braid at all times. This material, unlike mono, is allergic to any stone surface, snapping like cotton when drawn across it under tension.

A Wye wonder.

With all this knowledge taken on board, I unloaded the van and wandered across the flood plain toward the untamed energy I wished to control. I could see my destination as I crunched across a lunar landscape made up of tonnes of smooth pebbles dumped over centuries of floods on the inside of a bend. A derelict viaduct, although a shadow of its former self, still standing in defiance of the river, each stanchion forcing the flow to yield, which in turn drew the Wye back on itself, scraping out the gravel at the rear of the structure. Here, I hoped to find my quarry cosseted from the daily rigours of existing in a spate environment.

Pitching myself upstream, I aimed to target the run between the two central pillars but a spot of pre-baiting was required to catch the shoal's attention. Bait droppers have no value here given the snaggy bottom, so instead, I continued with a tried and trusted method. Six orange-sized balls of fishmeal groundbait laced with 6mm pellets were bombarded on to the surface and left to marinate the swim.

Then a 4oz lead, 14mm halibut pellet hookbait and a PVA mesh bag of similar free offerings was placed just downstream with a large bow of line let out, ensuring its position was held. All I had to do then was to watch the rod tip and hope for a sign.

One advantage with Wye barbel is that they are never slow in letting you know if you have got it right and within minutes the rod took on a life of its own, trying to leave the rod rests. Wanting to regain ownership, I grabbed hold of the butt only for the river to do its best in ripping it back out of my grasp. It seemed that I had underestimated the proximity of the viaduct and given the speed that the clutch was operating, I needed to do something quickly or the line would break. Jumping into the margins, I rushed downstream in a desperate attempt to get below the fish and prevent the brickwork from eating my tackle. Bamboozled by such a crazy manoeuvre, the barbel momentarily changed course, which enabled me to stay in direct contact as we both passed the stanchion.

The first obstacle had been avoided but I knew the deep hole below only too well and it was full of snags so this wasn't a time to release my grip on the situation. By keeping the pressure on, I ensured that the battle stayed close to the surface with huge explosions of white water and thunderous fin slaps. It seemed I had a tiger by the tail and I wasn't about to let go, allowing the hoop of carbon to suck away all the power. Then as a reward a fish etched with a thousand copper scales presented itself to me, prepared to succumb to the landing net. When safely inside, its proportions could be enjoyed; it weighed in at a new personal best for the Wye at 11lbs 2ozs and its capture was equal to any other barbel I have ever tamed.

With over 30 species of fish recorded as living along this ecosystem, it's hard to pick a favourite, although one seems to capture the river's essence more than any other. Wild and free, the Atlantic salmon returns to its birthplace after a voyage of epic proportions. The king of fish still seeks out the Severn Estuary and surges upstream despite being blighted by man, and it was here that I chose to meet this regal creature for the first time.

Having zero experience in this field I needed to seek guidance, especially as I wished to have my first encounter by wielding a fly which is a far from easy task. Fortunately, the links I have with the Wye & Usk Foundation provided me with a tutor, namely Simon Evans, an old hand at granting such audiences. First though I needed to be schooled in the art of Spey casting which entails a 15-foot rod and weighted line being whipped about one's head in an acrobatic motion until the time comes to launch the line in a controlled manner across the river.

Fortunately, Simon was prepared to exhibit a high degree of patience when teaching this coarse angler and by the end of the day I could cast after a fashion and was comforted by the words, 'the salmon never knows how the fly got there!' I was also witness to what I hoped lay in store for me, Simon's line being dragged across the flow with his reel struggling to keep up. Unfortunately, his knot slipped and a beaten angler sank to the floor in desperation while a bar of silver bade its farewells and continued the journey upstream.

A few weeks later, we returned to seek revenge and with two days ahead of us and the river in fine condition, the prospects looked good for the upper reaches. The first day found us working the water either side of an impressive arched bridge, treading the broken slate beds while wading waist deep. Splendid, swirling pools were investigated, with Simon's hand-tied bann shrimps worked under floating lines and long lengths of 12lb fluorocarbon. The day passed without an enquiry which wasn't a problem in the least as the delicious air of anticipation only served to cement my enthusiasm still further, overlooked by scenery to die for. That night, sleeping behind an old cowshed, I felt complete contentment and most importantly, I couldn't wait for dawn to arrive again.

A bird's-eye view.

Silver tourist.

Confident as ever, Simon guided me along a new section of river, which saw me perched on a felled tree, casting into a deep, dark hole with my imagination running wild as a silver shadow rose out of the gloom to intercept the tiny, feathered imitation. Alas, it was still not to be and we returned to where the adventure had begun to watch the sun fall in the sky behind the steep banks of the gorge that surrounded us. This time we avoided the well-worn areas and risked life and limb clambering through flood debris marooned under woodland and over slate as slippery as soap, eventually reaching a series of pools that remained untouched by rod and line.

On the second cast, something woke the rod tip making me flinch in anticipation but nothing manifested itself after this brief indication. Was this to be my only encounter with a salmon? I hoped not and the enthusiasm levels rose another notch. The next pool covered about 100 yards, which pulsed from a fractured rock formation rising above river level creating a small weir. I followed the instruction given to search out the water methodically, cast, take a step, and cast again. With each movement so the sky's saturation diminished as nightfall began to decend and with the sun's faltering grip, a salmon saw fit to react to my fly.

Halfway down the pool I felt a hit on the line, which resonated up into my fingertips before being replaced by another sensation as the plastic coating was drawn through them. Holding my breath and counting to five, I prayed nothing would change until the long rod I wielded was swept back and a connection made. Immediately, the salmon sought to break this bond by soaring high above the river and providing me with a memory that will last to my dying day. I shouted to Simon who was in the pool below, and he splashed through the Wye to stand at my side and offer advice. Only occasionally is an angler rewarded with a spine-tingling moment and this was one such time as I desperately sought to tame the salmon which leapt time and time again in the riffled water. When at last Simon did the honours with the net, I couldn't hold back the excitement, hugging the ghillie and saying 'thank you' over and over again. The specimen may have only been a grilse but it couldn't have meant more to me than if it had weighed 40lbs and I understood the addiction of chasing the silver tourist.

More in hope than expectation.

Eye of the storm.

I first became intoxicated by the pike on this river when, I chose to spend my 31st birthday on the bank at Hereford. A mild Christmas had given way to a true winter onslaught with local temperatures as low as -5°C. Even for a keen angler like me, it took some willpower to leave a warm bed but I was glad I did as despite the icing sugar-coated bankside, the river was in perfect trim with a green tinge. A sardine soon found its way into the water only to be consumed a short time after by a pike of 20lbs 12oz, which not only made my day but also cemented a new goal that would take years to get even close to. For if there was one fish I wanted to catch above all else, it was a 30lb pike from the river Wye. Tantalisingly, I had witnessed such a beast while roaming the river with friends, Terry Lampard and Tim Norman, and when Terry latched into a quite breathtaking specimen, I now knew where

my dream lived. The key question was, would the location remain secret so that Tim and I could return later in the winter?

Predictably, after Terry's fish was seen in Angling Times, the jungle drums started to rumble and with it a stream of likely locations suggested. I was told the picture's background had been studied and the game was up; the venue had been sussed. The three of us knew this game of cat and mouse well, though, and had played a double bluff to secure the stretch's identity. Selfish, maybe, and I freely admit to that mindset but also of paramount importance to me was the old girl's well-being as once the angling world descends on such a predator it usually ends in the fish's demise, for pike and pressure just don't go together. She had grown up unmolested to be queen of the river and she did not deserve a fate which would probably lead to her untimely death should her whereabouts become known to all and sundry.

I admit to a degree of double standards now, but a couple of months after Terry's encounter I concluded that one more trip that winter would do her no harm. It would be Tim's or my turn to do battle in the croc pit, given of course our assumption that we could catch her. Therefore, Terry received a red card from both of us and we headed west, leaving him behind.

As the car wound its way up the valley carrying two eager anglers, it was only then that the doubts began to ferment in my mind. We had become so focused on executing a covert operation that we had yet to consider the river itself. An agreeable assumption to our plan had been made on its behalf, which, as everyone who knows the Wye will be aware, was pure folly. Its moods can change on a whim, rendering it unfishable within hours as mud-stained water pours down from the Welsh mountains, but today it was showing us another cruel face. Low water exposed huge boulders to the winter sun and with this condition came a degree of clarity to the water not normally witnessed until the summer. Tim, of course, in his positive manner brushed it off while I, being a born worrier, was left to stew for the remainder of the journey.

Our date with destiny arrived some half-hour later as we pulled up in the lay-by and began to unload. My rods and rigs had been checked and double-checked and fresh traces whipped from a strong 28lb wire, which were connected to 40lb braid. I was determined that if fate were to smile on me I would not be found wanting. Then we were off along a muddy pathway, which had not become churned with heavy foot traffic from other expectant pike anglers. Thankfully, this also continued to the top of the bank, which peered down on to the swim that had last seen the monster show its face. In fact, we both agreed that it seemed as if no one had been there since our last visit. It appeared that we had succeeded in keeping the secret; could we now reacquaint ourselves with Her Majesty?

For a long tense minute, we didn't speak as I placed a herring on the trebles while Tim plumped for a sardine. Being mates, we both wanted each other to catch the pike but we both also knew a fish of a lifetime was within our grasp. Years ago, I would have made this journey on my own, selfishly assuring myself of 100% odds and I guess Tim would have done the same, but I'm glad I don't behave like that any more. The enjoyment of sharing success with a friend is far more rewarding, whoever catches, and I have come to learn what is really important. So who should cast first? This was the question that needed answering. I suggested tossing a coin but Tim came up with another solution. Generously, he insisted that I was to cast first and he would then choose another spot in the swim to position his sardine, knowing full well that the odds would swing to 60/40 in my favour. A true gentleman and one whose stature never fails to impress me.

Come to Daddy.

So it was, that with the assistance of a rope I clambered down the bank first and sent the bait sailing out downstream next to an overhanging bush. Tim's, meanwhile, hit the crease giving us two floats to keep a vigil over. Within a minute, it was Tim's orange tip that bobbed and sailed away; had Lady Luck rewarded his generosity? It would have been only what he deserved. Unfortunately, a strike gave the wrong answer, as a jack was soon being landed and unhooked.

Next came my date with destiny as the braid began to tighten before falling freely from the spool while below something gorged on the herring. Convinced already of the perpetrator's identity, I fumbled to re-engage the bail arm before sweeping the rod back. Momentarily, I hit the proverbial brick wall before the river bulged as down below a monster awakened. Like a mythological Greek creature, it headed upward into the light to see its opponent face to face, and as it thrashed across the surface, shock waves resonated toward me as I tried to tame its power on a seemingly inadequate thread of cotton. My god, we had clinically planned its downfall but I had been unprepared for this!

As the pike thrashed with all its might to trash the hooks, with gills flaring, Tim's presence was now more important than ever, steadying the ship and offering encouragement in his unflappable fashion. I couldn't face losing it, not now; the pain would be unbearable. I prayed to every god known to man as the landing net waited to tame her. Up she came, bigger than I could comprehend, sending events into a haze. Unbridled anger was etched across her jaws set in a prehistoric head, with a pair of eyes as dark as night fixing on me with a final indignant stare. A moment to make all of the winter's effort in search of big fish was about to arrive. First the head reached safety followed by the immense torso and finally the tail. It was then a whoop of delight from Tim which confirmed what I longed to know. A dream had come true with 32lbs of Wye pike.

All my dreams came true.

Camera: Canon EOS 40D - Shutter Speed: 1/250 sec - F-Stop: f/8.0 - ISO: 200 - Location: River Ness

CHAPTER 19

THE BEST OF BOB

As you mature, I think you begin to appreciate and value the friendships made during a lifetime of angling. I have been incredibly fortunate in meeting some great people and cherish all the time spent in their company but none more so than the relationship I have formed with the legendary Bob Church. He is a hero to many for his fishing prowess and skill with a fly rod, but for me it's not this trait but his generosity and humour that I treasure most, and you will go a long way to find a kinder person.

Brilliant Bob.

I have come to learn that catching big fish doesn't make you a good man and some very successful individuals fail abysmally on the humanity test. Bob, however, ticks both boxes with ease and I have never met such an enthusiastic character who always wants to go fishing, which has lead to some hilarious moments and fond memories.

A day fishing the river Ivel in Bedfordshire with my dear friend was too good an opportunity to miss and although the sport had been dire, the company had been anything but. We also had the delights of a big supper, home made by his lovely wife, Jeanette, to look forward to, a point I didn't fail to raise when the owner's wife (of the water we were fishing) also offered us dinner. Bob didn't want to offend so suggested that something light would be fine and he would ring Jeanette to let her know. Well, firstly, he had lost his phone and the call was never made and secondly, the snack turned out to be 'toad in the hole' with all the trimmings, plus a pudding!

Suitably full, we didn't walk but waddled back to my van to return to Bob's and this is where the story started to go wrong. Somehow, he put his shoes behind my van, intending to change into them from his boots, forgot to do it and then as I drove off, I ran over them! We both knew Jeanette would kill him, and only then did I ask if he had called her to cancel dinner. The blank expression said it all and we tried desperately to locate his phone, which turned out to have been in his pocket all along! 'Tell her the truth, Bob,' were my words of advice but the telling-off he received from Jeanette didn't see any such words pass his lips, and it got worse still when she made a point of telling us to get home or the dinner would be ruined. Now, Jeanette's dinners are never small and should really be called banquets.

"Please call her," I begged, but Bob stayed resolute.
"No, we will just have to act!"
How the hell do you act eating such a monstrous meal? Bob's panicked look and pasty skin confirmed to me that he knew there was no way back from this tricky situation. Arriving half an hour later in Northamptonshire, a concerned man rushed through the door to placate his wife; however, mud still clung to his boots.
"Where are your shoes?" she asked, and as the truth came out, she threatened to pour a jug of gravy over his head. Not the best of starts! Following orders, I sat waiting for my punishment and trying to look serious, but Bob's face was a picture as a lasagne the size of a snooker table was pulled out of the oven and I swear I heard Bob gulp!
"You don't deserve this," was offered by the cook, which only made the situation worse. Maybe it was the fear kicking in but both Bob and I began to giggle like schoolkids, which as you can imagine did little for Jeanette's mood. As her temper rose so our waistlines spread and with Bob looking fraught, the number of mouthfuls dropped to a snail's pace.
"Stop sulking, and eat," she said. Churchy was getting both barrels and he had no option but to clear his plate. I thought he would explode but the ordeal had one more terrible twist.
"You don't deserve this, either, but I can't see it wasted –

apple crumble and custard." Bob was a broken man over the next ten minutes and each tortuous mouthful saw me continue to giggle. Jeanette had had enough and after threatening to put the custard over Bob's head this time, she went to bed understandably upset. I will never forget the image of Churchy rolling around on the settee with a stomach ache – happy memories indeed!

Of course, the cornerstone of any friendship with Bob is fishing but it isn't just catching that counts; it's the introduction to his friends and the adventures encountered as a result that has been so special.

Through the mist, we could see two other boats silhouetted in the dappled sunlight, their location our destination. Eagerly, eyes flashed between the horizon and the echo sounder waiting for a sign. When it came, it was as if we'd passed over a wall of fish, as symbols, large and small, filled the screen. Even though the reservoir took up over a thousand acres, the shoals of silver fish found comfort in such huge groups, leaving vast areas barren; their hope, no doubt, to confuse and avoid a set of snapping jaws. Of course, my boat companion and I hoped the predators had also found what now lay below us.

So where was I, and perhaps more importantly what was I after? The answer to these questions was Grafham and zander. At the invitation of Bob Church and Mike Green, I had joined in the hunt for a leviathan predator. For years, whispers and rumours had spread from fly anglers, of fish pushing the record close to the boundaries of imagination. It was time to find out if these stories were true.

Let's first establish some facts and rewind a little to when Bob was in his pomp, and indeed a former fly fishing world champion on the reservoir where we now sat. To be exact, 15 years ago as seagulls dive-bombed the surface, gulping down hundreds of small dead fish that had been sucked into Grafham from the nearby Ouse. At first, Bob suspected one of the victims to be a ruffe but a closer inspection it revealed another spiny culprit, the zander. Although many perished, some made the journey along the pipe alive and so the seeds were sown.

With the passage of time and a suitable environment, these fanged creatures hid in the depths, away from attention, and grew fat on their new larder, rarely troubled by a fisherman's fly in water over 50 feet deep. Eventually, though, a mistake or two was made and anglers other than game fishermen like Bob and Mike began to explore the depths until eventually, Pandora's Box fell open with a place exposed to rewrite zander history. In a sport that today holds little to pioneer, this find could not be underestimated. This then was the reason I had made such a long journey east to join the gold rush.

While all around us a series of anglers wrenched rods up and down, imparting life to their rubber jigs in the closest impression of deep sea fishing I've ever seen inland, my companions' approach was a little more subtle. Weighted fly lines, stripped at a rate of knots from wide arbour reels, descended through the water columns until darkness fell across them and they became immersed in the gloom.

Game guru.

A pull from way above brought light to this shrouded world as two flies made their way erratically across the bottom. In a place that received no sun, the yellow feathers soon reflected in a watchful eye. In a scene that Stephen King would have been proud of, from nowhere, a set of monstrous jaws loomed large and the yellow was extinguished like a candle at bedtime.

Way, way above, Bob felt the energy surge into his fingers like electricity before a response was made and his pike fly rod bucked down, its tip smashing against the surface. In a game of cat and mouse, each opponent fought in different worlds until the two collided as a huge brown flank emerged into the sunlight, closely followed by its wide, underslung belly. Thirteen pounds, two ounces of zander was an impressive beast as Bob posed for pictures, proving as if he ever needed to, that at over 70 he was still a force to be reckoned with. Mike was next with a mere 10-pounder while yours truly stripped and pulled line like a mad man only to be rewarded with the grandchildren of their specimens! Grafham was teeming with baby zander and such was their number a double hook-up was far from uncommon.

Deep water demon.

Day one rolled by quickly, but suitably warmed up and ready to go, day two dawned, and once again, we went in search. Catching zander was not the issue but a big one was, as the morning kicked off as the day before. A five-second connection to a monster left me a quivering wreck before the hook sprung free and I cursed the loss of perhaps a fish of a lifetime. For me the 7lb barrier was impossible to break but I shall waste no more time on my exploits as Mike had a far more interesting tale to tell.

Partnering Bob on the second day, another double soon came to put a smile on Mike's face. A level of experience and skill far beyond mine enabled him to remain in closer contact with the target at such great depths. From my vantage point, I watched again as Mike's rod cranked down the nine feet of carbon, silhouetted against the brittle sky. Another grandma had been hooked and she was far from happy about being asked to play. With each surge the drum span, and with each lull Mike returned line to the spool. If a zander's mouth resembles that of a vampire then their hatred of sunlight is also shared. It was as if Christopher Lee had just been shown a crucifix as a head the size of a small dog thrashed on the surface in anger, desperate to rid itself of the hooks and return to the darkness. Mike, though, was doing an impersonation of Van Helsing and this one wasn't getting away!

My first glimpse came as the boat pulled alongside and it was obvious that something special lay within the net; 16lbs 14ozs of pure predator to be exact, as Mike's eyes bulged on stalks and his smile was finding it hard to remain inside the confines of his face. Great fishing with two great anglers and I nearly forgot a 14lb fish that was added by Bob, for good measure.

Despite the distance travelled since the salmon had last swum in the River Ness, when the call came to return it was impossible to ignore. Miles of ocean, though, needed to be traversed before their birthplace at the gateway to the Highlands could be reached. Dangers abounded on the journey but the urge to reproduce proved too strong for any obstacle to override this instinct. When at last this vast rift valley was entered, a switch over from salt to fresh water was unsurprisingly completed with the minimum of fuss by this incredible creature. Loch Ness now lay before them and home was close at hand. My hope was to intercept a fish on this final leg, in a bid to witness my own mythical monster that the Great Glen is fabled for. Nessie could wait; I wanted to see a silver, scale-clad flank launching free of the whisky-stained water, desperate to remove itself from my fly.

Although not as epic a journey, the miles between Chippenham and Inverness had meant catching a plane, but as soon as I made my way into the valley all the hustle and bustle of the airport was left behind. For a whole week, I could leave humanity, with the exception of a few like-minded souls, and one such person was waiting to meet me on the steps of a grand riverside lodge.

Churchy was, of course, the reason behind my visit, due to his tales of duels with Scottish salmon, and an invitation to join his yearly party in pursuit of these most enigmatic of fish couldn't be refused. An adventure with a game fishing legend lay in store so it was no wonder that I had been anticipating this moment for months. With a warm handshake, I received a guided tour of the amazing accommodation as well as making my acquaintance with the rest of the fishing party. Each one of them was to prove themselves true gentlemen, and tolerant of my inexperience. Unsurprisingly, though, it was the ness itself that captured my gaze. Lying a couple of miles downstream from the famous loch, this was prime salmon real estate, the Mayfair of angling, where plus fours and tweed jackets are the outfits to be seen in. Its powerful persona was softened around the edges by the bright yellow gorse and broom from which the psychedelic peacock butterflies flitted to and fro. Higher up, bracken lay with its green leaves now edged in beige, a sure sign of summer's doom. Finally, filling the horizon were banks of Scots pine, larch, ash and hemlock, completing the feeling of splendid isolation.

The river itself roared as it cascaded over rocks and boulders leaving only the largest partly exposed where lichen added to the 'time immemorial' feeling. Indeed this natural phenomenon had been occurring long before anglers had shown an interest and the rituals of Mother Nature outlasted even the longest memories, but had the migration begun? On cue, the spray-saturated air above the main weir suddenly became filled by the silhouette of our adversary, its form momentarily catching the sun and sending a sparkle across the valley. Sunday in Scotland sees no salmon fishing so, for now, a sleepless night lay in store.

Titanic tussle.

Dawn's misty arrival first saw a hearty breakfast devoured before we made our way to the fishing lodge and a rendezvous with the men charged to assist us with all our angling requirements – our ghillies; Gordon, Willy and Kenny. I hoped that between them they could unravel the mystery of Spey casting for me. Head ghillie, Gordon Armstrong's credentials were fortunately beyond reproach; he being a former world record holder despite being only 28. If he couldn't help me nobody could!

Have no doubt, Spey casting is an art form which, when executed correctly, is akin to striking a golf ball sweetly and there is pleasure to be derived from this act whether the salmon chooses to agree with your skill or not. Therefore, just being put through my paces saw the morning pass enjoyably in the nicest classroom I have ever attended. The level of competence achieved was an indicator that such a method is within reach of every angler. Dispelling myths should also include cost, as I would guess that the carp angler leaves the game fraternity in his wake when it comes to spending power. Obviously, after all the physical effort involved a rather large lunch was needed, which was going to become commonplace throughout a week that saw my waistline expand dramatically.

Angling is never predictable and once mixed with salmon, frustration follows closely. Hours upon hours of wielding 15-foot rods gave little in the way of reward, which may have been the reason that a copious amount of wine was consumed during the evenings, its magical healing properties soothing frustration and replacing it with renewed determination. Was it the high pressure sitting over us, water levels, or a bad year? A mix of everything, I guessed, but of course, for an angler there is always a good excuse!

Some of my colleagues fared a little better as the days passed, breaking their duck with just a single capture each and at least it allowed me to get a little closer to the Glen. The highlight was a magnificent, fly-caught 14lb hen fish that ripped line from the spool without mercy and spent more time airborne than swimming. It did seem that success with a fly this week was reliant on a great deal of good fortune, as better men than I had failed to trouble the scoreboard. The time had come to test my resolve; would I remain an angler or become a fisherman?

Due to the slow sport, Gordon decreed that we could resort to the ironmongery of a flying condom for one fish only, if we wished to break our duck. Retrieving a spinner was not difficult and the odds of success certainly increased. At this point, I would like to say I resisted, but a weakness for catching overpowered any moral dilemma I had, and before the day could draw to a close, a black and gold contraption tore through the water. This shimmering propeller blade tormented and tantalised the salmon and even those whose aggressive instinct had been placated by time spent in the river, took a shine to its movement.

A swift flick of the tail saw a flank of silver far shinier than any lure engage its propulsion system and a kype jaw brought fast judgement down on the flying 'C'. A treble hook snagged into bone and flesh and my braid tightened against the rod tip. I had come to Scotland to marvel at a fish whose life is nothing short of amazing and the brief audience I was granted didn't disappoint. With sea lice still attached to its skin, the salmon had left the Moray Firth only hours since. The fish's colouration was bold and bright with its head etched in pale blue and purple, bleeding into a metallic torso. It was a moment never to forget, leaving me to dream of a return next time the salmon see fit to grace Scotland with their presence.

Fresh from the sea.

How could I refuse?

The trip recounted not only saw the beginning of a new love affair with the salmon but also a friendship formed with the people in Bob's party, and when a call came to join them on another hunt for this enigmatic fish, how could I refuse?

Smoke poured out of the chimney of an old crofter's cottage with its whitewashed walls and slated roof desperately trying to retain the heat that Jack Frost wanted to steal. Outside, the landscape had already been taken prisoner, locked under an icy shroud. The river at the foothills of the Nithsdale valley had fared little better with fog engulfing its path, swirling down from the hill tops. A winter's dawn in Scotland can be a cruel affair although, as with any savage acts by Mother Nature, the outcome is nothing short of spectacular. Perched on an escarpment, the fishing lodge afforded me a grandstand view and now, with the sun's arrival on the horizon set to bring with it salvation, there was no place I would rather have been. A long journey north seemed a small price to pay and that was before I had even wet a line.

As a guest of friends, Ken Wheeler and John Rodger, my mission was to tempt a grayling, or a salmon, from the river Nith. This is a waterway that traverses a farmland flood plain, while tumbling over stony, rugged banks interspersed with Scots pines before pouring out into the Solway Firth at Dumfries; all under the watchful eyes of dippers, buzzards and occasionally the enigmatic osprey. Beneath the surface, life was equally splendid, if not harsh, given the river's cool temperature and pH level. Here, coarse fish had no foothold, giving way to Arctic species.

Ever generous, my friends sought to impart their game fishing knowledge to me and suggested a certain Raymond Fisher would be the best person to assist with the quest. Instantly, I took a liking to Raymond who certainly quashed any stereotypical ideas I may have had about salmon anglers! A Cumbrian lad, whose speciality was the black art of worming, schooled by his granddad since boyhood in methods some may have found unpalatable, especially river keepers, he had enjoyed a colourful education but nevertheless his credentials as a countryman were beyond reproach.

My apprenticeship started with bait collection, namely black headed worms, unavailable at tackle shops but found living under decaying cow pats! A poker is inserted into the ground six inches from the excrement before being gently vibrated, or rattled, for a few minutes. Then the same process is carried out next to the 'pat', the net result being up to 50 worms appearing out of the ground. With total certainty, Raymond informed me that they had been fooled by the vibration into believing he was a mole. The tricks of the trade didn't stop there; they had an overnight stay in sphagnum moss to toughen them up, as only then would we have the perfect bait.

First lesson over; next came the tackle selection for a would-be wormer. A barbel-style rod had its eyes threaded with 25lb braid before a running Jumping Jack was slipped on, followed by a bead and swivel, then two feet of 18lb fluorocarbon tied to a size 1 hook. The aim here is to use just enough weight to trip bottom, while keeping the rig moving at walking pace across the flow. Four to six worms were then threaded up the hook and on to the line. These would pulse temptingly like tentacles in the river.

Again, my teacher was matter of fact regarding this combination telling me to 'make it look like a squid and the fish will take it'. By now, I was ready to partake of the dark side so with a rod each, we waded out into the flow and began a methodical search for the silver tourist; a cast, a bounce through the swim and a step downstream before recommencing the process, until the pool had been thoroughly investigated. Angling in this manner allowed me to become lost to all outside thoughts and from the moment I began, I became intoxicated by the process. I could feel the river talking to me in a form of Morse code as the tip pulsed and the braid trembled, giving an air of constant expectancy, as I waited and hoped for a sign.

The notion of bait fishing being easy was quickly dispelled as both Ken and John troubled the scoreboard with the fly, while a take failed to materialise for us. At least our quarry's presence continued to be confirmed by the occasional salmon taking to the air in a leap of defiance, while below I imagined the cocks chaperoning their harem of hens over a redd in preparation for spawning.

Worming.

Wild, but wonderful.

Unperturbed, as the week wore on Raymond waited patiently for the climate to change and the balance to shift in our favour, while weathering the cold which tore through our waders, with copious amounts of hot 'tattie ash' (potato stew, for the uninitiated). A wet front needed to sweep over the west of Scotland, bringing with it the wind to ruffle the river and awaken the salmon. Occasionally, to pass the time, I changed tack and sought comfort with the grayling, which really deserved a more concerted effort, especially given their size. However, I had become obsessed and needed to connect with a fish that had roamed the Atlantic and covered thousands of miles while all the time having a destiny which was to cross my path.

The horizon's colour at first became just a little more saturated before a veil of cloud filled in the blue canvas. The once still air now gently pushed against reddened cheeks, building momentum. 'Marra (mate) we will catch yan (one) soon', was Raymond's response and my concentration intensified. The cast saw worms hit the surface but never find the riverbed, and the rod tip sent my brain a message as it thundered round. Spellbound, I watched as not only a hen salmon leapt with my braid trailing in its wake, but its cock companion also followed suit. Then in slow motion, the hook that was trying to hold it captive was flung free and my tenuous link was lost. Shell-shocked, I questioned whether I had imagined the whole event but concluded that it must have happened, given the stripped hook and limp line. This, though, wasn't the time to seek sympathy; the weather was changing and the salmon were beginning to run.

Together, Raymond and I stood in the river, unrelenting even in the face of a storm intent on battering us with wind and rain. Day took on the light values of night and waves more akin to the sea rolled down the Nith. There, in the commotion, fish head-and-tailed as the river came alive and in this maelstrom, I finally understood why there was so much fuss about salmon fishing. Their migration past me brought with it a constant shifting of targets. Alongside this was an air of excitement that I have never felt before and when braid was snatched out of my fingers and a strike made in response, the arc of carbon against the tempestuous sky liberated my mind from every worry and stress it had ever taken on board, bar one; would I land this salmon?

A time for tales.

Smiles all round.

Another couple of special people I have met through my dear friend, Bob, are Arnold and Spike, who welcomed me to their wonderful carp lake, which has supplied many a great trip over recent years. Funny, though, it's not a story of victory that has been my most vivid memory, but a tale of a great loss.

With high pressure and not a breath of wind across the lake, it seemed devoid of life. Cold nights, followed by bright, brittle sunlight, are no friend of the carp angler and today that was me. The water in question had once again played its trump card; the weather. On my two previous trips, the barometer had risen sky-high, sending my quarry into a torpid state. Lazing somewhere out there in the weed, though, were leviathans, for this was a Jurassic park. Rich pickings of bloodworm and daphnia had super-charged the carps' metabolism, enabling them to grow naturally to nearly 50lbs.

For now, it was hard to imagine that such monsters existed as not a single bubble broke the still surface, and as each bay was checked and crossed off the list, I became a little more despondent, hoping for a sign to lift my spirits. A shaded path gave way to sunlight pouring in through the canopy and warming my face; unquestionably, this was the warmest part of the lake. With carp being such sun worshippers, I wondered if this bay could finally break the duck and, sure enough, there were half a dozen grey shapes, lying motionless just under the pollen-covered surface. Transfixed, I came to an abrupt halt but it was what moved from my left that quickened the heartbeat; six submarines with a mullet like appearance drifted by, clad in giant copper scales. They were colossal grass carp at weights I found difficult to estimate; 30lbs, for sure, but that was just a guess for at the time, I had no experience with fish of such proportions. For now, the mirrors dozing in front of me could wait. I had bigger fish to fry, so to speak.

Spike's spectacle.

It was hard to contain the heady combination of excitement and panic as I broke into a jog back to the van to fetch my floater fishing tackle. Hastily, I bundled a few bits together and headed back to the bay. There, to my relief, the grassies still held station, occasionally breaking the scum-laden surface with pairs of huge white lips. The first two catapult loads of mixers rained down purposefully, a few feet short of the target so as not to spook them, but they were instantly aware. Without further ado, each biscuit began to disappear as a feeding frenzy commenced. I struggled to stay calm, madly trying to stab at the seal on the superglue, which would fix my hookbait in place. Overtaken by panic, I snapped a baiting needle sending the sharp end into my finger and immediately, blood oozed from the wound. 'For God's sake man, calm down,' I told myself, but still I fumbled around until somehow I could cast out.

The controller landed well over the back of their heads, and I pulled it back slowly into position. A shape the length of a broom handle broke ranks and headed straight at the bait; this was it and I struggled to hold the rod still. Down went the biscuit, followed by the controller and my response was to strike, but no! What had happened? The ensuing commotion didn't see the hook pull home, just a panicked shoal of fish! Falling to the ground, I closed my eyes and cursed – round one to the lake.

I needed some condolence and that evening, Spike, a friend, gave it as we sat behind a battery of rods and I tried to get myself back into the fight. In good company, my spirits were lifted but alas, the lake did not want to yield and with our alarms not waking us all night, she remained defiant. Spike left for work and I was once again on my own; if the heat drew any carp to the surface, I would be ready.

Thanks, Bob.

Twelve-pound line replaced the ten, a prudent move I felt, given the weed, and the terminal tackle was checked and re-checked. Unlike most anglers, I do not use a separate hooklength when floater fishing, as by using one continuous length of mono from the reel to hook, its maximum strength is maintained. The controller was fixed in place by float stops and a cocktail stick between two pieces of silicone, which also acted as an anti-tangle boom.

Midday saw my floaters taken with gusto but this time the mirrors had replaced the grass variety. A purple-pink flank rolled as the controller dragged sideways, and this time a strike did meet resistance but it was short-lived. Immediately, I felt the line grating against an unseen snag and all too soon the rod sprung back, lifeless. Another blow, and now I was against the ropes; even tempting a glorious, chestnut coloured fish of over 20lbs a short while later did little to steady me.

Evening arrived and Spike had to counsel me once more. I was hurting, but with a final night still ahead I figured it wasn't over until the fat lady had sung, although I felt that she was certainly now clearing her throat! With a lack of action on the bottom, we decided to place our baits by boat for perfect presentation. If it was going to be difficult we wanted to increase our chances and boldly, I selected an area some 200 yards away where the bottom rose out of silt into gravel, flanked on all sides by weed – a certain feeding area. Here monofilament would prove useless with its strength no match for the swim, so a replacement of 25lb braid was called for.

Each tiger nut bait was lowered into position with precision before a handful of hemp and pellets laced the areas, I hoped that any disturbance would be long forgotten come darkness. It did mean that any take would see me having to set sail, though, as it would be impossible to land any fish from the bank, given the weed situation.

It doesn't take a lot at 5am to confuse me and as the alarm shrieked I stumbled out of bed, bewildered as to how to respond. Grabbing the rod, I dived into the boat spinning it around and around. Snared now in a web of braid I could feel it tighten as the perpetrator of this commotion made off again. Being garrotted by a carp was definitely not part of the plan!

More by luck than judgement, I freed myself and rowed dementedly with a single oar, winding in any slack with the other hand. For now, I was Captain Ahab and Moby Dick was on the end of my line. As each weed bed was reached, I frantically ripped the braid free until at last I sat directly over my nemesis. A dogged, ponderous weight pulled back, and failure was not on the agenda; it was now my time for a knockout blow. Then, with no warning, my chin turned to glass as the hook pulled free! I stared at the rig in total disbelief, before my head fell into my hands and devastation ate me away inside. Happily ever after and angling don't always go together.

How can I thank Bob for these and so many other wonderful adventures? I owe him a great debt of gratitude and can only hope he remains as generous as ever for many more years to come.

A lost lump.

Camera: Canon EOS 40D - Shutter Speed: 1/250 sec - F-Stop: f/5.0 - ISO: 200 - Location: Oban

CHAPTER 20

LOCAL HEROES

During my travels, I have met many local experts who have formed a deep affinity with their environment. Andrew Allsop, the great shark hunter out of Milford Haven, explores the Celtic deeps for a chance of seeing the azure blue complexion of this magnificent fish and few understand their habits or set a trap for them better than he. While far north in the deep dark waters of the Firth of Lorne, Ronnie Campbell and Donald Maclean unlock its secrets with the capture of gigantic skate weighing 200lb or more.

Out of the blue.

Dave Harrell runs a float down his beloved Severn better than any man alive, but just like the men already mentioned, his bond to the place is so much more than what he catches. These people become part of the waterway, essential to its very fabric and as relevant to the area's history as any bridge or lighthouse. I could fill a book with local heroes and only just scrape the surface, which proves to me a social and economic benefit to angling, for how many people visit our seas, lakes and rivers to fish in the footsteps of their heroes when in all probability the local tourist board would never have heard of the angler in question? We stitch the countryside together as well as any tree, bird or building and that deserves to be celebrated. So cue John Everard (Evy), one of Oxfordshire's and the Thames' finest, who has dedicated much of his life to this historic waterway and is a man I'm proud to call a friend.

John is one of the most pessimistic characters I have ever met (sorry Evy). He would see it as being a realist, but although I have fished with him on countless occasions, he has never been happy with conditions or excited by the prospects ahead. Once, he nagged me for a year to explore a small side stream on the outskirts of Oxford for perch, and after risking a busy road and clambering down a steep, thickly vegetated bank, I asked what he thought. 'Rubbish', was the immediate response so I enquired what he thought we would catch and was told 'nothing!' So much for a positive mental outlook! Far from being depressing though, I like his character, combined with a dry sense of humour, and cherish our trips out on the river together as he has taught me much about fishing in Oxfordshire.

Happy Evy.

The Thames is a grand old man rising near Cirencester to become the country's second-longest river with a veritable cornucopia of locks, weirs, and bridges spanning the banks. An angler is spoilt for choice but it's Evy country that I find most interesting, where the tributaries energise the river as the Windrush, Thame and Evenlode spill out. Surface side it looks amazing but crays and cormorants have devastated the silver fish population, with poor water management combined with otters doing the same to the barbel. Fortunately, like me, Evy is schooled in the art of being an all-rounder so the sights can be adjusted and new goals set. Chub, therefore, sit at the top of his list and I can honestly say he has taught me more about catching this species than anyone else, so let me explain his art of cheese paste fishing and detail how refined a local expert's approach becomes.

Long before the river is even seen, the work starts in the kitchen with the preparation of the bait, beginning with a 50/50 combination of Cheddar cheese and stale white breadcrumbs. Once buzzed in a liquidiser, an amalgamation is formed that needs one more ingredient – a good dollop of margarine. This is to keep the bait soft even in the coldest of conditions as the oils help to prevent solidification. A dough is then formed to match the consistency of pastry and if it is too moist or dry any of the three ingredients may need to be increased before a final blending takes place. The core offering for the hookbait has now been made, but a vehicle to present it better is also required if the chub are to be fooled.

Balance it out.

Which one?

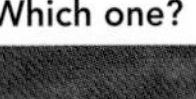

Floater cake is what is needed and this is made from a milk protein boilie mix, which receives double the recommended dosage of eggs and a firm whisking. By trapping air in the mixture it's on its way to floating, just like a sponge cake, but next it needs to be baked in an oven until a golden brown crust is formed. Then it's simply allowed to cool before turning out of the shallow tray it was cooked in and cut into inch squares. This is a most vital component to aid John's fishing but as always, only in conjunction with watercraft on the riverbank.

Location is, of course, the key factor when it comes to catching but on a fairly featureless river like the Thames it's easy to become confused. Here, I remember Evy's wise words, 'the bigger fish are always under your feet,' and combined with studying the water very closely, the straight Thames becomes filled with swims. It may be a tiny bush but in a barren stretch, the cover afforded here will be a chub haven and better still if it is combined with an undercut bank. This species looks for where the flow speeds up and kicks in causing erosion and then John's words can be taken quite literally. A surface disturbance, however insignificant, is created by something, and you can guarantee your quarry has investigated it as a home long before you. Close your eyes for a second; visualise the world below the surface and then project it into the swim you stand in; think like a fish and success won't be far away.

With a swim selected, it's then time for John to make preparations and that certainly doesn't mean casting out straight away. A drip feed of fingernail-sized pieces of paste for ten to 15 minutes will always be time well invested, to his mind, but it needs to be kept accurate as a spread of feed only serves to split the shoal. The same line is essential. A range of upstream and downstream baitings can have the advantage of bringing in new fish but to do this, mild conditions need to prevail when the chub will move further to feed. 'Think and think again about the situation faced', is always the approach he has.

Tackling-up can occur while this process is taking place, with an 11-foot quiver tip rod and a fixed spool reel carrying 7lb Drennan Double Strength providing his main tools. What is vital is an ability to interchange the test curve of the tip, for legering is not a case of 'chuck it and chance it' and needs to be carried out in a considered manner. The lightest test curve possible allows for minute bites to be seen but also offers an ability to balance the rig so it 'fishes' the river. A static bait is next to useless but by combining the softest quiver tip with a critically balanced amount of shot, he can create a 'shuffle' effect where his rig momentarily trips the bottom before re-anchoring, and it's during these moments that a bite is most likely to occur. He never just squeezes on a swan shot to his paternoster rig but plays around with AAAs and BBs to achieve the required effect.

The paternoster itself is not tied up using a water knot but instead calls on the services of a float stop. First, an 8-inch section of 10lb fluorocarbon is cut, which will form the boom. This is then pulled into the rubber widget at the same time as the main line. A knot is then tied into the fluoro to stop it pulling back through, before sliding it and the stop together up the Double Strength to the length of tail required, before a size 8-14 hook is connected in the normal way. The beauty here, for him, is that the hook length can be adjusted with ease to present the bait in a different manner if required, without damaging the mono. With pre-stretched products, this is vital to avoid unforeseen breakages, as is fishing it direct without any links. Last, but not least, comes the connection of the bait and this again needs to follow John's 'balanced' approach. Paste is smeared around the shank before a tiny piece of floater cake achieves almost neutral buoyancy, removing the weight of the hook. The more natural the presentation the more fish you will catch, is the philosophy.

Testing the Thames.

Time for Evy to cast out then; be in no doubt, a mistake can easily be made now that will scupper all the planning. So he thinks carefully and works the swim from the top to the bottom so a chub never has mono cross its path before it's offered a piece of cheese paste. Once touchdown on to the river has occurred, he pays out a big bow of line immediately, so the fish, when it bites, never pulls directly on the quiver tip and drops the bait because of resistance. Also, due to this process, the 'shuffle' effect will look natural and trundle downstream in a straight line. Only by following these guidelines, combined with a good deal of concentration, can big Thames chub be captured. Each local expert has refined his approach in a similar manner, adjusting the tackle to suit conditions and I absolutely adore travelling the country meeting these characters and learning their techniques. In a sport filled with bolt rigs and bite alarms it will be a tragedy if the work of such craftsmen is forgotten, for however ruthless modern ways are, a trip out with person like Evy is never to be missed, and each winter I find myself heading toward the Thames to rendezvous with him.

Frost and ice.

No longer did the grip of snow melt strangle the prospect of sport on the river; for weeks the water had been stained brown as freezing ice melt seeped into it from surrounding fields and ditches. Combined with rock salt and frosts, this formed a deadly combination which suppressed any fish's appetite. Hunkered down, the chub shoals that proliferate in the Oxford area decided wisely to ride out the icy blast wherever the strong flows abated. Undercut banks, fallen trees, and lock cuts provided safe havens, anywhere in fact that kept the fish out of the main force of the flow. These congregations, while providing their salvation would also, I hoped, prove to be their undoing. If I could time my arrival for when the colour had slipped away, but the river's pace still herded the chub together, then I could tempt bites and enjoy sport that the water and air temperatures suggested was impossible. A call to John was in order to meet on the banks of his beloved Thames even if, true to form, he did think it would be a waste of time!

During the 50-minute drive from my home to the river, I went over and over the game plan which would see me search out slack water and entice its occupants with a steady drip feed of paste. As already explained, on such a wide venue many anglers have a tendency to cast into the middle and miss the biggest fish, which sit under their feet. Virtually every chub over 6lbs that I have tempted from this waterway has come from less than a rod length out, so unsurprisingly, this is where I would be targeting the fish.
The warmth of the van's heater had made me even more susceptible to the arctic blast and my face reddened immediately as I stepped out into the Oxfordshire countryside and shook Evy's hand, who still cursed the conditions. Ice thick enough to walk over, sealed up the puddles of the muddy track that wound its way down to the river and the hedgerows, which skirted the path, were noticeably devoid of life. Cloud cover had suffocated the weak sun and with this loss of energy, every animal and bird had decided to stay at home. The river itself still surged from its increased velocity, forcing it to roll over on itself in places, creating mini vortexes on the surface. On a positive note, brown was no longer the dominant colour to its complexion and if I looked hard enough, a tinge of green was evident. In addition, the level of clarity had reached at least a foot, meaning that if we could find a chub, catching would be a possibility.

His beloved river.

Just there.

In many ways, location becomes a simpler task when conditions are difficult and hotspots stand out like sore thumbs. Where we stood, the bank cut in forming a recess along an otherwise straight course; the result, we guessed, of cattle during the summer months wanting a drink. A slack had been created here and better still, at the tail end, a series of overhanging bushes provided that all-important cover and undercut bank. "No self-respecting chub," Evy pronounced, "could have ignored this prime real estate." So, this would be the swim that the quest would begin from. For 15 minutes, fingernail-sized pieces of paste hit the water directly in front of me regularly, in a bid to awaken the fish, all to a backdrop of my mentor offering encouragement and advice. Only when we thought the chub were on the move did I make the first cast. Out of the main flow, the quiver tip yielded slightly but I still ensured a large bow of line was paid out in a bid to keep resistance to a minimum. Under the water, the combination of a three-foot tail and the critically balanced cheese paste ensured a natural presentation.

A tiny but discernible tap on the tip alerted me and caused my hand to hover over the reel which soon turned to a grab of both it and the rod's handle as the movement grew. As I struck into a solid resistance, the carbon took up its fighting test curve followed by a thump and a release of line from the clutch as the safety valve kicked in. Despite the bleak landscape which surrounded me, I had managed to make a connection to nature and for that priceless moment I was, and always will be, happy to endure the worst that winter can throw in my direction. As I looked round at Evy, he said, "I told you so!" with a big grin on his face.

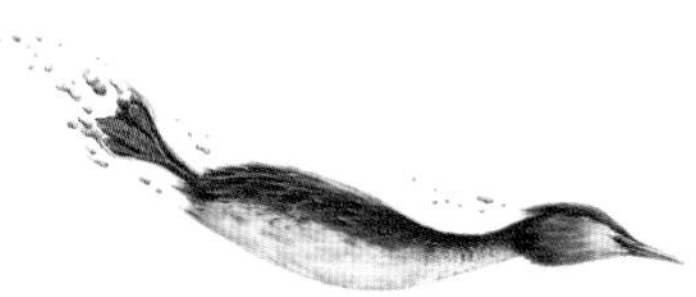

The Thames was also the meeting place with another local expert although this time it was a match man of some repute – Gary Barclay. What he was to teach me fundamentally changed my approach to angling, even if initially I treated it as a joke. Why would a specimen hunter need, or wish, to use a pole, I mused? My prejudice came to the fore when I had arranged to meet Gary for a magazine article with this angle to it, at the ungodly perch hour of 10am. What was I doing? Any self-respecting perch would have long finished its dawn breakfast, I chortled. Pushing my tackle-laden trolley down the path, I sweated under swathes of gear. "Do we really need all of this?" I groaned. A quiet man, Gary kept his counsel, but he must have regretted getting involved with a 'specimen hunter' at this point. Eventually, we came to our swim where the river widened slightly, creating a bay directly in front of us. It looked great but the sun was now high overhead and I was still to be convinced that anything worthwhile could be caught.

The plan was for Gary to set up his outfit while I watched, and then I could do the same with my own tackle under his guidance. His first task therefore was to position his box and platform for total comfort. "In pole fishing, it's vital to have your legs positioned at 90 degrees or you will not fish correctly," were his words of wisdom. The pole, at this point, seemed an incredibly long, unwieldy contraption so no wonder he needed all the scaffolding, I laughed to myself. Choosing his rig from the numerous winders situated in his box, a 1.5g float was selected with the tip altered from its original thin cane for a thicker version. This would help to support the lobworm better and make the float easier to see, I was informed. Main line was a 4lb, pre-stretched version, with the bulk weight provided in the form of an olivette sitting at three-quarters depth followed by two no. 9 dropper shot. The hook was a size 14, which was also connected to 12 inches of 4lb Double Strength. A spade end model was chosen over its eyed brother, for finer presentation that only a crude specimen hunter would try to fish with!

"I told you so!"

A change of mind.

It was all very technical and a world away from my normal approach at the time, of that there was no doubt, and I tried not to laugh out loud as I mused how ridiculous it all was. Unperturbed by his pupil's attitude, Gary shipped out the tackle to 13 metres and proceeded to plumb the river. "If a pole has one major advantage, it's this," my teacher told me. "You can check the depth with incredible accuracy, compared to rod and line."
He intended to fish three inches over depth and allow the worm to drag bottom. Once the measurement had been set, it would be marked on the pole, using a Tippex pen. "Therefore, whatever the session may bring, you always know your original depth," Gary offered by way of explanation.

At last, the tackle was ready and it was now a case of selecting the hookbait and feeding the swim. On today's menu was 100 lobworms, 100 dendrobaenas, two pints of caster and two pints of white maggots with a handful of reds added for good measure. Half a lobworm would be the hookbait, with the rest of the worms chopped up with the caster to make up the feed. So the worms were removed from the earth and washed in a sieve; these were then placed in a large pole cup and chopped into half-inch segments. To this an equal amount of casters were added and Gary stressed the importance of only chopping up enough worm for each feed to help to keep it in tip-top condition. The concoction was now fed into the swim using a bait dropper, which had been carried out over the water on a cable tie connected to the pole, before being released. Feeding, like plumbing, can be incredibly accurate in this manner I was told, and Gary's dropper landed at a 1 o'clock position with minimum disturbance; the plan being to re-feed after every two or three fish caught, or when bites ceased.

It was now my turn to tackle-up and with a little guidance and an eternity of messing around, I was ready to tempt a perch. The trouble was, it was already heading towards lunchtime, and I was certain this whole fiasco was bordering on insanity.

Hooking on half a lob at the broken end, I also nicked on a caster to stop the worm spinning over the point. Sitting no more than 10 metres apart, we both shipped out our baits and waited for events to unfold. Damn! I must have

You must be joking!

too much shot on, I thought, as the float sunk away. As I lifted the pole, the fluorescent yellow bungee shot out of the tip and, shocked, I found myself connected to a perch. As I looked upstream toward Gary, I could see that amazingly, he too was into a fish. Incredibly, we had both begun playing 2lb perch within seconds of commencing. Surely, this was a fluke, but no, bites continued and I'm not talking small fish either. Fish just short of 3lbs tired under the strain of pole elastic and filled the keepnets.

Four hours later, we drew proceedings to a close. Over 40lbs of perch had fallen to our tactics and I can honestly say that I was gobsmacked. Without the pole, I wouldn't have caught one, let alone a dozen, and the possibilities raced through my mind as I digested the information gleaned. There certainly was no laughing at Gary or the method now!

Every winter from then on has seen me behaving like a match man and I have lost count of the number of big fish I have caught because of the pole. If I hadn't been willing to explore the wide gambit of techniques on offer, or learn from the generosity of Gary, I would have been none the wiser. Long may my path cross with the local heroes that are the lifeblood of our sport and who have enriched so much of my life.

Pole power.

Camera: Canon EOS 300D - Shutter Speed: 1/200 sec - F-Stop: f/6.3 - ISO: 100 - Location: Southern Ireland

CHAPTER 21

TALES WITH TERRY & TIM

Enjoying an angling adventure with friends is something I relish, particularly when it ends in the capture of a big fish. This wasn't always the case. In my younger years, a degree of selfishness prevented any possibility of sharing such a trip but fortunately, maturity brings with it a less single-minded approach. It gives way to a more philosophical point of view and two anglers that I have spent many enjoyable days with are Terry Lampard and Tim Norman.

Terry.

Ironically, I think we have actually caught more because of this companionship, encouraging each other to stick with it even when the going gets tough and then, when success presents itself, taking it in turns, where possible, to capitalise on the harvest. In every sense of the word, we put in a true team effort and contribute our own skills and assessments to any given situation before pulling together to achieve success.

Terry is, without doubt, the most prolific catcher of big fish that this country has ever produced, with a level of dedication few can match. This intensity has lasted not for five or even ten years, but the whole of his life and he fishes virtually every day of the week. Combine this with natural ability and a range of prolific waters at his disposal, and it's no wonder his number of Drennan Cup wins resembles a cricket score! Tim, on the other hand, invests far less time in his angling. He has a business to run and a family to keep happy but he's still an equally exceptional angler. Another trait that's different to Terry is Tim's gregarious nature, which coincides with an incredibly positive outlook. To me this is the most valuable asset he brings to the team and I can honestly say that I have never seen the man in a bad mood. Above all else, both men are true all-rounders, a rare commodity these days, adapting and altering species and tactics as dictated by the seasons. This is why I do not refer to them as specimen hunters, as most of these, however successful, struggle to cope with a range of methods – float fishing, for example, is an alien concept and many rely solely on some form of bolt rig tactic a lot of the time. Not that I'm knocking anyone's approach here; the sport is enriched by this diversity. It's just that the three of us find our pleasure in an ever-changing diet.

So, for whatever reason, Terry, Tim, and I have struck up a companionship that has seen an array of specimens falling to our rods, from carp to catfish, perch to mullet and nearly every other species in between. I could recount many tales, but two of my favourites are my first 7lb chub and a trip to Ireland after giant rudd – both proving that teamwork brings not only rich rewards but fond memories, too.

Tim.

Treasured memories.

Terry, the teacher.

I'd never caught a 7lb chub and this was my target for the winter of 2007-8. As always though, other challenges cropped up and once again, the chub I desired looked like it would have to wait for another season. Without fish of this calibre being available on my local river, a well-planned trip was required and I didn't think I had the time to fit it in. That was until a gap opened in my diary and I knew which direction to point the van – the Dorset Stour, arguably the country's finest chub river and certainly home to my dream. The added bonus was that I'd get to team up with Terry and Tim, who were more than willing to show me the ropes.

With the river running at a normal height and the water clear, I was told to pack only one outfit. A 17-foot rod was combined with a small fixed spool reel loaded to the gunnels with 4.4lb monofilament. Next on the list came an old favourite, the loafer float, carrying up to four swan shot, and finally, a strong size 18 spade end hook to a 2lb 8oz bottom. The tackle was in place but what about the bait? It was, of course, red maggots and I'd been told to bring lots - a gallon, to be exact. The hope was that a constant trickle throughout the day would send the chub into a frenzy, a tactic my companions had always found successful on the river in question.

Being mid-week, we were fortunate to find the normally popular free stretch relatively quiet and I didn't need to be asked twice to place my tackle in a swim that I was told had a good chance of containing what I dreamed of. The easy part of the adventure had been completed; the next part, the catching of my goal, might well prove trickier!

Fortunately, I already knew maggots would be the answer. A constant stream of grubs fed for half an hour before wetting a line is a sure-fire way of triggering a feeding response, so while I set about rigging up the tackle, 'pultfuls of bait were continually rained on to the river's surface. I could only guess what the response was down below. Perhaps that big old chevin I so desired was drifting across the flow, with its huge white mouth, swallowing maggot after maggot. It was a thought that got the adrenaline coursing through the veins. Meanwhile, Tim and Terry had decided to share a swim directly below me and were applying similar tactics.

Eventually, the time had come to cast out and with a sideways motion I flicked the float three-quarters of the way across the river, feathering the spool continuously in an attempt to avoid a tangle. Once I'd mended the line, the float could begin its journey alongside a set of overhanging bushes and the sharp bob halfway down the trot told me everything I needed to know - there were chub present and they were taking maggots. If I kept the feed going in, a bite wasn't far away. Following the script, some ten minutes later a fish of 4lb headed into my landing net, followed by another of similar proportions shortly afterwards. Each one spewed out a mulch of red grubs, a sure testimony to their attraction.

The stretch I was fishing wasn't the most splendid example of the Stour but it's amazing how catching fish blinkers you from the rubbish and road noise. I have to admit, the scenery on this occasion was of a secondary concern to the angling possibilities. Maybe half an hour had passed before the next bite manifested itself and

Cruel twist of fate.

Luckiest angler in the world.

from the outset I knew this fish was different, mainly because of the way it bored away to the far bank, remaining heavy as it did so.

It was definitely a big fish and I needed to guide it downstream to calmer waters. The chub had a similar idea but some 50 yards later it still remained stubbornly in mid-river. No chub could fight this hard, so by now I thought it was a barbel. I was desperate to gain a glimpse, and piling on as much pressure as I dared, I began to gain line until a huge, dark torso rolled in front of me; it was a chub and it was massive! My elation immediately turned to horror as I got a better look. No wonder it had fought so hard! There, as clear as day, was my hook and bait in its dorsal fin. The fish of my dreams had become a nightmare. How could I possibly have foul-hooked it? Eventually, 7lb 4oz of chub sat in the landing net, caught but not by fair means. I could do nothing else but slip the monster back without adding it to my personal best list. How unlucky could I have been? I knew full well that it was eating the bait with gusto when I struck, and if I hadn't foul-hooked it, then I would have stood a good chance of tempting it fairly! Tim and Terry offered their condolences, amazed by the cruel hand of fate.

The next hour of fishing hurt, and I was sick to my stomach. Destiny had played a cruel trick, allowing me a glimpse of what I desired then snatching it away, shattering the dream. With little interest in fishing, I did no more than go through the motions and continued the stream of maggots going in. What was the point though? Lightning never strikes twice. As I kept control of its path, the loafer float entered the hotspot before, on cue, dragging under. I struck, made contact, and was immediately forced to yield line, which prevented me from engaging the bail arm. All I could do for 30 seconds was to hang on and control the pressure with my fingertip. At last, it relented, enabling me to spin the handle and at least gain a better level of control.

Straightaway, I knew something was wrong, as the thumps appeared to be resonating through an underwater obstruction. Rushing downstream, I tried to get below the fish and was pleased to find that the ruse worked. I freed the line and found myself in direct contact once again.

With the first obstacle overcome the chub then decided to implement Plan B by sweeping aggressively toward me. Normally, this wouldn't have been an issue but unfortunately between the fish and me was danger! During the recent floods, a tent had been washed downstream, becoming snagged on a near bank bush, and it now wafted in the flow like a giant parachute. Plunging the rod under the water I hoped that the chub would remain out of harm's way but to my horror, it became entangled at the tail end of the canvas. From my vantage point, I could clearly see a large, dark shape being dragged from side to side with the line firmly stuck. What could I do? By now Tim and Terry were by my side; in fact, this drama was being played out at the top of their swim. For a while, we debated the best way forward, although Lamp's furrowed brow said it all. He did his best to tell me it was just a small fish but we both knew otherwise. Tim, being the leader in our gang, was about to take control of the situation.

By shipping out the landing net, he hoped that it would become snagged at the top end of the tent that was festooned with debris. He could then drag the whole lot back to within grasping distance and, in turn, pull in the chub. Executing this plan though, turned into a Laurel and Hardy moment. The landing net head did indeed grab hold but as it was pulled back, the mistake became apparent. The top half of the pole had a six-inch removable section and as it was yanked, this and the net freed itself. Dumbfounded, we watched as my landing net now tumbled down the parachute while Tim was left clasping a useless pole. As the mesh came across the chub it swallowed up the dark shadow which in turn wrenched my rod down under extreme force. Before I had time to think, the line sprang back and I felt certain that it had broken, but immediately a new pressure returned. Somehow, the net had freed the fish from the tent, but both were now heading down the Stour! Making contact again, I knew I needed another miracle and it came as the chub swam free from the mesh. No matter what the chub did right and we did wrong, being caught was its destiny. So despite another couple of minutes of valiant battling, Lamps soon scooped up a 7lb 3oz fish. Laughter and handshaking abounded with Tim summing it up best: "The unluckiest angler in the world has just become the luckiest in the space of an hour!"

Without my friends' help this capture would never have happened and the same could be said when we visited the Emerald Isle with Peter Drennan, after its glorious rudd.

Madness!

The stern of the ferry left behind the rocky outline of Wales, its hilltops shrouded in mist, and four anglers remained on deck to dream of adventure and the Irish gold that we hoped lay ahead. This treasure couldn't be locked away in a chest but was free to roam the crystal clear water of the country's loughs, occasionally revealing itself to a lucky soul. It was the possibility of catching giant rudd that compelled my companions and I to make the voyage across the sea, full of optimism, and the hope of returning with tales to tell. As the long journey continued from the sea and up through 40 shades of green, I remembered battles with the species on the Bedfordshire brick pits. Peter Drennan smiled as towns passed by, the names acting as reminders of boyhood holidays and memories of trips with the late Peter Stone. Terry and Tim also had a track record in Ireland, with thoughts of our destination and its jewels soothing the long hours on the road. Eleven, in total, passed us by until daydreams started to turn into reality.

One hundred acres of sparkling expanse lay at our feet, occasionally broken by banks of reeds. We had arrived in big rudd country, a place where the legendary Hugh Gough had made his name decades before, proving that Irish blarney was indeed fact. How we hoped that we would indulge in such fishing but this evening it could wait a little longer, as a hot meal and a warm bed was in order for this band of weary travellers. A drop of Guinness, of course, helped to fuel the imagination still further. What we needed at dawn the following day was the promise of sunny, calm weather to begin the quest but, alas, the gods only bequeathed a moderate offering made up of a mixture of sunshine and showers, combined with a stiff breeze. Spotting our target would be challenging if not impossible, but our first day's fishing was not the time to be negative. If there were rudd in the lough we felt sure that one of us would find them, whatever the conditions.

We had brought two 10-foot, flat-bottom boats with us on the long journey, and these would enable every nook and cranny to be reached during our mission. What we needed first was a game plan. So initially, the electric motors powered both craft around the water enabling observations to be made and depths recorded. Two circular areas, taking up approximately half of the acreage, saw depths to over 40 feet and we all struggled to see how such a place would prove hospitable to our target. The remaining water was much shallower, in places less than a couple of feet. Here, on these limestone flats, rush and reed beds broke up the landscape as well as providing the demarcation point for the darker, deeper water. Our combined experience told us that this was the area on which to concentrate. Now all we had to do was decide how to tackle the place.

Along the junction found between the dramatic depth change, four marginal spots were primed with a bombardment of groundbait, pellets, and corn. Although not a typical rudd tactic, it would at least give us swims to try should the primary and more mobile approach fail in the conditions we faced. Once completed, we prepared to go afloat again with tackle suitable to fish a sprayed maggot tactic.

Emerald Isle.

Heading home.

Loaded crystal wagglers presented close to the strips of vegetation in the vast areas of shallows was where we would begin, so while our pre-baited areas were left to stew we made the first casts.

Having showered the fluorescent float tips with grubs, the game plan was continually put into action and with each new reed bed fished, our hopes rose before falling as the reality dawned on us that no rudd were at home, or at the very least were unwilling to feed. In the poor light and rippled water, spotting fish was impossible and in such an expanse it didn't take long to realise that we were facing a needle in a haystack situation. Every time we returned to the bankside for refreshments, neither party had anything of note to report. Looking to the skies I could only hope that the cloud cover would break, remove the lough's veil that had blinded us and turn it into an aquarium instead. Our first day was rapidly passing us by without a score on the board and we needed help. Would Ireland smile on us and lift the spirits?

Tim and Terry had once again anchored against some reeds without success when suddenly, the surface sparkled as a shard of light cast its spell after breaking through. Instinctively, Tim stood up to survey the scene and from thin air, eight shapes materialised dead ahead. Struggling to get the word out, in a stammer, he managed 'R-r-r-rudd', belatedly alerting Terry to their presence. Now, through the shadows, the rudd shone and they were

Golden glory.

upon them. With a pair of windmill arms, frantic efforts were made to cast and feed maggots at the same time. As the loose feed hit the surface, every golden torso flashed its approval and the inevitable transpired. Tim began his battle, while Terry rushed to feed another pouchful of bait to the rest of the shoal to keep them occupied.

The ploy worked perfectly. No sooner had the landing net secured Tim's reward than his companion faced his own duel. Both men remained tense throughout the fight until the last twist and turn faded away and another elusive prize from the Emerald Isle was beaten. Peter and I had witnessed the success from afar, but keen to share the moment we all made our way to the bank to take a first look at what we had come for. Two handfuls of gold, adorned with ruby red fins, sat in Tim and Terry's palms, weighing 2lb 9ozs and 2lb 14oz respectively. The grins said it all; the treasure chest had been prised open to reveal its contents. For a few seconds, we took time to marvel at nature in all its glory before they were returned to their rightful owner, the lough. Was the rest of the shoal still in the area? While this was a possibility, it would have been foolish to ignore such an opportunity. A quick committee decision led to Peter joining Tim in a boat that headed back out to the hotspot. Fishing in our team meant not only sharing information but fish too. The aim from the very beginning had been for everyone to have an equal share of the bounty. Self-interest had no place on this trip.

Back you go.

As quickly as the sun had appeared, it now began to soften along the horizon of the green hills. In these last embers of the day came Peter's chance. A single rudd moved near the bait, perhaps separated from the shoal by the recent skirmishes. With a careful introduction of maggots, isolation began to fade from its mind and greed kicked in. Snaring a single fish is never easy but eventually it made a mistake and the float sank away. Peter, too, had got his hands on some treasure – a burnished bar of 2lb 8oz. The trip had kicked off in style and it seemed certain that my time would come, but even as Peter smiled at the camera the storm clouds were gathering out west, sweeping in from the Atlantic. Gales and rain battered the land for two long days making it impossible to get back on the lough.

Other places sheltered from the worst of the weather were visited but our hearts and minds remained with the rudd. It didn't look good and I needed to face up to the reality that with one day left I could be the Jonah who missed out. Would the fish gods desert me completely? This was the question at the forefront of my mind when I drew the curtains on the final morning. My prayers were answered as a clear sky greeted me and, more importantly, the treetops remained unruffled. The storms that had battered Ireland for two days had passed, leaving behind the conditions all rudd anglers pray for. My companions were equally buoyed by the weather and as we made our way to the lough the talk, at last, returned to what we had travelled here for.

The only ripples on the water's surface were made by our boats as we slipped them quietly in. We decided that Terry would accompany me and because I was still to catch, we would pitch up alongside the reed bed that had produced the three rudd to my companions on the first day. Propelled by an electric motor, we crept into position and slowly nestled against the vegetation, dropping a mud weight over each end to provide an anchor. The tactics remained the same, with a constant drip-feed of maggots while the hookbaits sat under crystal wagglers.

Happy holiday.

In my experience with rudd, tackle selection rarely holds the key to success because they are bold feeders. Instead, the priority is location and we could only pray that our pitch was on their patrol route. Little could be done for now except to remain patient hoping that the shadows would cast their shapes across the yellow limestone shallows.

Half an hour ticked by, then an hour, and with each glance of the watch, I began to feel the frustration build. Terry was feeling the same way and the point was fast approaching when our patience was going to wear out. Peter and Tim also failed to report any activity, leaving us all bemused by the lack of action in seemingly perfect conditions. Had we got our choice of lough terribly wrong after all? Maybe the fish population was sparser than we presumed. Enough was enough. If we were to fail, we would at least go down fighting. Our game plan was going to change. We were going to search every inch of the shallows in this quest for treasure.

Four-leaf clover.

Upping anchor, we headed for a huge area of water no more than a couple of feet deep and while Terry concentrated on controlling the boat, I balanced on the raised front of the craft to gain maximum height over the water to increase the chances of spotting a rudd. Looking left and then right, I swept my vision across each and every stone as, little by little, the acreage was covered. I needed a sign quickly to avoid a blank and this was the thought at the forefront of my mind when a disturbance on the edge of my peripheral vision called for a closer inspection. Excitedly, I drew Terry's attention to the series of backs that were rising clear of the water in a porpoising motion, intent it seemed, on capturing the sedges trapped in the surface film. We agreed that it had to be rudd and we changed our course rapidly to investigate.

Holding station ten yards away from the scene of the disturbance, we waited patiently for another sign but cruelly, it never came. Had we imagined it? The fish were no longer there and I guessed our presence had scared them. In such shallow, open water it didn't matter how careful we were in our movements, because it was always going to be transmitted to the rudd long before we could reach them. Maybe the bank of reeds 50 yards in front of us had offered the shoal some sanctuary. We crept along the outer stems and I peered intently through a pair of Polaroids hoping to be stopped in my tracks. Momentarily, I raised my gaze only to see the water boil back on the shallows exactly where we had just come from. Flies were once again being devoured in a feeding frenzy. Responding to my frantic pointing, Terry began to steer the boat in their direction.

"Stop! Rudd in front of us!" were my next words as half a dozen shapes nearly ran into the boat. Instinctively, the motor was put into reverse while I catapulted maggots into the water. The response was immediate as the surface rocked, caused by the rudd darting into the grubs. I grabbed hold of the rod and cast beyond the feed, fired another 'pultful out and drew the float into them. Without hesitation, it then pulled under and was dragged sideways. A rapid strike set the fight in motion and from the relative calmness of a minute previously, all hell broke loose!

I wanted the rudd in the landing net and it wanted to visit the reeds – 2lb 12oz of nylon would be deciding the outcome. Twice I thought it had successfully made its bid for freedom only for the rod's alarming curve to relent at this critical moment. Terry stood by me, waiting with the landing net, forgoing his chance at the shoal because he was so keen to see me succeed. A huge flank boiled in front of us, normally the signal for the fight to finish but in a final throw of the dice it charged for the cover of the boat, hitting the net's spreader block in the process. Panic reigned for a few seconds before sense prevailed and we got back to the task of landing the rudd. A whopping 3lb of wild Irish magic presented itself, previously unmolested by man and shimmering in the summer sun. This beauty then fell into the safety of the mesh and turned the trip from personal failure to resounding success in a single bite.

The final afternoon lay in front of us and our spirits remained incredibly high. We felt sure that more rudd would come our way; the conditions allowing stalking to be part of our armoury. Each boat criss-crossed the lough on the lookout for another prize but mysteriously they vanished once again. After a few hours of relentless searching, the sun's power began to lose its grip and with this battle between night and day a huge hatch of sedges skipped and danced on the surface. Would the rudd begin to gorge again? Terry and I stood guard over the shallows waiting for a sign but away in the distance, we noticed Peter and Tim's body language change suddenly and become more animated. Even from our long-range vantage point, it was obvious that rudd had at last been found again. Slipping anchor for the umpteenth time we headed in their direction, watching both men tussle with big fish as we made our journey.

On arrival we were greeted with Tim's enthusiastic words, "Get your rod out, Terry!" At least 20 monster rudd, with widths of immense proportions, sat alongside a reed bed in less than a foot of water. The two captured fish from the shoal had already weighed a mighty 2lbs 13oz giving an indication of the potential which lay before us. Terry, of course, hadn't needed a second invitation and within a minute, he too was embroiled in a fight with our target; a battle that resulted in another victory for him. It was my turn next and the pleasure of the bite turned to pain as a bronze flank twisted and flashed in its frantic bid to avoid making my acquaintance.

"Terry," I said, "my legs have turned to jelly!"
With a grin, he replied, "So have mine!"

Ireland was in a generous mood and I joined the gold rush. Unsurprisingly, the rudd had by now begun feeling unsettled but still they decided to give Peter a parting gift before bidding farewell and vanishing from our view forever. All that was left for four happy anglers was to grin for the camera and reflect on a special day. The curlew had greeted us on arrival and its distinctive call waved us off in style. We had experienced wild Irish fishing at its very best.

Memories are made.

Exploring the estuary.

There's no doubt that my angling life would have been considerably poorer without sharing so many adventures with this pair. Even when our trips end in failure, there is always a smile on our faces because we love the sport so much, especially when it's laced with a degree of humour. This was definitely the case with the trials and tribulations faced when we first tried to catch the dastardly mullet. I say 'tried' because attempting to catch these creatures can turn a sane man mad. In fact, I could easily be penning these words from the safety of the rehab clinic for washed up anglers and it's only by sharing the problems we faced that I can let the healing process begin!

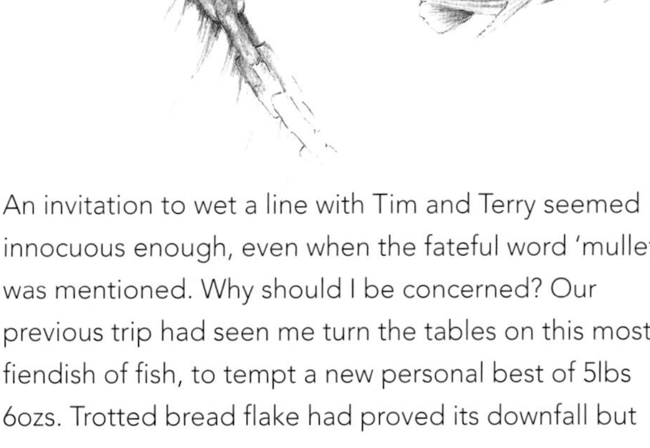

An invitation to wet a line with Tim and Terry seemed innocuous enough, even when the fateful word 'mullet' was mentioned. Why should I be concerned? Our previous trip had seen me turn the tables on this most fiendish of fish, to tempt a new personal best of 5lbs 6ozs. Trotted bread flake had proved its downfall but only after demented surges had failed to break the link which held it captive. How could such a small fish exert so much pressure? In the world of tails, scales, and fins, their fighting qualities are unsurpassed. Combine this with a mindset I am yet to fathom out and you have a tricky opponent indeed.

Tim would be in charge of the trip and that would entail a maiden voyage of his new boat. The vessel was perfect for our normal escapades in the sedate Christchurch Harbour but could it cope with going where no mullet angler had gone before? Ahead lay a potentially treacherous 90-minute voyage through the waves to a spot that he promised held monsters beyond imagination. Although it seemed rather a long distance, I was reassured by Terry's quiet nod of approval and if the stories could be believed a grey ghost of double-figured proportions would more than make up for the time invested in the journey.

The following morning, three of us prepared for the voyage ahead at the old slipway that serviced the tidal river. From here, we would follow the last of its course before navigating the gigantic harbour until the sea was nearly reached. In the placid weather window of dawn there was little to trouble us on the trip, even the huge sea-faring ships had yet to mobilise. As we pushed on, the expectations rose for the sport ahead and the petrol engine occasionally misfiring did little to dampen our collective enthusiasm.

Staying sane.

Skipper Norman.

A pointed finger and a beaming smile from our skipper, Norman, told us that our date with mullet destiny had nearly arrived and as the horizon drew closer a gull-infested landing stage came into view.

With the salt content rapidly rising in the estuary, a zesty, fresh scent filled our nostrils and against the pitted wooden station, waves lapped with erosive energy, trying their best to prise off the limpets. Here, alongside the timber, was the mullet's home and by anchoring a short distance away a hook baited with bread could be cast to them with ease.

We dropped anchor and prepared the tackle, quiver tip rods replacing our normal float fishing equipment. We hoped that line of 7lb breaking strain would be strong enough, while feeders filled with mashed bread would tickle their taste buds. With everything prepared, three splashes heralded the beginning of the contest. Patiently, we sat and watched the water level ebb away as the tide rushed back out to sea. Slowly but surely, our surroundings became more apparent and with it the presence of hundreds of mullet. Was this a good omen? They were certainly present but seeing them was equally depressing. Had it just gone to show how inadequate our tactics had been until now?

Before we could begin to debate the situation, Terry's rod was dragged round savagely and line screamed from his clutch as he reacted with a strike. With gob-smacking power, the mullet tore under the boat, tangling itself around the anchor before heading back to the landing stage and smashing the line, all in a matter of seconds. Battered and bruised, Lamps wound in the limp line, which unfortunately for him, was only a prelude to another battle that saw the mullet come out on top again. I know I shouldn't have chuckled at Terry's predicament and I rued my behaviour even more when I, too, failed to overcome our adversary. A bowstring-tight line being ripped across gnarly, old wooden pillars was always going to end one way but how the hell do you stop something that moves with the force and speed of a bullet?

Meanwhile, Tim had to fight his own demons, despite not making contact. We had warned him not to stare directly into the eye of the fish as 'mullet madness' would be the outcome but he paid no attention. The glazed expression and pale skin told us all we needed to know. The thrashing of water with a variety of tactics that followed came as no surprise but, of course, the fish ignored every single one of them. We had come to conquer and instead could only leave with our tails between our legs. Failure had been our only bedfellow for eight hours but despite this being manageable for three hardened specimen hunters, we were now faced with something much worse – the journey home.

During our fishing frenzy, we had failed to notice the wind speed picking up and while our angling pitch had placed us in calm water, white horses needed to be traversed if we were to reach the safety of the river. However, before we hit the full force of this obstacle, ferries blocked our path. In typical gung-ho fashion, Tim ignored our wimpish concerns and headed straight for the vessels in a manner more akin to a Somalian pirate. Why, I asked, did they continuously sound their horn?

"It's nothing to worry about!" came the reply, just a sign, I was told, of friendship between seafarers! Don't ask me how but we made it through this obstacle course, only to be led into another rollercoaster ride! If the CIA thinks it knows how to carry out water boarding then they need to come on a boat ride with Tim and Terry! Waves continuously broke over the hull and while getting wet was okay, sinking was an entirely different matter. The only option open to us was to get out of the wind, but this meant heading for and traversing the shallow sandbanks! As he probed the depth with an oar, Terry was the only thing keeping the motor from being smashed to pieces. I hope he will forgive me when I say I wasn't reassured by this tactic! For two hours, we battled the elements until somewhat fortunately, three shell-shocked souls docked back at the safety of the slipway. Bedraggled, I clambered on to terra firma and headed off to seek counselling. What happened to my companions? I'm unsure but I do remember men in white coats and a couple of straitjackets!

Mullet madness.

For those reading these words who have faced the same trials and tribulations, take heart in the fact that eventually even we got our act together with this species, the only problem being that Terry has the bragging rights over Tim and I with a colossal fish scaling over 8lb! This is a point of which he's never slow to remind us every time we launch the boat in search of mullet. Long may the madness continue with these two great friends.

Camera: Canon EOS 300D - Shutter Speed: 1/30 sec - F-Stop: f/5.6 - ISO: 100 - Location: Oxfordshire estate lake

CHAPTER 22

OFF THE BEATEN TRACK

In a world full of mobile phones and the Internet, angling faces the prospect of being sterilised. Every fish has a name, every venue can be Googled and the chat rooms seem to know a fish has been landed before it's even returned. Technology is often seen as progress, but at times I feel it can interfere with the very essence of our field sport. To put it simply, we know too much and no species suffers from this syndrome more than carp.

Out of the rat race.

Busy venues, rotas and syndicates proliferate in this side of angling and for those just wanting to get away from it all, finding the right venue is becoming harder and harder. This is why I cherish and guard as much as possible the waters that afford me this luxury. Is that an act of double standards given my media profile? Yes, but sometimes it's nice to escape the 'rat race'.

The Oxfordshire estate lake in question is quite probably the nicest venue I've ever fished. Sculpted by the hands of Capability Brown, the place has an aura of grandeur and nobility where fishermen are granted an audience with royalty. Mature oaks, chestnuts, and elms stand guard over this jewel, their age testament to that uplifting feeling that grabs me on every visit as I enter a bygone era. No matter what the season, a splash of colour awaits me along the pathway to the lake; snowdrops or wild flowers on the complex may change with the calendar but never the level of beauty. Midsummer reveals opulent flowers perched on lily pads against a jade background, framed perfectly with a border of bulrushes. Fresh mint is crushed underfoot, releasing its menthol vapours and combines with the delicious scent of mown grass to surpass even the finest perfume. Have no doubt, a masterpiece has been created, and this is without mention of the carp that sift through the silt and send up plumes of mud along with sheets of bubbles.

Many years ago, each fish was hand picked to create a chocolate box selection of commons and mirrors with scales the size of apple slices. Their weight may not rival that of a boilie-guzzling brute, but that hasn't stopped them being revered time and time again. Countless magazines and films, from 'A Passion for Angling' to 'Catching the Impossible' has sought to portray them and I, too, have tasted success at the estate lake many times. My favourite capture, though, was while recording 'A Fish for all Seasons'.

Conditions were perfect, being mild, overcast and with a gentle south-westerly pushing against the immature pads, but there had been no sign of a carp. Patience, I'm told, is always a valuable asset for an angler but given that I was here to make a film, you can understand why Jacko, the cameraman, looked thoroughly disillusioned. With deadlines in place, time was one commodity that I didn't have. The carp here didn't rely on the copious amounts of bait fed to them and I guessed this was part of the problem – they were free to roam at their whim not mine! With the bay fed with a sprinkling of boilies and pellets I'm afraid, like it or not, I would have to just wait and hope something showed up.

Far away.

Half a dozen times I left base camp to investigate the water's edge, peering over the reed bed but nothing of interest appeared. In such a perfect place, awash with a dazzling kaleidoscope of bluebells and rhododendrons, it would be cruel never to let the camera roll, I mused. Fortunately, salvation was close at hand and on visit number seven, the bottom was no longer visible, as sediment began to be stirred up. From my vantage point, I counted up to six fish being responsible for the disturbance, which had arrived it seemed, out of thin air but were now determined to make their presence felt. Lips grabbed at the mud trying to extract nutrients, and giant rudders waved in approval creating tiny vortexes on the surface. Unsurprisingly, I beat a hasty retreat to get the tackle and pass on the good news to Jacko.

An advantage with lightly fished waters is that complicated tackle isn't required, just a simple straightforward approach.

For bottom fishing, I rarely look beyond a snowman rig, combining a standard boilie and a pop-up. This helps to disguise the fact that I'm using a large hook – a size 5 in this case. A length of coated braid hooklink and a semi-fixed, 1.5oz lead gave me everything I needed, with the main trick being able to get the hookbait in place without making the carp aware of any disturbance. Creeping back to the scene of the crime, I bided my time until the shoal decided to go on a circuit of the bay, and I flicked out the lead. It landed well past the spot before I gently dragged it into position, allowing the rig to sink on a tight line. I then paid off plenty of slack to ensure line bites would be minimised. The rod was then hidden in the reeds with only the tiniest section of tip protruding to avoid causing alarm.

Three fish that had branched off from the group promptly swept back into view and resumed their feast. Given the hookbait's placement, a bite could only be seconds away from materialising, but seconds soon turned to minutes and once the remainder of the group joined in the fun, I became perplexed by the situation. Being rig-shy certainly wasn't the issue; it had to be something a little more complex than that. The substrate we fish over has a huge impact on what is caught, and silt, to my mind, is one of the hardest challenges of all. It seemed sensible to assume that the carp had been encouraged to feed on this spot due to the bait I introduced, but once the feeding began the bottom started to shift, revealing tiny food particles like bloodworm. This soon led to a preoccupation with filter feeding and the boilies became superfluous to requirements. What, then, could I do? The answer was to move the hookbait's position to a zone where this preoccupation hadn't occurred. If the carp passed by a bait out of the cloud, maybe the memory of what triggered the feeding frenzy in the first place would still remain. Carefully, I reached for the rod, unplugged the lead, and pulled it into position until it sat almost under my feet. From observation, I knew that this was part of their patrol route and a crossing of paths wouldn't be far away.

Two shapes broke away from the pack and headed toward me, one distinctly bigger than the other. I soon had a chance of closer inspection, showing the pair to consist of a mid-double mirror and a big common, with scales that appeared to be straining to keep its belly contained. More than that, it was a fish we had sought from the very inception of the film. Which one I wanted to catch was obvious, and when a mouth the size of a bucket opened and headed in the boilie's direction it seemed like all my prayers were to be answered. Then, without justification, it closed it again and waddled off, not panicked, just uninterested. Wincing, I cursed the beast and puzzled over the failure without getting an adequate answer. Before eyes could engage the brain, it was back staring directly at what it had chosen to ignore. Again, the huge mouth opened; only this time fins propelled it downward, forcing each lip to block my view of the bait. Then the suction commenced, lifting the bait and the razor-sharp hook into the carp's mouth, where the point turned and snagged the flesh.

It's a wrap.

For a second, the common tried to fathom out what had gone wrong then, in annoyance, its head was flicked from side to side in a bid to free itself from the rig. As reality dawned, an urge to leave became the overriding instinct. Luckily, given the proximity of the pads, my reactions were equal to that of the carp and before its tail had time to build up power, the rod I wielded toppled it on to its flank, making the common stall. Like a man with a beer belly stepping into a ring with Mike Tyson, there was only going to be one winner and a quick conclusion to the fight. Sure enough, 34lb of carp soon sat inside the landing net, as I enjoyed the victory, hoisting her up to the camera, where her beauty seemed totally in keeping with this magical place, and the television production found a fitting finale.

Finding a water that contains large virgin carp is no easy task, and it's compounded in a busy angling county like Oxfordshire. A stroke of luck came my way in the summer of 2004 while exploring a 20-acre gravel pit for tench. Over a period of a few weeks, John Everard and I had each baited a marginal swim along the bank that received the warm winds. Here in my selected spot, a tree had fallen in the water, above a gravel slope which slipped away quickly under the canopy. Combined with its close proximity to one corner of the lake, this certainly had all the makings of an ideal carp, as well as tench, swim.

Carp had never been on the radar here though, until recent times, and given that the last carp to be banked had been a 20lb common in the 1970s, you can understand why. This was a fish believed to be one of only four residents, but I came to the conclusion later that the odds were even worse, with only two carp present. Adam Penning had targeted the fish for the last couple of seasons and I knew from all the blanks that had occurred that it would be a very difficult task to catch one.

It was only when Evy reported spotting two large shapes ghost in over the pre-bait on a balmy summer's evening that my interest levels lifted; to such an extent that I told him, to his disbelief, that when a south-westerly next arrived I would be carp fishing the pit.

The wind in question took another week to arrive but as I unlocked the gate and drove across the open field that led to our swims, I could already see the water gently lapping towards me.

Lost in nature.

Fortunately, I also knew that the areas we had chosen would have remained unmolested because, at the time, John and I had exclusive use of the venue. Everything was perfect and it needed to be, given the ridiculously low stock levels and the limited 24 hours I had to catch one.

Keeping things very simple, I rigged up two identical outfits each with 15lb line, a 3oz semi-fixed lead, six inches of 15lb coated hooklength and a size 8 hook. Only the bait was different, with a tiger nut on one rig, and the other holding two grains of fake corn. Their placement was obvious, and once I had guided each rig down on to the gravel slope, the spot received a few handfuls of hemp and maize. I also ensured that the main line was pinned to the bottom, by squeezing on a lump of heavy metal putty. Each rod was then positioned on a buzzer well back from the water's edge to prevent them from being spotted.

Likewise, the bivvy couldn't be positioned directly over the swim and I hid it behind a bush, which unfortunately, meant that I couldn't watch the water. However, I thought this would work to my benefit, as constantly traipsing up and down the bank had to alert these wild creatures. I knew my swim was being visited and felt, given the conditions, a return seemed likely, so I now needed to keep my head down and remain patient.

For once, I was grateful for nightfall. Staring at a bush while confined to barracks can be a wearing affair. All that I had while I tried to sleep through the sticky, humid hours, was my imagination, and boy, was it in overdrive! Untroubled by man, and kings of their lake, it was only they who decided which whim to follow, sucking on snails laced inside the rich Canadian pondweed or gorging on the beds of silt full of bloodworm. Then again, could the new, nutty scent of hempseed attract their attention? The dream was never to reach a conclusion because the next time I opened my eyelids I squinted, dazzled by the early morning sun. The urge to look in the swim was stronger than ever but given the hookbaits I had chosen, it would serve no purpose and maybe destroy all the good work I'd put in so far. So instead, the kettle went on in a bid to distract me but no sooner had the flame kissed its metal surface than an alarm sent out a cry for help in a single, constant shrill. Ever the pessimist, my immediate thought was of a swan snagging the line around its neck, although this didn't stop me from diving off the bed and rushing round to the other side of the bush. What was I about to find?

Suddenly, the reality of the situation kicked in when nothing wearing white feathers could be seen, so logically it had to be, my God, a carp. Diving on the rod I set about implementing the game plan I had devised should this moment ever arrive, and that meant running down a steep bank and straight into the lake up to my waist. There was a method to this madness, because I knew if I put myself between the carp and the fallen tree from the outset, it would never become a problem, especially as whatever I was connected to seemed intent on finding another snag first.

Unbridled panic had grabbed hold of the carp and an 80-yard run was the response before it smashed head first into the largest weed bed it could find. Until this moment, all I could do was hold on and only once the carp thought sanctuary had been found did I start to impose my will on the situation.

Next came a moment of stalemate under a constant pressure of a fully-loaded rod, before I felt the individual stems begin to snap and I started to prise open the fist of weed a fingertip at a time. Then, lifeless, the mass started to shift in a single lump and I started the winching process, retrieving all the line that had been taken from me.

Unmolested.

Progress was slow but constant and soon came the question of whether or not my carpy present was still inside the green wrapping. Twenty yards offshore, I got the answer as a giant black tail shook off three-quarters of its straitjacket, leaving just the hood in place, which only served to assist me still further. Reeling in became easier but the carp still remained docile within the darkness of its shroud. Only when the landing net was shipped out in its direction did concern cross its mind, but in a series of jubilant movements I slipped the mesh under its frame, lifted, and punched the air!

I had in my grasp a truly special fish that had remained unmolested all its life. A flank of chestnut browns, reds and purples was interspersed with slices of gold around its gill cover and tail - and what a tail - huge, powerful, and as black as a crow's feathered crown. On its torso dozens of tiny starburst scales lit it up like comets in a night sky. Incredible! The fish's head was the pièce de résistance, appearing to be sculpted in mahogany, with its barbules and lips exhibiting nothing except perfection. Cradling her in the mesh, I staggered back up the bank to record her weight, and at 37lb 4oz, I thanked the angling gods that our paths had crossed.

It seemed, then, that the story was complete; but fate had another card to play. I had called Evy out to assist with pictures and once completed, our attentions turned back towards tench. With all the commotion I'd created, I felt the common carp that still remained uncaught in the lake would be a million miles away so I was happy to break camp with a job well done and explore a few of the other pits in the area.

Over the next few hours, we tried in vain to locate any sizeable tench and somehow we ended up back where we had started, with Evy heading up the bank towards his pre-baited area. Unconcerned and just happy to enjoy the day, I decided to creep back to the scene of the capture and flick out a float, fished lift-method style, supporting a single grain of corn, hoping that a tench or two had returned. Almost immediately, the float began to dance to the tune of the fin-wash being created below. Then, as John crept up behind me, the float lifted with purpose before lying flat. A strike made a solid connection that soon turned into an uncontrollable surge of energy, hitting rod, reel, and then my arm. The centrepin's drum span like a Catherine Wheel, as line was removed at an incredible rate, sending fireworks shooting through my mind. This wasn't any tench so it had to be the only remaining carp which, given the estimations made, was a common of over 40lb! Ridiculously outgunned, I watched as the coils of line reached a critical point on the spool before making the only choice I had – to clamp down in a last-ditch attempt to stop the beast. 'Crack!' A gunshot sound gave me exactly the opposite conclusion and the rod returned to its lifeless, straight form. Evy and I looked at each other and then burst out laughing. You can't win them all!

Into the unknown.

Does an almost unfished venue of 100 acres, with a sparse but hefty population of carp to 45lb, sound good to you? Well, it did to me, although, as with most dreams there are always one or two stumbling blocks to overcome. Firstly, access was extremely difficult to obtain. One third of the water was out of bounds due to holiday homes, while powerboats propelled water skiers up and down the lake all summer and there was no night fishing. All this before I established that the carp population numbered no more than a handful.

A few years previously, after a summer of fishing, a holidaymaker on site had extracted an upper 20, a 30 and two 40s, one of which he caught twice, giving an indication that although fewer than a dozen fish existed here, each was of significant size. They were therefore highly prized, with every one's life remaining uncharted by the carp world, and big enough to see me embark on a project that would take place over the course of three years.

A lucky break came in the form of a friend called Basil. He had fished the venue for years, being the last remaining member of a small group that had been granted access some time back. Making known my desire to join his depleted ranks, I was excited to hear that, as a favour to Basil, the owner would meet with me and, if I proved to be acceptable, allow me to fish the lake. Again, I got over this hurdle but I knew immediately that any thoughts of carp fishing would be put on the back burner, given the summer onslaught of boats. To a dyed-in-the-wool specialist this would have been a disaster but I was more than happy to learn about the lake while indulging in extracting its tench from under a float.

The pea-shingled banks slipped into clear, rich, weedy water with the horizon broken by three long islands running down its spine, while another sat alone closer to the bank, before a large area of barren shallows rose to almost touching distance of the surface, providing an interesting vista full of wildlife. The park's holidaymakers never once troubled me, seeming to be from another dimension, as I focused on the enjoyable fact that I was the only angler locked behind electric gates.

During this time, I also formed a friendship with the maintenance manager, Trev, whose kindness was about to unlock the carp for me. Realising I had to leave each evening and seek somewhere to sleep because I was not a local, he said he would ask permission of the owner for me to stay overnight. Fortunately, I must have proved myself to be trustworthy and the following season I was allowed to stay and, better still, if I chose a spot, Trev would be happy to bait up for me three times a week during March in preparation for a spring assault.

All did seem perfect except for one big problem – the devastating floods of 2007. With this tidal wave of water, the lake, like several in the area, broke its banks and poured into surrounding ditches. Unlike many that suffered far worse, the water exiting the lake remained shallow, although a ditch was built to help to release the pressure; but had my hopes been flushed through it? It was a worrying turn of events, especially given the stock levels. However, come the following March I still dropped off 30 kilos of Spicy Prawn boilies to Trev's workshop with the instructions that I had selected a narrow gravel bed three-quarters of the way toward the small island. I hoped that this feature would be part of any patrol route and the bait would soon turn it into an area worth visiting regularly for the carp.

The door had opened.

Plans were made.

Trev's diligence was, to my mind, as instrumental to success as any fishing prowess I might have shown. So, after two years of waiting, I made my first casts, with all three rods supporting chod rigs placed over the areas I had earmarked.

The peace was shattered by the frantic call of the alarm. This set off a chain reaction; my eyes opening, a scramble to free the zip on the sleeping bag, a dive out of the side door of my van, and a rush without boots toward the source of the upheaval. Life struggles to be any more exciting and with a heartbeat that threatened to smash out of my chest, I grabbed for a rod that a carp of unknown proportions was attached to. Under that starry sky, I became a religious man more than once, and only gained some level of self-control when the battle had been won.

Until I switched on the head torch, I had absolutely no idea what lay in wait, but there, under the illumination sat the prize – a 29lb carp with a leathery complexion. Neither its weight nor its appearance was particularly inspiring to anyone else, but I felt such jubilation at making contact with the pit after all this time. It seemed as if I had cracked it, with bigger and better fish surely to come. Wrong! Eighteen more trips came and went that spring without another sign. On reflection, I don't think it was anything I did wrong, but a repercussion from the flood of the previous year. Vast exchanges of water had occurred, bringing ditches, rivers, and lakes in contact with each other and after a winter to incubate, bacteria were now rampant. This, in turn, sickened the fish and as the temperature rose, it got worse; hence my early carp being followed by nothing. Sanity should have kicked in at this point, but I found it hard to forget this place and continued to dream of mirrors with purple-blue complexions that were as fat as pigs, meandering through a forest of Canadian pondweed. So, all winter I glanced regularly at the picture of my one and only success and contemplated whether or not to return.

The answer, of course, was yes; how could I ignore the challenge? So once again, as carp up and down the country began to move and feed, my baiting campaign recommenced. A drawing of last year's clear spots was reexamined and correlated against the marker float's findings. It seemed that the weed had still to infringe on the area, giving me a platform for a boilie bombardment. Six kilos of Spicy Tuna and Chilli baits were earmarked, once again for introduction every week, made up of three separate baitings. This would continue for a month, by which time I hoped every fish in the lake would be aware of the free food. It seemed a perfect plan but thoughts that I had already caught the only carp crept in. Was this really possible in nearly 100 acres of water?

Concerned but undeterred, the baiting campaign continued unabated until at last came the moment of truth. A predicted mild day with no wind gave me the best possible conditions and from my bankside view I was convinced the clear spots had grown. Testing each of the three areas with a lead, brought a 'donk' response from the rod tip, giving me at least hope of something feeding. Alas, my pessimistic side soon questioned this positive. Carp needn't have been the perpetrators, as tench and birds also have a penchant for boilies. Arguing with myself, I retorted that the 20mm baits used should have at least slowed these thieves down, and the coot, which not only guarded her nest but also the water in front of it, might well have kept the tufties at bay.

Tackle in such a place needed to be faultless and with a lack of angling pressure, simple as well. Six feet of leadcore and a chod rig seemed the logical answer and a reasonable drop was all that was required to know that my baits were presented well. A year on and the search had begun once again.

As night fell, something below was keeping unsocial hours too and it crashed out, drawing me back from my dreams and causing the coot to send out a distress call. I strained my vision against the silhouetting sky to scan for a carp on the prowl. I knew full well that a dozen fisheries within a stone's throw of where I now sat could offer more in pure pounds and ounces, but all in a sanitised environment. This pit, while relatively unproductive, had allowed me to step back in time a little, to where the spirit of adventure was alive and well. For this, I had sacrificed a guarantee of not just catching but the existence of carp, but that was a deal I was happy to strike. Settled in a position surrounded by an air of anticipation, it was a decision I was glad I had made.

A warning would have been nice to save my heart from the shock of the reel's spool that came to life as it frantically tried to keep up with the line being demanded from it. I had forgotten to switch on the alarm so the now singing loose clutch was the only audible warning. Before I had even touched the rod, I knew that no tench could do this and that fact immediately raised the stakes. Excitement and fear mingled in my mind to provide a heady cocktail that intensified as I picked up the rod. How a fish can do this to a grown man I have difficulty rationalising, although I'm happy it does. It produces an adrenaline rush like no other that, for a while, allows real life to fade away, replaced with the most exhilarating primeval hunting instinct. With each surge, I prayed to remain in contact as weed teamed up with the carp to do its best to scupper me until, gut-wrenchingly, it wrapped up the fish I was so desperate to see, in a cocoon of vegetation. Taking a calculated gamble I put the rod back on the rest and frantically reeled in the other two. If I were to stand any chance now I would need as few obstacles as possible.

Back on point, I arced the carbon as much as I dared, hoping to break the bond between carp and weed, but it quickly transpired that this would be impossible. A strand at a time was the next option and that required me to lift and lower the rod in a series of short, sharp movements, thus forcing the taut mono to act as a saw.

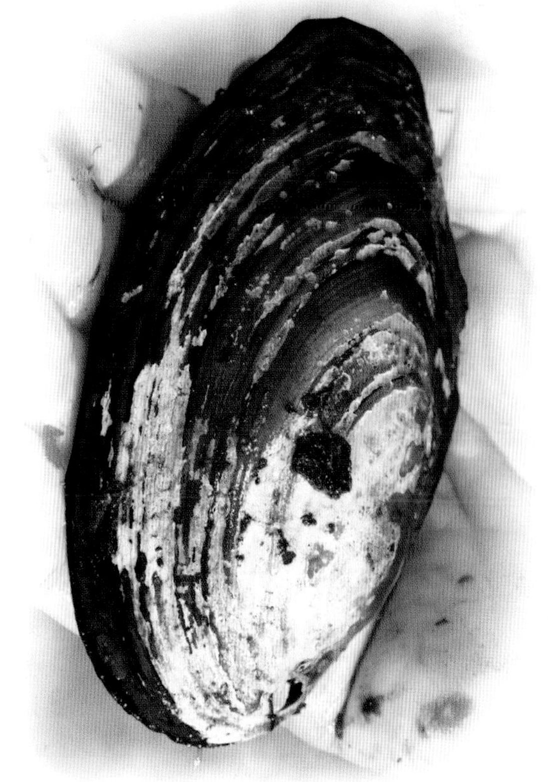

Far from the madding crowd.

Progress came slowly but with each stem broken, I prised apart the dense ball of weed and, with one last sweep of the rod, the bond was released and I had direct contact. She rose through the water column, sending out a huge bow wave across the surface in a final act of defiance. Closer and closer, the straining tackle drew the fish until, in the gloom, I dipped the net and waited for a gulping pair of lips to hit the spreader block. Then, with an eager lift, I ended the battle. For a few seconds I took time to savour the moment and dream of what I had caught before taking a look. Was it the same fish as last season? Was it a mirror or a common? How big was it? Returning to the job at hand I opened my eyes and switched on the torch, and 37lb 8oz of unmolested mirror carp lay before me, tempted more out of hope than expectation.

Unlike the previous spring, this wasn't to be the only carp, with a new specimen of 28lb 6oz slipping up, followed by the 30 again at 34lb 14oz. Its scratched body and weight loss testimony to a frantic spell of spawning. All too soon, the lake switched off again as an influx of boats and holidaymakers took hold. It left me with one, single question; were the 40-pounders still present? One day I hope to find out.

Another 100 acres of windswept gravel pit sprawled in front of me. A brisk south-westerly pushed in toward my bank, providing respite from the intensity of the sun. If I were a carp, I know where I would have been, but with fewer than 30 fish present in this vast expanse, it was like finding a camouflaged needle in a field full of haystacks. Chucking and chancing didn't seem very appealing, so donning the Polaroids, I headed off down the windward bank. Every 100 yards I would pause for five minutes, scanning the pit and hoping for a sign. A huge boil close to the margin lifted my hopes, but they were quickly dashed by the sight of a cormorant hitting the surface. Half an hour later, I had reached the far corner and I sat down for a breather and a sip of water as I gazed out at the pit.

Waves lapped in, bringing with them copious amounts of loose Canadian pondweed. My immediate margin saw this vegetation stack up on itself so much that it stretched out into the lake for 30 yards, and such was its density that a swan struggled to paddle through the tangled stems.

For a while, all appeared quiet, with the weed bed lifeless, save for the occasional pond skater going about its business. Then a silhouetted triangle drew my gaze, intensifying when it sank from view momentarily before reappearing. It was the unmistakable sign of a carp's dorsal fin! Now focused on the area, I began studying it closer. Although the weed was dense, there were occasional clearer patches, no larger than a football. The carp were behaving like seals with ice holes, appearing to flex their fins to feel the sun's warmth before sinking from view. Their presence was confirmed but how the hell do you catch them from a floating weed bed that resembles the centre court at Wimbledon?

I needed a plan. Heading back to the van, I made the quick drive to the village shop and prayed they would have what I required.

"Last one left, sir," the girl replied when I asked her.

"I'll have it," I replied, passing over the money and grabbing hold of the fresh white loaf, like a starving man.

Armed with my secret weapon, I headed back and began assembling the tackle. A 2lb test curve rod was combined with a centrepin and 15lb line straight through to a size 6 hook. Filling the rucksack with bits, I also pulled out my solid-framed barbel net. In such thick weed, a bow-framed version would prove useless, assuming of course that I was lucky enough to hook something. Now ready, I headed off on the arduous walk, sweating from head to toe. Back in the bay, a dorsal immediately erected itself, waving like a flag as it tempted me to have a go. I duly slipped into the water and began to push my way through the weed. It was incredibly thick, grabbing hold and tangling around my legs, which made gaining headway a slow business. Finally, I came within a rod's length of the hole that had seen the disturbance. A huge grey back rose into view and pushed weed upward around its perimeter, such was its dimensions.

Creeping closer.

A bluey flank interspersed with silver scales showed, which revealed that a mirror was at home and carefully, I squeezed on a lump of flake and gently pushed out the rod. Holding my breath, I ticked line off the 'pin until, with hardly a ripple, the flake broke the surface. A giant eyeball scanned the situation. In turn, I tried not to stare directly into it, fearful of some primeval instinct kicking in and spooking the fish. Was it the bread, me, or a lack of appetite? I'll never know but with a flick of the tail and a shuffle of the shoulders, the hole was left empty.

I scanned the rest of the weed and spotted another dorsal flick upwards, glinting in the sun. Exiting on to dry land, I stalked along the margin before heading back into the pit. I could feel the bands of temperature clearly; my feet remained cool while my thighs were bathed in lukewarm water. Once again, I slowly displaced the weed, beating a path to my quarry. Some ten feet away, I stopped and placed the net by my side. From my new vantage point, I peered into the hole and waited for a carp to reveal itself. A pair of lips drifted out of the shadows, gulping eagerly in the weed. Then there was another, and another...three heads in no more than a couple of square feet!

Trembling, I reached into my pocket and scooped out some flake from against the crust. I carefully squeezed it onto the hook's shank, ensuring that the point remained exposed, and held my breath until the bait reached its position. The response was instant - freshly made dough triggered the taste buds. The carp pushed upwards and the weed began to heave as it tried to force a way forward. Suddenly, a huge head rose above the surface, lifting the flake clear out of the water. With my hookbait suspended on top of its head, laced with a wreath of weed, the carp frantically gulped air. Frozen to the spot, I watched as it bounced up and down in a desperate bid to eat the bread. Then it was gone; bait, fish and all. What had happened? Did it suck it in? My brain overloaded with each quandary. Seconds ticked by and still I stalled before a rush of sanity kicked in. I struck hard, the water erupted and the carbon lunged over.

Mercy was not an option and the do-or-die battle commenced. It was winner-takes-all. A tackle failure would mean freedom for the carp, but keeping my bottle would mean getting a picture taken. I clamped down on the 'pin and refused to budge an inch. Trapped in a tomb of weed, the carp's enormous tail failed to kick-start and as I plunged the net forward a leviathan's head hit the surface with its tail trailing three feet behind. I dropped the rod, frantically scooped at the beast, and for a split-second, it began to slip from my grasp, but with a final thrust, the tail flipped into the net and the game was over. Gently, I pulled the frame toward me. Inside, sat a shimmering goliath of wild, untamed common carp - all 39lb 4oz of it! Screaming, I punched the air and said 'thank you'.

A man, a rod, a piece of bread flake and a carp - an epic encounter indeed. I have caught bigger carp but none any better!

Bread flake brute.

Camera: Canon EOS 5D - Shutter Speed: 1/80 sec - F-Stop: f/13.0 - ISO: 100 - Location: Parlour Pool

CHAPTER 23

CONSTABLE COUNTRY

Rising east of the Wiltshire town of Devizes, a river begins a journey that will see it develop into one of angling's most enigmatic fisheries; a place where legends have been made and records broken. First, though, this trickle has to be fuelled by tributaries like the Nadder, Ebble and Wylye before turning it into the country's most popular chalk river known as the Hampshire Avon, a place where dreams can be made reality.

Salisbury, therefore, sees its potential as a coarse fishery really develop and there is a good argument for saying the finest fishing is to be found in Wiltshire not Hampshire as you would expect given its name. England's finest romantic artist, John Constable, found inspiration from the river and water meadows here, which even today still typifies what is special in our great countryside. Nevertheless, the journey of this fast-flowing river cannot be stopped as it surges to meet the Channel and much of the history behind our field sport has been created along its route. Tales of monster fish living in the tap water-clear environment has captured many an angler's imagination for centuries, and I was certainly no different when I first gazed upon the Avon.

Moving to within striking distance of the great river a decade ago made it a place not of a yearly pilgrimage, but a river in which to engross myself regularly, and with all the variety of sport available, there was one that sent my pulse racing more than any other; barbel, the prince of the river. I, too, could follow in the footsteps of many of my angling idols and try to carve my own slice of history in a place that has always been legendary in angling circles.

The old suspension bridge bounced as I traversed its span to cross the river, loaded with tackle and full of expectation. A couple of days previously I had scattered a pound of caramel flavoured boilies over a gravel run close to the bank which was flanked on either side by ranunculus weed, its pretty white flowers swaying to the pulse of the river. Here under this wonderful canvas I hoped the barbel would appear, be drawn to the bait, and indulge in a feeding frenzy. Then, when all their suspicions were lost, I would reappear to plunder the shoal – well, that was the plan anyway!

No sooner had the tackle come off my shoulder and the bucket been put on the floor than I was peering into the swim, expecting to see that marvellous sight of shadows drifting across the bottom just as the text books had promised me. Alas, despite my confidence, the barbel did not appear to be of a similar mindset. Nothing, not even a chub held station and pangs of doubt started to eat away at my perfect plan. Had the Burgate barbel evacuated the area or were they just sheltering from the morning sun under the vast weed beds that filled the Avon downstream as far as the eye could see? In a bid to find out, I decided to introduce another half-pound of bait and then explore upstream for an hour while it stewed and, I hoped, grabbed the fishes' attention.

Wandering the banks of the river was a joy but I was struck by what a small population of fish it actually held. I could wander for five minutes before stumbling on a group of chub, and the barbel were even far less frequent. Recent years had seen poor water management wreak havoc on the population but I did question the river's suitability for the species as well. Ask an angler to conjure up the image of a perfect barbel river and the Avon would come pretty close to it. That's not to say, though, that the barbel thinks the same and if I look at large, coloured rivers such as the Trent or Severn, the species seems to colonise here much more successfully. Perhaps this environment is closer to the one inhabited before the British Isles broke away from the landmass that is now Europe. Then, the Rhine was a typical river for barbel to live in and this has little in common with our southern chalk rivers. Whatever the truth, on my jaunt upstream I failed to spot a single barbel and apart from a few chub, the river appeared devoid of life; it was time to head back.

Parting the nettles and reeds, I cleared a view enabling me to stare into the water and through to the gravel bed below. A huge grin spread across my face telling its own story, as there before me, twisting and turning, were at least nine barbel, six of them of specimen proportions. Even with the displacement caused by such a fast flowing river, I could see several sets of lips grabbing at the bottom in a frantic bid to extract a boilie from the boulders and gravel. What a marvellous sight! It was one I took time to enjoy as rushing to fish in such a scenario only serves to spook the shoal; far better first to study their behaviour and tease them with regular but smaller introductions of bait.

Watching sometimes can be as exciting as catching and this is what I chose to do for another hour while preparing the tackle. Its components were 10lb main line to a large, 4oz flat lead and 15lb Dacron hooklength with a size 10 hook tied using a knotless knot, enabling a hair to be formed. Then, quite simply, a 12mm boilie was skewered and pulled in place, followed by a paste wrap to add extra attraction. Very simple indeed, but boilies were relatively new to the river then and once the barbel had lost their self-control, even crude tackle failed to put them off.

The time had come to fish and I waited for the shoal to drift to the back of the swim before lowering the rig on to the gravel at the top of the run. By now, the barbel were already working back up toward me, hoovering the bottom, and I knew a bite was imminent. My heart pounded and my body shook as the tension tightened every muscle in anticipation. Below, one of the smaller fish arrived on the scene, spotted the hookbait immediately, and sucked it in without hesitating. The instant snagging of the hook in the bottom lip probably made it wish it hadn't, though, and regardless of how much it shook its head there was no escape. Grabbing the rod, I took further control of its destiny and watched as it charged up and down to no avail. I had caught an 8lb barbel but with bigger fish to fry, my main concern was the mindset of the remaining shoal and immediately on wielding the landing net I threw in another handful of boilies. Without hesitation, and while I unhooked the fish, barbel started to regroup and recommence feeding; it seemed as if spooking the shoal wouldn't be a concern today as they had lost their minds to greed.

Quintessentially English.

A 10lb 10oz fish came next, closely followed by its identical twin weighing in at 10lb 4ozs and still they demanded more bait. By now the fish had decided to sit high up in the water at the bottom of the run with their backs almost breaking the surface. At such close quarters and against a green backdrop, their scales sparkled like golden sovereigns each time the sun broke free of the cloud cover and clashed with the water. What a sight! Even better was to come when I threw in another handful of bait, which of course, was spiked with my hook. The feeding orgy recommenced and resulted in a familiar conclusion; hooked barbel. Two more fell foul to greed and the scales recorded weights of 11lb 1 oz and 11lb 3oz. What a day!

Burgate barbel.

Certainly, I had no right to catch any more but the grand finale was now on its way.

I had just watched the biggest fish of the day impale itself on my hook and it nearly pulled the rod in before I could get to it, such was the anger and power of the barbel, and when I compressed the Avon rod fully, it was even less impressed with the situation. Line surged off the clutch and for a while, there was nothing I could do but hang on. A grating sensation could be felt through the line, which saw me wince until everything went solid as the fish buried itself completely in the vegetation. Next, it was my turn to try to gain the upper hand, straining the rod as much as I dared, to drag the barbel free of its refuge.

As each stem was severed by the taut mono, I gained an inch until the tipping point came and the ranunculus released its grip. Free again, the bronze battler exploded each time I sought to win the day and its huge rudder powered it down toward the gravel run. Patience was indeed a virtue in this situation, allowing the tackle to take the strain and slowly suppress the power. Easier said than done, though, when the stakes are so high, and given the Avon's clarity I knew exactly what they were, so when at last a big white belly hit the surface, indicating that my opponent was throwing in the towel, I tried to calm myself a little in preparation of doing the final job with the net correctly. As I strained with one outstretched arm, the frame struggled to cope with the fish's length until it gave a little and flopped inside. The big old warrior was beaten and mine for a while, to admire as well as record at 12lb 12ozs. A day's fishing quite simply couldn't get any better as the Hampshire Avon welcomed me with open arms. I was going to enjoy Constable's country.

The Avon is a place to get lost in the cradle of nature. Here, a barn owl will ghost past you at dusk as it quarters the meadow, or the talismanic salmon greets you as it breaks free of the water and takes to the air. This, and so much more, is what I have come to expect and so my first footsteps on the hallowed banks of the Royalty Fishery came as a big surprise. Set against an industrial backdrop, the green canvas is replaced with bricks and mortar, but after the initial shock, beauty is really in the eye of the beholder. Here, the river seems to go into feature overdrive with bends and bays coming thick and fast, which helps create a plethora of famous swims, and maybe more than anywhere else, barbel hold sway, leading to local experts honing their skills in pursuit of such magnificent prizes.

During my first tentative steps with this fishery, two men, Ray Walton and Chris Holley, took on the task of teaching me the art of rolling meat, which if put in expert hands is a deadly method for fooling the prince of the river. I knew I couldn't have better tutors and if I paid attention, an understanding of this tactic would be mine.

The Royalty.

The principle behind this way of angling is to get a piece of luncheon meat to roll down the riverbed in a natural manner, so inducing a barbel to eat it. This is easier said than done and requires both concentration and skill. Casting upstream, while keeping a bow in the line and maintaining control over the bait's path, can only be achieved by an expert, so both Ray and Chris agreed to spend the day kindly giving up their hard-won secrets to me. After a crash course, and much patience, we eventually came to the most prolific period for tempting a bite, twilight, and I had by now managed to move on from novice to amateur, which at least gave me hope that a reward might come my way. Following a well-worn routine, I stood in the shadow of the famous railway bridge, its dominance of the river ever growing as the sun sank from view, and prepared to cast.

A size 2 weighted hook helped me to propel both the meat and the braid out upstream into the middle of the river. Careful to keep the balance between tension and slack, I allowed the first run-through to commence and the meat bounced over the bottom tantalizingly. I had, of course, hoped that a barbel was in residence but even when this became fact, I was slow to acknowledge its presence. Yanking the braid a little harder, I cottoned on at last and struck, forcing the rod to buckle and the reel to sing. For a while, I couldn't quite believe that my world and that of the barbel had collided, especially while using such a traditional tactic that I had only just mastered. Overjoyed with this fact, I paid little thought to the size of the barbel until it swirled in front of me and I gained a strained glimpse in the half-light. Such a big fish seemed a rather generous reward for a day's training, but I certainly wasn't going to be ungrateful. At 12lb 5oz she was a Royalty monster for the time, although what I will always hold most dear is how I caught her.

Overjoyed!

As I've said before, the Hampshire Avon is quite possibly the most enigmatic of England's rivers. The very mention of it conjures images of giant fish drifting over polished gravel beds exposed by the crystal-clear water while streamer weed pulses in the flow. Topside, it's always sunny and the landscape is made up of lush water meadows filled with all manner of wildlife. In fact, think of an angling cliché and it's probably been used to describe this river, but in reality, does all the romanticising match the truth, or is it all hype?

Well, let's get one thing straight; the Avon is not paved with fish. In fact, I would class it as a difficult river from which to extract a specimen, but it does meander through three of the country's most splendid counties; Wiltshire, Hampshire and Dorset, which you would have to be soulless not to enjoy. Most importantly, though, it's one of the few places where the history is almost tangible.

Enigmatic Avon.

Old mills, bridges and weir pools make up many of the vistas along the Avon's path and it's not hard to imagine the ghosts of anglers from a bygone era taking the same footsteps along the river bank as we do now. Yes, I admit I'm one of those romantics who swoon over the place when maybe its stock levels don't deserve it. So when colour seeped into the river at last, I didn't have to think very hard which direction to point my van, hoping that the sport I would encounter could match the river's persona.

The rain of the previous days had revitalised the Avon. Creases had begun to reform, weir pools thundered again and weed racks had something to catch. In such conditions, only one fish grabbed my interest; the barbel, which I knew would be enjoying the change that had taken place. The secret would be to find my opponent and on such a large waterway, this inevitably leads to a lot of walking. Still on the plus side, it would allow more of the magnificent views to be enjoyed as I pottered about searching out likely looking lies.

Holly trees laden with rich, red berries did more to remind me of Christmas than any television advert while a dozen shades of copper, yellow and brown easily made up for the loss of green vegetation. High up and now exposed, the rookery was filled with squawks and occasionally, its inhabitants would see fit to take to the air and harass anything that crossed their paths. At ground level, I first sought to tame the white water which swept through fully-opened sluice gates, although it didn't take long to see the error of my ways. A washing machine full of debris is an unpleasant affair which neither I, nor the barbel, wanted to tolerate, so I felt it was best to search out calmer waters.

A washing machne.

What I was looking for was a smooth, unbroken surface that would provide a comfortable home and with the introduction of colour, this didn't necessarily have to coincide with cover. The swim I chose next had this quality and more. The bottom, I knew, also dropped away deflecting the Avon's pace and giving an additional reason for a barbel to take up residence. The rig landed in an unwieldy manner, although I was not overly concerned as the fast flow would straighten out the tackle and present it as I had designed it to be. Likewise, the rod became engaged with the river, yielding to its power with a bent tip. By letting out a large bow of line, I could make its entry point into the river very close to the bank, which assisted with avoiding the never-ending stream of flotsam. The vigil had begun and for the next five minutes everything remained connected, then without ceremony, the tension was released, indicated by a slack line before becoming reinstated, in a more forceful and savage manner.

The Avon was no longer responsible for this energy surge and my response changed to match. Striking, I

Wishful thinking.

completed the process that had already begun, driving the hook home and ensuring the 12 feet of carbon I held remained stressed. This process didn't agree with the barbel that had stolen my pellet and it had no compunction in letting me know its displeasure with the situation. The clutch of the reel was the only thing now between me and a broken line, as it soaked up surge after surge, punctuated occasionally with stalemate, as the barbel turned broadside and hung in the flow. Patience was the key for the time being, allowing the tackle to do its job, and biding my time to turn the tables.

Inevitably, even with the fish's and the river's combined strength, the moment came when I began to take control and the surface was broken for the first time in this desperate struggle. What I had suspected from the off was confirmed as I watched a beast of impressive proportions weave up and down the margins, bristling in anger with the situation. Twice, I tried to test its resolve with the landing net only to be denied until at last it succumbed, rolling over in defeat and exposing its white underbelly. There, inside the mesh, sat 13lb 14ozs of barbel and for once, the Avon wasn't just a place for wishful thinking.

There is another, less expected, quarry that has the power to test tackle to the limit on this river, and over the last few years, I have found it hard to ignore this enjoyable challenge.

Peering over the high, steeped bank into the clearing winter water of the Avon, I found what I had been looking for. Immediately upstream, a long run of withered reed stems were deflecting the main flow allowing a slack bay to form where I could now see a series of sizeable shadows drifting about. Given the venue you could be forgiven for thinking that they were barbel or even monster chub but not so; carp were the cause of my excitement.

Constable country.

Over the years, literally hundreds have escaped from their stillwater homes during times of flood, taking up residence in the country's rivers. Despite this intrusion, I couldn't be happier with their presence giving an air of mystery to the next bite. Not only does the size vary considerably but also the strain, supplying a real chocolate box scenario from ghosties to commons and mirrors to leathers. So, not knowing exactly what lay in front of me only served to increase the adrenaline levels still further.

Reaching into the bait bucket, I introduced 100 chocolate malt boilies and a couple of handfuls of halibut pellets as this would allow me to gauge what interest, if any, they had in feeding. Predictably, the initial disturbance saw the shadows push out into the flow where I lost track of them, but not for long. Obviously, hunger overrode the need for caution as a dozen shapes swept back into view, only this time great plumes of silt and bubbles accompanied their movements. This was a no-holds-barred feeding frenzy with boilies and pellets rapidly disappearing into the carps' mouths. Time, I felt, to get the gear ready, so with another few handfuls of bait thrown in to keep them occupied, I set about that task.

Keeping things very simple but strong is the number one priority with river carp, so 20lb fluorocarbon fished directly through to a size 8 Continental Boilie hook seemed appropriate in this scenario. If at all possible, I never like to have a monofilament hooklength only, as this material gains a lot of its strength from its ability to stretch. Remove the fixed points, swivels, in this case, and these physical properties will be greatly enhanced. Knowing this, I use a series of float stops and a link bead to attach my lead and a smaller back lead. One downside of using fluorocarbon directly to the hook, though, is how it sits next to the bait if you use the same line as a hair material. The hook will actually ride off the bottom in an ungainly fashion, allowing the carp to spot it easily. Therefore, I used a braided material for this job and due to its supple nature, everything stayed nice and snug to the bottom. The final part of the rig came in the form of an AAA pinched on the line, one inch from the hook. At first glance it looked like a pop-up rig but it was not there for the boilie's buoyancy; it was to help pull the hook into the bottom lip when a carp sucked the bait in.

Suitably confident in my approach, I crept back to the vantage point to confirm that the shadows were still moving across the bay. The feeding, it appeared, had continued and if anything it had increased, so with no further ado, I nicked on a PVA mesh bag of pellets to complement the boilie and flicked it out into the mêlée. Firstly, I allowed the lead to land on a tight line after which the backlead would be keeping everything nicely pinned to the bottom. Switching on the reel's free spool, I ensured the rod tip didn't extend over the riverbank and, in fact, a good few metres of line actually draped over the reeds, reducing the risk of spooking my target.

Understandably, five minutes passed without a sign until the calm was shattered by a bow wave heading across the Avon and a rod bent in desperation to follow it. As I grabbed the reel's handle, I swear smoke was coming from it!

A welcome intruder.

Disengaging the free spool, I fared little better at stopping line from being removed at a rapid rate. With a weir just downstream adding to the river's force, I had only one option; to run downstream with it and hope it didn't disappear into the white water. Due to the distraction, I hadn't noticed Pete, the river keeper who I had fished with previously on the Avon and then tempted carp to 25lbs, walking through the meadow to be by my side. I was glad of the assistance as he grabbed the net and followed me in hot pursuit, especially as he had previous form with the species.

Once I was directly opposite it, I could do no more than get the carp to hold station, waiting for the next move. I had no doubt it was in control and only a mistake on its part would allow me to land it. Fortunately, its strength was not matched by its intellect as it proceeded to head back upstream and into the bay. From a dire situation, the fight now came under my control, and despite the carp's best efforts for five minutes there was no escape. With a final heave, a linear sporting a brown and purple complexion became tamed by the landing net. What a thrill! No sooner had this battle ended than I was eagerly awaiting the next.

Two more fights were to follow that afternoon with similar-sized fish and I had to admit that I had become firmly addicted, so much so that dawn the following day saw me back on the river, only this time at the entrance to a side stream which was directly opposite the dangerous weir. Could I possibly stop a carp in time with the sill being in such close proximity? I was about to find out.

Hold on tight!

Immediately, the game plan of not giving line went out of the window with the rod bucking against my grip. Across the flow, the carp surged until it actually cut in front of the weir. Frightening as this was, it was better than disappearing down it! Never once did I feel in control of the situation and for a good while I was given the run around looking doomed to fail. I felt sure the carp could smash me at any time. Perhaps then, it was out of pity that it allowed itself to be netted, displaying a classic winter colouration of staggering beauty. Strangers they may be, but I can see a future that definitely includes more of this type of angling.

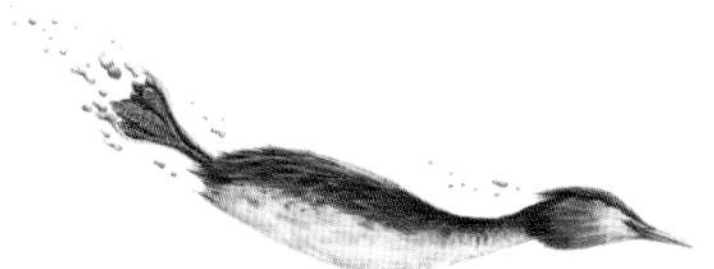

Allow me to return for one last story about the barbel, which have provided me with so many tales to tell, and celebrate all that is special along this splendid waterway. Is there a better view of England than that of Salisbury Cathedral from the Hampshire Avon's water meadows? John Constable certainly didn't think so when he was inspired to create a series of masterpieces in the 1800s.

His brush strokes may have captured the imagination of the general public but to all anglers it's the fish which lie beneath the blue part of his canvas that captivates most. Situated in Wiltshire, the county really does lay claim to the finest parts of the river, and one of the county's jewels is the Britford section, controlled by the London Angler's Association.

Here, in the cathedral's shadow, are roach I would happily swap any masterpiece for; fantastic creatures of gargantuan proportions dressed in a silvery-blue livery. Sadly, it's only this stretch and the Longford estate below where it's possible to angle for such fish with any realistic possibility of success. Why? Without keepers, of which there is a dearth on the river, the black plague (cormorants) swarm up the valley annihilating every silver fish in their path. The simple, sad truth is that without the protection of a gun, vast swathes of the river have been left barren; shameful, when you consider the Avon's historic pedigree.

Wiltshire then may be the final bastion of the roach, but nevertheless the population still doesn't suffer fools gladly, and I was one such clown when I took to the banks on a late autumn day. Quite why I packed only a quiver tip rod, I don't know, but a debris-strewn river made it impossible to hold bottom and I was forced to retreat, cursing the lack of float tackle. At this stage, it would have been easy to head for home, but instead my mind turned to another of the river's favourites - barbel. Their proportions may not match that of their cousins on other southern rivers, but the power they display in the fast flows makes up for this in spades.

In the shadow of the spire.

Leaving the roach and the spire behind, I wandered along the banks of a pacey section, introducing small quantities of pellets into likely looking spots to see if anyone was at home. Even with the tinge of colour, location wasn't an issue as the feed began to work its magic. Unusually, a silty, lily-strewn slack came up trumps and such was the fishes' greed, great plumes of dirt were kicked up in desperation for food. Chub, carp, and most importantly, two big barbel, were the culprits and, in all, perhaps 30 mouths hoovered up the bottom. It was beyond doubt that I had found a suitable place to return to in the morning with more adequate tackle. The question was how to extract the biggest barbel in all the commotion? Fishing visually would, on the face of it, seem the sensible option but given the substrate the fish were feeding over, I knew I would quickly lose contact with the bait, which in turn would inhibit seeing it being picked up. I needed to sleep on it and come up with a plan.

It was mid-morning when eventually, I strolled along the bank again pushing past a herd of nosey cattle and alarming a group of swans intent on ripping out the final remnants of a ranunculus bed. Today, the river looked in a sombre mood, created by a blanket of slate-grey clouds that had been pushed in overnight by a low-pressure front. It's wise, though, not to judge a book by its cover and I knew such conditions were conducive for feeding fish.

Dropping the tackle some way back from the bank, I crept into the swim where I had spied the fish the previous day, and scanned the water. A couple of moderate carp and a shoal of chub milled around in the weed and despite the lack of barbel, I remained positive. I guessed they were safely tucked up downstream enjoying the comforts of some streamer weed.

It was time to put my plan into action, which was based more around the chubs' cunning rather than that of the barbel. Chub, you see, are far more adept at spotting terminal tackle and I knew that by using a braided hooklength as opposed to a nylon one, I would be unlucky to get a bite from a chevin. The carp, though, were an altogether different story and here I needed to rely on greed. By mixing sweetcorn into the droppers full of pellet and hemp I intended to feed, I hoped that the visual stimulation of such a bait would divert attention from the hookbait, giving the barbel time to find the pellet which they, in turn, always seem to prefer. It sounded good in principle, but I knew full well that with so many variables involved it could quite easily go horribly wrong.

So, after popping the pellet offering into a solid PVA bag accompanied by a few free baits, I lowered it on to the silty, clear patch below and this was followed by four dropper loads. For this special situation, I wasn't going to allow any fish to feed first, to gain confidence before fishing; to do so would have only compounded still further the situation of catching an individual fish.

Retreating behind a set of reeds, I began keeping vigil and noticed almost immediately a pack of chub arrive, circling over the food with intent. Minutes later, half a dozen carp of assorted shapes and sizes also came on the scene but they had even fewer table manners. Straightaway, plumes of mud heaved upward and the surface was peppered with fizzing bubbles. It was obvious that the barbel had to arrive quickly for me to stand any chance.

Biting both lips, I looked at my watch and saw that five minutes had passed; a barbel should have arrived by now. Then, through the gloom, a coppery orange flank momentarily materialised. Was that what I thought it was? Straining, I waited for another glimpse and sure enough, it came in the form of a barbel and as an added bonus it was also the biggest fish I'd seen the previous day. It seemed judgement time had arrived.

No sooner had the barbel disappeared again than the rod tip bounced and the reel's clutch sung out its tune. Surely, I couldn't have been that lucky, that quickly? As I struck, a series of bodies headed in all directions but my line only cut through the water to one. A big, pristine, copper clad barbel of 13½lbs. With fish like this on offer inside a theatre of dreams, how can I ever ignore the call of the Avon?

Personal best.

Camera: Canon EOS 40D - Shutter Speed: 1/1000 sec - F-Stop: f/8.0 - ISO: 640 - Location: English Channel

CHAPTER 24

NEVER ENDING

The road I have walked because of angling has certainly been a diverse one and not always directly associated with catching fish, but a love of our field sport has always been at the forefront and this is why I found myself entering the area of angling politics.

"Why," I asked one of the sport's shrewdest operators, "don't you get involved?"

"Well," he replied without consideration, "I'm always the first to shout 'bollocks' and that doesn't win you many friends, and you will be exactly the same." Oh, how I wish I had heeded his advice.

For our children.

It was during a sponsors' open day at Yateley Angling Centre that my path crossed with the owner, Ruth Lockwood. She is a serial angling politician with an infectious belief that a difference can be made, and if we all cared as much as her, our world would be a better place. Disappointed in the direction our sport was going, I allowed myself to become entwined in her argument and by the time I left the shop I had become a member of the media-named 'Magnificent Seven' alongside the likes of Keith Arthur, John Wilson and Danny Fairbrass. We would save angling and lead it into a new era. How foolish I was to think this would ever be possible.

Be it trawlers, beavers, otters or cormorants, fish get a raw deal with little protection, and if birds or mammals suffered in a similar vein there would be public uproar, but for an ecosystem hidden below the surface, no one but an angler cares. Many of the marvellous fish displayed within this book are no longer with us after falling foul of would-be environmentalists and their crazed policies. In fact, the entire contents of chapters 5, 7, 16 and 17 have ended up shredded by otters without a whimper from the world inside and outside of angling; we seem scared of our own shadow at times. After paying out over 25 million pounds in the form of a rod licence tax, you would have thought we might value it a little more and the government collecting the cash would help us with the problems faced. We are the only group of people taxed to go into the countryside while canoeists and bird watchers go free, so I think, quite rightly, that we should expect to take priority over those who follow these pursuits.

'The antis are coming' is a common cry if you put your head above the parapet and express these opinions, but this is a myth perpetuated by the parties who wish - no, need - to keep you in your place. When was the last time a shop, lake or angler felt the public's wrath for angling? Once in a blue moon at worst, so we should feel free to speak out with no fear of our field sport ever going the same way as fox hunting. Not convinced? Well, I can think of at least 25 million reasons why it won't. These and many other issues were the reasons I was willing to help Ruth, but in the end I found out that you could only take a horse to water, not make it drink.

Arrogantly, convinced that angling could unite and rise up against the injustices, I set about the tree huggers with vigour, those who would rather schmooze in suits along the corridors of power than climb out of their trench and fight a battle in the name of angling, and it's this attitude that has lead us to a point where the environment we all love is under threat.

For an aggressive stance to work, it does still need unity. Any skilled politician will use the 'divide and conquer' technique to keep any uprising at bay and, alas, what makes our sport special is also what makes it so weak – diversity. A carp angler shows very little interest in the plight of a sea fisherman, or that of a salmon angler, which in turn, is reflected in each of their attitudes to someone living in a bivvy. Now factor in the countless meetings with people who love to talk instead of act, with the sole conclusion each time being the arranging of another meeting, and you end up getting nowhere!

I opened the lid and found a pit of vipers but instead of slamming it immediately shut, I decided to argue with them. At each meeting I attended, I don't believe I ever gained a new friend, probably just a few enemies. At times, my passion explodes and that doesn't sit well with dyed-in-the-wool committee members who, to my mind, haven't got a clue what they're talking about. Angling is in the Dark Ages, so why keep it there by behaving as meek as a mouse to any group or government that crosses our path, feeding not at the top table with the likes of the RSPB but existing on scraps off the floor and then being forced to say 'thank you'.

As I hope I have demonstrated, my persona and confrontational attitude was perhaps a little shocking, but what really got my goat was the insistence that such a vocal stance and lack of corporate behaviour would get me nowhere. 'Who would listen to you?' I was asked. Well, that was like a red rag to a bull.

Let's keep it this way.

The big boss.

Leading up to the 2010 general election, my path crossed with the fisheries minister in waiting, Richard Benyon, who I found to be a thoroughly decent man; who was straight talking, without an agenda and a person who I felt understood the countryside. So, fellow anarchists, John Wilson, Tim Norman and Chris Logsdon, plus journalist Steve Partner, and I, side-stepped the angling politicians and met with him to discuss the issues we felt were affecting the sport. The meeting went well, in fact, so well that Richard decided I should take the message to his boss, David Cameron. Angling had never had such a high profile meeting and getting an audience with the Prime Minister-in-waiting wasn't going to be straightforward, even if Richard was keen on it.

The first date was scuppered by President Sarkozy of France, but two weeks later, and after a lot of effort by both Richard and I, we entered Westminster. Accompanying me was Steve Partner and Lloyd Rogers of Angling Times who would be covering the meeting, and of course affording the Conservative Party a good deal of publicity. To meet with the main man there needed to be a pay-off, but the chance to air our issues with the soon-to-be most powerful man in Britain was too good an opportunity to miss. I also took seriously the responsibility afforded me and had come up with an angle that I hoped would help him to understand the plight of our waterways, as well as connecting with him on a personal level.

Witney being his constituency, attracts an awful lot of tourists and money into the area due to carp fishing, namely Linear Fisheries, which was news to him, and demonstrated the economic benefits of the sport that had been happening right under his nose for years, which typically, we had failed to promote or celebrate. Once hooked, I then needed to highlight the plight of our waterways and here, the river Windrush was the perfect candidate, being again in his constituency; it has been ravaged by red signal crayfish, cormorants and otters, like so many of our lowland waterways. It was lateral thinking and surprisingly, an angle all our leading angling politicians missed - or worse still, were unaware of!

I can talk for England as you may have guessed, but as I wound my way up the oak beam staircase my mouth dried while my hands sweated profusely; this was the big league, of that there was no doubt. Then, without ceremony, a surreal moment occurred as David bounded out of this office to greet us, shaking us all vigorously by the hand. Schooled in the art of small talk, he set us all at ease and invited us into his office for a 20-minute conference which felt more like 20 seconds. He listened, took stock of every issue, and didn't flinch once when the subject of cormorants and otters was raised, remaining sympathetic at all times.

Obviously, he wanted us to write a positive story but, to me, it was his eagerness to hold a meeting that was the true triumph. Surely angling shouldn't be afraid to hold its head up high and speak its mind if he was willing to associate himself and his party with the sport? Do you really think that in the lead-up to a general election he would allow such a link with a vote loser, or an issue that would divide the country? This, to me, was vindication of my argument that we shouldn't be constantly looking over our shoulders and, in fact, should speak out without fear whenever necessary. Do you know, as I shook his hand and posed for pictures, I couldn't see any of the people who wished to temper my aggressive attitude to defending the way of life we all love. I guess they were busy arranging another meeting!

Glorious game fishing.

After so many years of coarse fishing, a desire to understand more about the game and sea angling side of the sport has become stronger recently, especially with the predation spoken about so much in this book affecting many of the waters I cherish. Standing in the river Spey under the snowy peaks of the Cairngorms is truly inspiring, as is sitting on a boat enjoying the ocean waves. In such a large expanse of water, the mystery remains and the adventures now come thicker and faster than ever before.

When the Nazi U-boat raised its periscope, locked on, and fired a torpedo, it seemed that life was about to be extinguished from the destroyer forever. With its hull torn open and boarding water rapidly, the descent to the seabed was swift and it lay on its side in the darkness for decades. Nature, though, had plans for the tortured and tangled metalwork. Humans had abandoned it, but other life could still put it to good use: first as a collection point for a range of crustaceans, followed inevitably by small fish to feast on the fresh larder. As this colony began to grow, it became coveted by predators who wished to colonise it to service their own needs. No longer would this sleeping ship be a safe haven – the serpents had arrived writhing across the barren underwater plains to take charge of the situation, and there they lay in ambush, kings of this castle daring anyone to cross their path.

Fast-forward 70 years, travel 30 miles due north, and you arrive at a bustling scene of locals and holidaymakers going about their business in the harbour town of Dartmouth. On the face of it, despite the two worlds sharing the same planet, a link between them seems almost impossible. Four men, though, sitting on board the catamaran Gemini had made it their mission to plot a collision course with the wreck in a bid to do battle with the conger eel. The glum faces showed that all was far from well. Plans and preparations had been made to the nth degree, but what couldn't be controlled was the wind and swell that lay in ambush as soon as the safety of the natural bay was left behind. Only the skipper could make the call to press on with the quest. Dave Harrison, one of the country's finest conger hunters spoke to fellow seamen on the radio before pondering once again.

On deck, three anglers nervously twiddled with the tackle and kicked their feet, hoping for a positive outcome. I had been joined by my good friend, Kev Newton, and experienced sea fisherman, Mike Concannon. With Kev and I being inexperienced with the species, it was to be Mike's task to guide us through the intricacies of catching the eel, which judging by the tackle on show seemed to be a brutal affair. Fifty-pound class boat rods coupled with large multipliers loaded to the gunnels with 60lb braid to cope, not only with the sheer strength expected to be inflicted on us, but also the 200 feet-plus depth in which our goal was to be found. Huge leads of 2lbs or more would sit on heavy mono rubbing leaders before finally, 250lb mono hooklengths were crimped to 10/0 super-strong hooks. Baits lashed to these would either be cuttlefish or mackerel, which still needed to be caught on feathers during our voyage; if, of course, it was ever to take place.

"We are going for it," were the relief-filled words Dave offered to us at last before firing up the engine and making a break for the open sea. Running for almost three hours through the waves would not be pleasant but weighed against the prospect of fishing, it was worth enduring, especially as our arrival at the wreck would see the tide subside, meaning the battle it fought with the wind would reduce, as would the swell.

Laughing out loud.

Perfect pollock.

Then, and only then, could the anchor find a strong grip, providing a steady platform close to the wreck. If the truth were known, this would be the most skilful part of the day which needed to be carried out with pinpoint accuracy to optimise the chances of a successful trip, hence our selection of Dave. Anglers may be the ones with the smug grins and an armful of fish in the photos but it's the man at the helm who makes it all possible when sea fishing.

Mackerel catching was our first port of call, which didn't take very long given the overloaded rods and lines full of iridescent green fish, so with the job done we pressed on and ignored the waves that buffeted the boat. Mike took us through the procedure required to tame a conger which was obviously going to require more than a little sweat and elbow grease to prevent a fish that can swim backwards from snaring its tail around a pole, doorway or radio mast, helping to smash up an angler's tackle. With all the excited chitter-chatter the voyage, despite its length, soon passed by. Our skipper's concentration on the echo sounder's screen, and careful movement of the wheel, was a sign for us to prepare the hookbaits. Expertly, Dave took into account all the factors trying to prevent him from placing the boat perfectly, before dropping the anchor to leave us only a few rod lengths from the wreck.

Eagerly, we split our bait choice between mackerel and the inky flesh of the cuttlefish, ensuring that the hook remained proud whatever the selection. Then with 2lb of lead clipped on, they were transported down to the darkness of the seabed. Scent oozed from the corpses, causing an overpowering stench before being carried away with the underwater tow, to infiltrate the portholes of the broken metal structure which lay a short distance away. At first, all seemed calm but any tranquillity was soon to be shattered. An easy meal does not remain unmolested for long in such a harsh environment and inside the hull, monsters stirred. No longer was the ship lifeless; it now writhed like Medusa's head, with huge, grey tentacles protruding, each one with a set of snapping jaws. We had awoken a nightmare and now we would begin to pay the price for such folly.

Mike's fate was sealed first, followed closely by Kev, as braid ticked slowly off their clutches as something wanted to return to its home with fresh flesh.

Engaging in combat was the only option to prevent broken braid and I watched in awe as two broomsticks folded over like wimpish wands. Each man fought his own battle which was a strenuous affair indeed; primeval and brutal. Why, you may ask, would anyone want to endure this? Well, given the broad grin on each man's face, this form of self-harming seemed a pleasurable experience to me!

Six-foot long sea beasts were hauled on board with both captors excited to pose alongside the magnificent conger. A gaff in the bottom lip could seem barbaric and uncaring but nothing was further from the truth. It allowed the moment to be safely recorded and the eel returned alive. I was pleased for both men but also desperately wanted to make my own connection.

Two congers did accept the cuttlefish I had lovingly impaled but came adrift halfway up, leaving me the exhausting and unrewarded task of reeling them back in and the, by now, 4lb of lead required to hold station. Down the bait went again, and soon I felt a tug before a slow, steady pull. I didn't intend to make another mistake and set the hook home with a solid strike; my time had come as the reel tried desperately to contain the serpent. When a fish can exert as much strength as you, it's always a wonderful experience and this fight didn't disappoint. With arms full of lactic acid, cramped fingers, and out of breath, I waited for Dave to do his job well with the gaff, as he had done all day.

With the conger lying at my feet, I took a few seconds to admire the creature rather than being fearful of it. Reassessing any prejudice, I came to realise that evolution had not created a monster but a marvellous apex predator, and a total of five fish over an estimated 60lbs up to 75lbs, gave all of us a chance to come to that conclusion. Everyone making the mark, to become a fully-fledged member of the British Conger Club reinforced the tremendous sport.

Sea fishing has become a new addiction and I am like a kid at Christmas each time I charter a boat and head out toward the horizon.

Portraying my passion for angling is important to me and writing or creating a magazine feature has never been a chore; in fact, I love it. Maybe my editor was right when he said I was obsessed, and now I have a new toy to play with in the form of films. After serving an apprenticeship with Hugh Miles, I couldn't ask for a better introduction into the world of television, although I did have a mountain to climb to make anything that approached Catching the Impossible, and at first, I swore I would never try to. Well, for a few days anyway, until I started my own film production company and embarked on a new testing voyage, much to my wife's dismay.

Sea serpent.

To succeed, I knew it would take the same level of obsession that I had with Catching or maybe even more, as without Hugh and Bernard to fall back on, all the decisions fell on me, but I was willing to rise to the challenge. A Fish for All Seasons started production to coincide with this book of the same title. Cue business partner and cameraman, Jacko, who would now be the person who would have to cope with any madcap ideas I came up with to help push the limits further than ever before. Surprisingly, a baptism of fire on board a microlight didn't finish the relationship before it had really begun, although I sensed the next adventure could well achieve it.

'The worst snowstorm for 30 years' and 'emergency travel only' were the words spoken on all news channels and radio stations to describe Oxfordshire's plight over the next few hours. So guess where Jacko and I were heading? Better still, we intended to sleep outside for the night; obsessed, yes, sensible I'm not. With tackle hastily bundled in the van, I embarked on the first task, a rendezvous with my partner at Oxford's Park and Ride to dump the van before transferring everything into Jacko's wagon. For anyone considering driving a rear wheel Mercedes Vito in the snow, all I can say is don't; it truly is a death trap. The withering look from my friend as we greeted each other said it all, and wise to my ramblings, the Dunkirk spirit speech didn't cheer him up much either. Never mind, we still headed to the estate lake with the grey, angry skies following in our wake although for now we were granted a stay of execution inside the eye of the storm.

Best friend.

As always, the lake wrapped us in a cloak of history with its ancient fauna living proof of its time immemorial status. For once, though, the water didn't dazzle, with 99% of its surface entombed in ice, the sun unable to shimmer across the surface. At least swim selection would be straightforward with little choice but an area the size of a tennis court in the lee of an island. Hurrying, I made my way into position for if the weatherman was to be proven right, the worst arctic blast for decades would hit us in a matter of hours.

Given the limited amount of open water, the use of only two rods seemed logical for if a miracle did occur in the form of a bite, the last thing I wanted was a set of tangled lines. As ever, terminal tackle was simple, implementing a length of anchor tubing, safety clips with a 3oz lead and a size 6 hook. Bait choice was also straightforward with a banana-flavoured pop-up combined with a PVA stringer of half a dozen dense boilies. The base of the marginal slope from the island appeared to be the best choice to place these rigs, so without further ado, casts were made into the freezing waters.

Getting the camp up was equally, if not more, important to ensure survival through the night as sensational temperatures of -20°C were predicted across Great Britain. Once satisfied I had done all I could, there was little left to do but wait with the air of expectation not connected to the rods for once, but the skyline which was rapidly filling in, with a huge cloud bank devouring all the light laid out before it. A monster had set a course for us it seemed. Jacko and I joked about our predicament with much bravado but the first snowflake silenced conversation and we gulped as fiction turned to fact. At first, it was light flurries and even up to dusk little had settled on the ground although the temperature drop was tangible and I watched, horrified, as ice began to eat the last remaining section of open water. For a while, I ignored the obvious until only an area the size of a snooker table remained. Our situation had just become even more insane as I was forced to reel in the rods with our fate sealed, for by now a white carpet of snow filled the landscape preventing a retreat.

I must be mad!

Fishing was no longer on the agenda, only survival, and two sad souls sat inside the bivvy, with just the flicker of a lantern across the frost-starched and tortured nylon, preventing the world from being consumed by gloom. The gas stove was uninterested in helping with the situation as the canister struggled against the cold, so we sought solace in a small hip flask of whisky. For a time, the light-headedness even caused us to consider the carps' plight – as still as stone, mid-way up the water column, with only leeches for company as all other inhabitants hibernated, but as the malt ran dry so did the warmth, and once again the conditions made us wretched. Was this worth a picture or a moment on screen? I surely hoped so, for only the obsession would keep me going. Time for sleep as Jacko headed to his van with a moment Captain Scott would have been proud of, swallowed up by the blizzard as he embarked on the hazardous journey into the jaws of the beast in an attempt to reach his vehicle. As I zipped the bivvy door down, I could only hope that he made it and prayed that my sleeping bag would be able to stave off hypothermia.

The silence was deafening and filled my first awakening sense. Lifting my head off the pillow, I gingerly touched my face to confirm that I hadn't shed my mortal coil, and muttered a 'thank God'. As I tugged on the bivvy door zip it felt heavy from a force pushing against it and only when I prised it open did I comprehend; the height of drifting snow had turned the tent into an igloo. There, to greet me, was one of Britain's finest and most rare sights; pure white snow, untainted and coating every grass blade, branch and berry. I had, it seemed, been transported into a fairytale that supplied views even spring couldn't match. Better still, Jacko was there to greet me with the camera and we set about recording a once-in-a-lifetime event. Effort, as they say, equals reward, and whatever the critics write about the films we have made, they can't say we haven't tried.

So we come to the end of this book, but not the adventure which I hope will last to my dying day. However, I do not want to finish with a story about myself, but rather a celebration of what inspires me, and thousands of other anglers, as the natural history to be found within the British Isles is truly breathtaking. Nowhere else on planet Earth will you find such diversity of landscape, and as anglers we are well placed to enjoy the best that this wonderful country has to offer. Despite over 60 million people living within this relatively small land mass, a few hours by its lakes, ponds or rivers can see you escape into your own secluded world where only nature will be your companion.

This special landscape, covering over 121,000 square miles, was separated from mainland Europe thousands of years ago, leaving us an intimate country that allows every inch to be explored by means of a simple car journey. Of course, angling gives a further excuse to 'loaf around' in the countryside, but with this field sport comes a passion as strong as that of any conservationist or bird watcher, for Great Britain and its wildlife.

The British Isles.

Our coastline supplies us with a massive amount of water in which to cast a line. Indeed, with over 11,000 miles of shoreline to fish, you cannot live more than 75 miles away from this breathtaking scenery. Throwing a lure for bass on a rocky outcrop in Cornwall, or trying to winch up a giant skate in over 600 feet of water from Scotland's Firth of Lorne, and every saline pursuit in between, gives us more than we could explore in a lifetime, and we haven't touched freshwater fishing yet!

Rivers, streams, and many stillwaters originate from the last ice age, which left a network of waterways in its wake. Added to this is a human influence that has created further homes for fish: namely canals, estate lakes, and gravel pits. It's no wonder that we are spoilt for choice with the species we can catch. The mighty salmon still explores our rivers, where gentlemen with fancy casts and a kaleidoscope of flies wait patiently to make their acquaintance, while on gravel pits in the south of England sit anglers who come from an entirely different social class but are as equally schooled and passionate about their quarry – carp. Indeed, no other fish evokes such single-mindedness or dedication. Obsession is another word that springs to mind here, where marriages are broken and jobs lost in pursuit of a fish! Madness, maybe, but where better to lose your mind than among the blood-red dawns and shimmering surface of a favourite lake.

Every region brings with it a different tale. There's the South-West and the possibility of sharks marauding just offshore, or maybe a mullet happy to drift between both fresh and salt water. Southern England is the home of the carp, with impossibly large cyprinids feeding in the seclusion of a bed of lily pads Not that this is the only choice a fisherman has, far from it, with the area's chalk streams and rivers hard to beat. It could then be a trout supping down a mayfly on a balmy evening, or a roach at last deciding to intercept that carefully presented piece of flake at dawn, that takes your fancy here.

The East of England is dominated by fenland and we have much to thank the Dutch engineers for, who created such a tapestry of dykes. Mention our most fearsome predator, the pike, and the word 'fen' won't be too far away. A punt slipped into the water on a misty morning, its owner keen to reach the reed beds that criss-cross this wetland arena, is evocative enough, but then the calm is broken as a brightly coloured bung is wrenched downwards, leaving a set of rings on the surface, and the battle commences. How is it possible to find a more exciting moment laid out against such a magnificent vista?

Central England brings with it two mighty waterways; the Severn and the Trent, both home to the prince of the river, the barbel. Once you have engaged in battle with this fish, little else can match its fearsome charges. Also scattered throughout this region are large, man-made reservoirs which have been colonised by trout, giving the angler a chance to test his, or her, talents against this adversary with only insect imitations and a weighted line to win the day.

As we travel higher, Northern England comes next, where the Lake District of 886 square miles dominates the scenery. All manner of species live here but it's the predatory pike and perch that prove most popular. How could you refuse to take up the invitation of a bent rod and screaming clutch against the backdrop of mountains and ravines? Canals seem a world away from this scene but they, too, offer something in this part of England. The fish may not be big but they are prized all the same, for they offer a chance of relaxation near to the industrialised towns and cities.

Wales follows, if we head west, and I can think of few finer places to go than the Wye Valley. Its gorges see a river cascading over boulders and sweeping unhindered along gravel beds, offering numerous challenges for a rod and line, all of which will leave you spellbound by not only what you catch but also where it took place, no matter what the season you choose to visit.

Over the sea, Ireland awaits with monstrous tope, huge hauls of bream and the biggest prize of all for the Emerald Isle, the fabled rudd that live in the clear and forgotten loughs, shielded from prying eyes by a barrier of reed beds where only a boat will grant you a way in. All, of course, toasted with a pint of Guinness or a tipple of whiskey and maybe both if a Red Letter Day needs celebrating.

Finally, we come to another Celtic province - Scotland. Coarse fishing, although possible, doesn't hold sway here. Instead, you are more likely to book an appointment with the sea, or if freshwater takes your fancy, the mighty salmon, fighting-fit, and ready for battle.

The choice is endless if you are not pigeonholed and held back by a species or label. The words 'coarse', 'game' and 'sea' are simply a barrier to enjoyment. There is no difference; just water, fish, a rod, reel and an angler wanting to catch. Great Britain, if you let it, will give you more fishing adventures than you ever dreamed possible, and it's only a cast away.

A special sport.

Never ending.

GONE
FISHING